Learning Three.js – the JavaScript 3D Library for WebGL

Second Edition

Create stunning 3D graphics in your browser
using the Three.js JavaScript library

Jos Dirksen

BIRMINGHAM - MUMBAI

Learning Three.js – the JavaScript 3D Library for WebGL

Second Edition

First published: October 2013

Second edition: March 2015

Production reference: 1250315

Published by Packt Publishing Ltd.
Livery Place
35 Livery Street
Birmingham B3 2PB, UK.

ISBN 978-1-78439-221-5

www.packtpub.com

Credits

Author
Jos Dirksen

Reviewers
Adrian Parr
Pramod S
Sarath Saleem
Cesar Torres

Commissioning Editor
Kunal Parikh

Acquisition Editor
Kevin Colaco

Content Development Editor
Arwa Manasawala

Technical Editor
Humera Shaikh

Copy Editors
Sarang Chari
Relin Hedly

Project Coordinator
Danuta Jones

Proofreaders
Simran Bhogal
Maria Gould
Paul Hindle

Indexer
Hemangini Bari

Production Coordinator
Melwyn D'sa

Cover Work
Melwyn D'sa

About the Author

Jos Dirksen has worked as a software developer and architect for more than a decade. He has a lot of experience in a wide range of technologies, ranging from backend technologies, such as Java and Scala, to frontend development using HTML5, CSS, and JavaScript. Besides working with these technologies, Jos also regularly speaks at conferences and likes to write about new and interesting technologies on his blog. He also likes to experiment with new technologies and see how they can be best used to create beautiful data visualizations, the results of which you can see on his blog at http://www.smartjava.org/.

Jos is currently working as a consultant for a large Dutch financial institution and has just finished a function as an enterprise architect for Malmberg, a large Dutch publisher of educational material. There, he helped to create a new digital platform for the creation and publishing of educational content for primary, secondary, and vocational education. Previously, Jos worked in many different roles in the private and public sectors, ranging from private companies, such as Philips and ASML, to organizations in the public sector, such as the Department of Defense.

Jos has also written two other books on Three.js — *Three.js Essentials*, which uses an example-based approach to explore the most important feature of Three.js, and *Three.js Cookbook*, which provides a recipe-based approach to cover important use cases of Three.js.

Besides his interest in frontend JavaScript and HTML5 technologies, he is also interested in backend service development using REST and traditional web services.

Acknowledgments

Writing a book isn't something you do yourself. A lot of people helped and supported me when I was writing this book. Special thanks to the following people:

- All the guys from Packt who helped me during the writing, reviewing, and layout parts of the process. Great work guys!

- I, of course, have to thank Ricardo Cabello, also known as "Mr. dò_ób", for creating the great Three.js library.

- Many thanks go to the reviewers. They gave great feedback and comments that really helped improve the book. Your positive remarks really helped shape the book!

- And, of course, I'd like to thank my family. I'd like to thank my wife, Brigitte, for supporting me, and my two girls, Sophie and Amber, who always can find reasons to pull me away from the keyboard and computer.

About the Reviewers

Adrian Parr is a BAFTA-winning freelance frontend developer from London, UK. He has been creating interactive content since 1997, starting with CD-ROMs in Macromedia Director, websites using tables, mobile sites using WAP, and coding games in Flash 4. With his experience in developing content and managing technical teams, he has been hired by many London agencies, large and small. After a long period of specializing in the Adobe Flash Platform as an ActionScript developer, he is now focused on open web standards (HTML5, CSS3, and JavaScript). He is currently playing with AngularJS, D3, Phaser, SVG animation, Processing, Arduino, Python on Raspberry Pi, and, of course, WebGL using Three.js. Outside of work, he enjoys cycling, windsurfing, and snowboarding. You can connect with him using the following platforms:

- Blog: www.adrianparr.com
- Twitter: www.twitter.com/adrianparr
- CodePen: www.codepen.io/adrianparr
- LinkedIn: www.linkedin.com/in/adrianparr

Pramod S has more than 8 years of experience in the field of graphics programming using OpenGL and WebGL. He has worked on a few game titles for PC, console, and mobile platforms.

He is currently working as a technical leader in one of the Fortune 100 companies in the area of 3D visualization.

> I appreciate our predecessors who have worked intensively to make graphics and the 3D library what they are today.

Sarath Saleem is a JavaScript developer with a strong background in web application development. With years of experience from various organizations in the IT industry, he has gained immense expertise in creating large-scale web tools, performance optimization, and JavaScript architecture.

At present, he is working for a web hosting company in Dubai besides pursuing his master's in software engineering from BITS, Dubai. During his free time, he polishes his passion for blending technology and the arts to enable creative growth. He is passionate about interactive data visualization, web 2D/3D graphics, and theoretical physics. He maintains `http://graphoverflow.com`, a collection of visualizations; you can connect with him on Twitter at `@sarathsaleem`.

Cesar Torres is a computer science PhD student at the University of California Berkeley. His research projects explore digital fabrication technologies as exciting, critical new media. Using frameworks such as Three.js, he builds computational design tools that aim to expand aesthetics and design practices as a vehicle for more engaging STEM education.

www.PacktPub.com

Support files, eBooks, discount offers, and more

For support files and downloads related to your book, please visit www.PacktPub.com.

Did you know that Packt offers eBook versions of every book published, with PDF and ePub files available? You can upgrade to the eBook version at www.PacktPub.com and as a print book customer, you are entitled to a discount on the eBook copy. Get in touch with us at service@packtpub.com for more details.

At www.PacktPub.com, you can also read a collection of free technical articles, sign up for a range of free newsletters and receive exclusive discounts and offers on Packt books and eBooks.

https://www2.packtpub.com/books/subscription/packtlib

Do you need instant solutions to your IT questions? PacktLib is Packt's online digital book library. Here, you can search, access, and read Packt's entire library of books.

Why subscribe?

- Fully searchable across every book published by Packt
- Copy and paste, print, and bookmark content
- On demand and accessible via a web browser

Free access for Packt account holders

If you have an account with Packt at www.PacktPub.com, you can use this to access PacktLib today and view 9 entirely free books. Simply use your login credentials for immediate access.

Table of Contents

Preface

In the last couple of years, browsers have become more powerful and are capable platforms to deliver complex applications and graphics. Most of these, though, are standard 2D graphics. Most modern browsers have adopted WebGL, which allows you to not just create 2D applications and graphics in the browser, but also create beautiful and good performing 3D applications using the capabilities of the GPU.

Programming WebGL directly, however, is very complex. You need to know the inner details of WebGL and learn a complex shader language to get the most out of WebGL. Three.js provides a very easy to use JavaScript API around the features of WebGL, so you can create beautiful 3D graphics without having to learn WebGL in detail.

Three.js provides a large number of features and APIs that you can use to create 3D scenes directly in your browser. In this book, you'll learn all the different APIs Three. js has to offer through lots of interactive examples and code samples.

What this book covers

Chapter 1, Creating Your First 3D Scene with Three.js, covers the basic steps you need to take to get started with Three.js. You'll immediately create your first Three.js scene and at the end of this chapter, you'll be able to create and animate your first 3D scene directly in your browser.

Chapter 2, Basic Components That Make Up a Three.js Scene, explains the basic components that you need to understand when working with Three.js. You'll learn about lights, meshes, geometries, materials, and cameras. In this chapter, you will also get an overview of the different lights Three.js provides and the cameras you can use in your scene.

Chapter 3, *Working with the Different Light Sources Available in Three.js*, dives deeper into the different lights you can use in your scene. It shows examples and explains how to use a spotlight, a direction light, an ambient light, a point light, a hemisphere light, and an area light. Additionally, it also shows how to apply a lens flare effect on your light source.

Chapter 4, *Working with Three.js Materials*, talks about the materials available in Three.js that you can use on your meshes. It shows all the properties you can set to configure the materials for your specific use and provides interactive examples to experiment with the materials that are available in Three.js.

Chapter 5, *Learning to Work with Geometries*, is the first of two chapters that explores all the geometries that are provided by Three.js. In this chapter, you'll learn how to create and configure geometries in Three.js and can experiment using the provided interactive examples with geometries (such as plane, circle, shape, cube, sphere, cylinder, torus, torusknot, and polyhedron).

Chapter 6, *Advanced Geometries and Binary Operations*, continues where *Chapter 5*, *Learning to Work with Geometries*, left off. It shows you how to configure and use the more advanced geometries provided by Three.js such as convex and lathe. In this chapter, you'll also learn how to extrude 3D geometries from 2D shapes, and how you can create new geometries by combining geometries using binary operations.

Chapter 7, *Particles, Sprites, and the Point Cloud*, explains how to use a point cloud from Three.js. You'll learn how to create a point cloud from scratch and from existing geometries. In this chapter, you'll also learn how you can modify the way the individual points look through the use of sprites and point cloud materials.

Chapter 8, *Creating and Loading Advanced Meshes and Geometries*, shows you how to import meshes and geometries from external sources. You'll learn how to use Three. js' internal JSON format to save geometries and scenes. This chapter also explains how to load models from formats such as OBJ, DAE, STL, CTM, PLY, and many more.

Chapter 9, *Animations and Moving the Camera*, explores the various types of animations you can use to make your scene come alive. You'll learn how to use the Tween.js library together with Three.js, and how to work with animation models based on morphs and skeletons.

Chapter 10, *Loading and Working with Textures*, expands on *Chapter 4*, *Working with Three.js Materials*, where materials were introduced. In this chapter, we dive into the details of textures. This chapter introduces the various types of textures that are available and how you can control how a texture is applied to your mesh. Additionally, in this chapter, you are shown how you can directly use the output from HTML5 video and canvas elements as input for your textures.

Chapter 11, Custom Shaders and Render Postprocessing, explores how you can use Three. js to apply postprocessing effects to your rendered scene. With postprocessing, you can apply effects such as blur, tiltshift, sepia, and so on, to your rendered scene. Besides this, you'll also learn how to create your own postprocessing effect and create a custom vertex and fragment shader.

Chapter 12, Adding Physics and Sounds to Your Scene, explains how you can add physics to your Three.js scene. With physics, you can detect collisions between objects, make them respond to gravity, and apply friction. This chapter shows you how to do this with the Physijs JavaScript library. Additionally, this chapter also shows you how you can add positional audio to a Three.js scene.

What you need for this book

All you need for this book is a text editor (for example, Sublime) to play around with the examples and a modern web browser to access these examples. Some examples require a local web server, but you'll learn in *Chapter 1, Creating Your First 3D Scene with Three.js*, how to set up a very lightweight web server to use with the examples in this book.

Who this book is for

This book is great for everyone who already knows JavaScript and wants to start with creating 3D graphics that run in any browser. You don't need to know anything about advanced math or WebGL; all that is needed is a general knowledge of JavaScript and HTML. The required materials and examples can be freely downloaded, and all tools used in this book are open source. So, if you ever want to learn how to create beautiful, interactive 3D graphics that run in any modern browser, this is the book for you.

Conventions

In this book, you will find a number of text styles that distinguish between different kinds of information. Here are some examples of these styles and an explanation of their meaning.

Code words in text, database table names, folder names, filenames, file extensions, pathnames, dummy URLs, user input, and Twitter handles are shown as follows: "You can see in this code that besides setting the `map` property, we also set the `bumpMap` property to a texture."

A block of code is set as follows:

```
function createMesh(geom, imageFile, bump) {
  var texture = THREE.ImageUtils.loadTexture("../assets/textures/
    general/" + imageFile)
  var mat = new THREE.MeshPhongMaterial();
  mat.map = texture;
  var bump = THREE.ImageUtils.loadTexture("../assets/textures/
    general/" + bump)
  mat.bumpMap = bump;
  mat.bumpScale = 0.2;
  var mesh = new THREE.Mesh(geom, mat);
  return mesh;
}
```

When we wish to draw your attention to a particular part of a code block, the relevant lines or items are set in bold:

```
var effectFilm = new THREE.FilmPass(0.8, 0.325, 256, false);
effectFilm.renderToScreen = true;

var composer4 = new THREE.EffectComposer(webGLRenderer);
composer4.addPass(renderScene);
composer4.addPass(effectFilm);
```

Any command-line input or output is written as follows:

```
# git clone https://github.com/josdirksen/learning-threejs
```

New terms and **important words** are shown in bold. Words that you see on the screen, for example, in menus or dialog boxes, appear in the text like this: "You can do this by going to **Preferences | Advanced** and checking **Show develop menu in menu bar**."

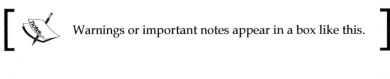

Warnings or important notes appear in a box like this.

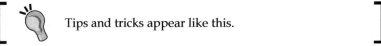

Tips and tricks appear like this.

Reader feedback

Feedback from our readers is always welcome. Let us know what you think about this book—what you liked or disliked. Reader feedback is important for us as it helps us develop titles that you will really get the most out of.

To send us general feedback, simply e-mail feedback@packtpub.com, and mention the book's title in the subject of your message.

If there is a topic that you have expertise in and you are interested in either writing or contributing to a book, see our author guide at www.packtpub.com/authors.

Customer support

Now that you are the proud owner of a Packt book, we have a number of things to help you to get the most from your purchase.

Downloading the example code

You can download the example code files from your account at http://www.packtpub.com for all the Packt Publishing books you have purchased. If you purchased this book elsewhere, you can visit http://www.packtpub.com/support and register to have the files e-mailed directly to you.

Downloading the color images of this book

We also provide you with a PDF file that has color images of the screenshots/diagrams used in this book. The color images will help you better understand the changes in the output. You can download this file from https://www.packtpub.com/sites/default/files/downloads/2215OS_Graphics.pdf.

Errata

Although we have taken every care to ensure the accuracy of our content, mistakes do happen. If you find a mistake in one of our books—maybe a mistake in the text or the code—we would be grateful if you could report this to us. By doing so, you can save other readers from frustration and help us improve subsequent versions of this book. If you find any errata, please report them by visiting http://www.packtpub.com/submit-errata, selecting your book, clicking on the **Errata Submission Form** link, and entering the details of your errata. Once your errata are verified, your submission will be accepted and the errata will be uploaded to our website or added to any list of existing errata under the Errata section of that title.

To view the previously submitted errata, go to https://www.packtpub.com/books/content/support and enter the name of the book in the search field. The required information will appear under the **Errata** section.

Piracy

Piracy of copyrighted material on the Internet is an ongoing problem across all media. At Packt, we take the protection of our copyright and licenses very seriously. If you come across any illegal copies of our works in any form on the Internet, please provide us with the location address or website name immediately so that we can pursue a remedy.

Please contact us at copyright@packtpub.com with a link to the suspected pirated material.

We appreciate your help in protecting our authors and our ability to bring you valuable content.

Questions

If you have a problem with any aspect of this book, you can contact us at questions@packtpub.com, and we will do our best to address the problem.

1

Creating Your First 3D Scene with Three.js

Modern browsers are slowly getting more powerful features that can be accessed directly from JavaScript. You can easily add video and audio with the new HTML5 tags and create interactive components through the use of the HTML5 canvas. Together with HTML5, modern browsers also started supporting WebGL. With WebGL, you can directly make use of the processing resources of your graphics card and create high-performance 2D and 3D computer graphics. Programming WebGL directly from JavaScript to create and animate 3D scenes is a very complex and error-prone process. Three.js is a library that makes this a lot easier. The following list shows some of the things that Three.js makes easy:

- Creating simple and complex 3D geometries
- Animating and moving objects through a 3D scene
- Applying textures and materials to your objects
- Making use of different light sources to illuminate the scene
- Loading objects from 3D-modeling software
- Adding advanced postprocessing effects to your 3D scene
- Working with your own custom shaders
- Creating point clouds

With a couple of lines of JavaScript, you can create anything, from simple 3D models to photorealistic real-time scenes, as shown in the following screenshot (see it yourself by opening http://www.vill.ee/eye/ in your browser):

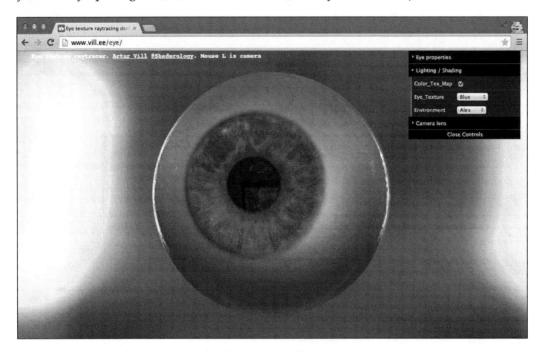

In this chapter, we'll directly dive into Three.js and create a couple of examples that show you how Three.js works, and which you can use to play around with. We won't dive into all the technical details yet; that's something you'll learn in the following chapters. In this chapter, we'll cover the following points:

- Tools required to work with Three.js
- Downloading the source code and examples used in this book
- Creating your first Three.js scene
- Improving the first scene with materials, lights, and animations
- Introducing a couple of helper libraries for statistics and controlling the scene

We'll start this book with a short introduction to Three.js and then quickly move on to the first examples and code samples. Before we get started, let's quickly look at the most important browsers out there and their support for WebGL.

At the time of writing this, WebGL works with the following desktop browsers:

Browser	Support
Mozilla Firefox	This browser has supported WebGL since version 4.0.
Google Chrome	This browser has supported WebGL since version 9.
Safari	Safari Version 5.1 and newer installed on Mac OS X Mountain Lion, Lion, or Snow Leopard supports WebGL. Make sure you enable WebGL in Safari. You can do this by going to **Preferences | Advanced** and checking **Show develop menu in menu bar**. After that, go to **Develop | Enable WebGL**.
Opera	This browser has supported WebGL since version 12.00. You still have to enable this by opening **opera:config** and setting the values of **WebGL** and **Enable Hardware Acceleration** to 1. After that, restart the browser.
Internet Explorer	Internet Explorer was for a long time the only major player that didn't support WebGL. Starting with IE11, Microsoft has added WebGL support.

Basically, Three.js runs on any of the modern browsers except older versions of IE. So, if you want to use an older version of IE, you've got to take an additional step. For IE 10 and older, there is the *iewebgl* plugin, which you can get from `https://github.com/iewebgl/iewebgl`. This plugin is installed inside IE 10 and older versions and enables WebGL support for those browsers.

It is also possible to run Three.js on mobile devices; the support for WebGL and the performance you'll get will vary, but both are quickly improving:

Device	Support
Android	The native browser for Android doesn't have WebGL support and is generally also lacking in support for modern HTML5 features. If you want to use WebGL on Android, you can use the latest Chrome, Firefox, or Opera mobile versions.
IOS	With IOS 8, there is also support for WebGL on IOS devices. IOS Safari version 8 has great WebGL support.
Windows mobile	Windows mobile supports WebGL since version 8.1.

With WebGL, you can create interactive 3D visualizations that run very well on desktops and on mobile devices.

 In this book, we'll focus mostly on the WebGL-based renderer provided by Three.js. There is, however, also a CSS 3D-based renderer, which provides an easy API to create CSS 3D-based 3D scenes. A big advantage of using a CSS 3D-based approach is that this standard is supported on almost all mobile and desktop browsers and allows you to render HTML elements in a 3D space. We'll show how to use the CSS 3D browser in *Chapter 7, Particles, Sprites, and the Point Cloud.*

In this first chapter, you'll directly create your first 3D scene and will be able to run this in any of the previously mentioned browsers. We won't introduce too many complex Three.js features yet, but at the end of this chapter, you'll have created the Three.js scene you can see in the following screenshot:

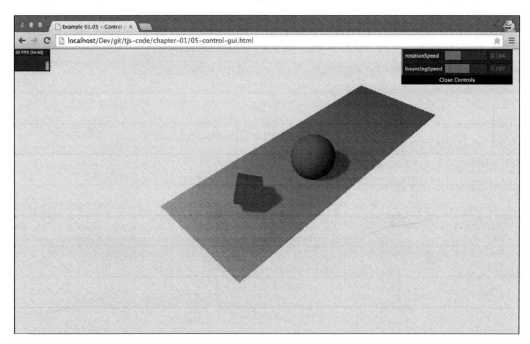

For this first scene, you'll learn about the basics of Three.js and also create your first animation. Before you start your work on this example, in the next couple of sections, we'll first look at the tools you need to easily work with Three.js and how you can download the examples shown in this book.

Requirements to use Three.js

Three.js is a JavaScript library, so all you need to create Three.js WebGL applications is a text editor and one of the supported browsers to render the results. I would like to recommend two JavaScript editors, which I've started using exclusively over the last couple of years:

- **WebStorm**: This editor from the JetBrains guides has great support for editing JavaScript. It supports code completion, automatic deployment, and JavaScript debugging directly from the editor. Besides this, WebStorm has excellent GitHub (and other version control systems) support. You can download a trial edition from `http://www.jetbrains.com/webstorm/`.

- **Notepad++**: Notepad++ is a general-purpose editor that supports code highlighting for a wide range of programming languages. It can easily lay out and format JavaScript. Note that Notepad++ is only for Windows. You can download Notepad++ from `http://notepad-plus-plus.org/`.

- **Sublime Text Editor**: Sublime is a great editor that has a very good support to edit JavaScript. Besides this, it provides many very helpful selections (such as multiple-line select) and edit options that, once you get used to them, provide a really good JavaScript-editing environment. Sublime can also be tested for free and can be downloaded from `http://www.sublimetext.com/`.

Even if you don't use any of these editors, there are a lot of editors available, open source and commercial, which you can use to edit JavaScript and create your Three.js projects. An interesting project you might want to look at is `http://c9.io`. This is a cloud-based JavaScript editor that can be connected to a GitHub account. This way, you can directly access all the source code and examples from this book and experiment with them.

> Besides these text-based editors that you can use to edit and experiment with the sources from this book, Three.js currently also provides an online editor itself.
>
> With this editor, which you can find at `http://threejs.org/editor/`, you can create Three.js scenes using a graphical approach.

I mentioned that most modern web browsers support WebGL and can be used to run Three.js examples. I usually run my code in Chrome. The reason is that most often, Chrome has the best support and performance for WebGL and it has a really great JavaScript debugger. With this debugger, which is shown in the following screenshot, you can quickly pinpoint problems, for instance, using breakpoints and console output. This is exemplified in the following screenshot. Throughout this book, I'll give you pointers on debugger usage and other debugging tips and tricks.

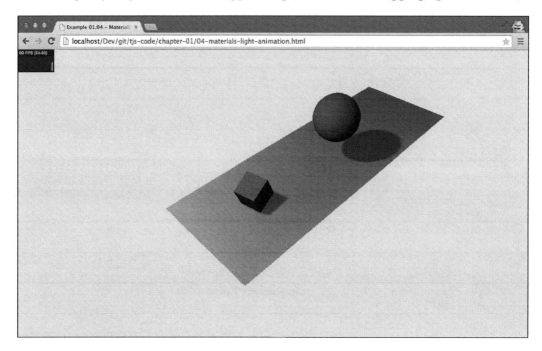

That's enough for an introduction to Three.js for now; let's get the source code and start with the first scene.

Getting the source code

All the code for this book can be accessed from GitHub (https://github.com/). GitHub is an online Git-based repository that you can use to store, access, and version source code. There are a couple of ways that you can get the sources for yourself:

- Clone the Git repository
- Download and extract the archive

In the following two paragraphs, we'll explore these options in a bit more detail.

Using Git to clone the repository

Git is an open source distributed version control system that I used to create and version all the examples in this book. For this, I used GitHub, a free, online Git repository. You can browse this repository by `https://github.com/josdirksen/learning-threejs`.

To get all the examples, you can clone this repository using the `git` command-line tool. To do this, you first need to download a Git client for your operating system. For most modern operating systems, a client can be downloaded from `http://git-scm.com`, or you can use the one provided by GitHub itself (for Mac and Windows). After installing Git, you can use this to get a *clone* of this book's repository. Open a command prompt and go to the directory where you want to download the sources. In that directory, run the following command:

```
# git clone https://github.com/josdirksen/learning-threejs
```

This will start downloading all the examples, as shown in the following screenshot:

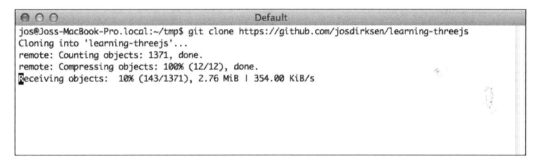

The `learning-three.js` directory will now contain all the examples that are used throughout this book.

Downloading and extracting the archive

If you don't want to use Git to download the sources directly from GitHub, you can also download an archive. Open `https://github.com/josdirksen/learning-threejs` in a browser and click on the **Download ZIP** button on the right-hand side, as follows:

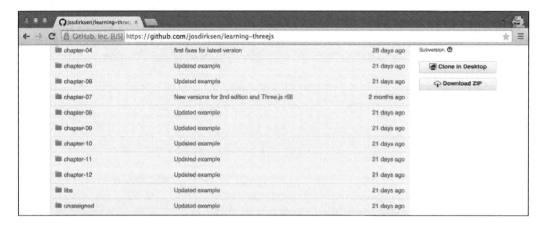

Extract this to a directory of your choice, and you'll have all the examples available.

Testing the examples

Now that you've downloaded or cloned the source code, let's do a quick check to see whether everything is working and make you familiar with the directory structure. The code and examples are organized per chapter. There are two different ways of viewing examples. You can either open the extracted or cloned folder in a browser directly and look at and run a specific example, or you can install a local web server. This first approach will work for most of the basic examples, but when we start loading external resources, such as models or texture images, just opening the HTML file isn't enough. In this case, we need a local web server to make sure the external resources are loaded correctly. In the following section, we explain a couple of different ways you can set up a simple local web server for testing. If you can't set up a local web server but use Chrome or Firefox, we also provide an explanation on how to disable certain security features so that you can even test without a local web server.

Setting up a local web server is very easy depending on what you've already got installed. In here, we list a couple of examples on how to do this. There are many different ways to do this depending on what you've already got installed on your system.

Python-based web servers should work on most Unix/Mac systems

Most Unix/Linux/Mac systems already have Python installed. On those systems, you can very easily start a local web server:

```
> python -m SimpleHTTPServer
Serving HTTP on 0.0.0.0 port 8000 ...
```

Do this in the directory where you checked out / downloaded the source code.

Npm-based web server if you've worked with Node.js

If you've already done some work with Node.js, there is good chance you've got npm installed. With npm, you have two simple options to set up a quick local web server for testing. The first options uses the `http-server` module, as follows:

```
> npm install -g http-server
> http-server
Starting up http-server, serving ./ on port: 8080
Hit CTRL-C to stop the server
```

Alternatively, you can also use the `simple-http-server` option, as follows:

```
> npm install -g simple-http-server
> nserver
simple-http-server Now Serving: /Users/jos/git/Physijs at http://
localhost:8000/
```

A disadvantage of this second approach, however, is that it doesn't automatically show directory listings, whereas the first approach does.

Portable version Mongoose for Mac and/or Windows

If you haven't got Python or npm installed, there is a simple, portable web server, named Mongoose, that you can use. First, download the binaries for your specific platform from `https://code.google.com/p/mongoose/downloads/list`. If you are using Windows, copy it to the directory containing the examples and double-click on the executable to start a web browser serving the directory it is started in.

For other operating systems, you must also copy the executable to the target directory, but instead of double-clicking on the executable, you have to launch it from the command line. In both cases, a local web server will be started on port 8080. The following screenshot encapsulates the discussion in this paragraph:

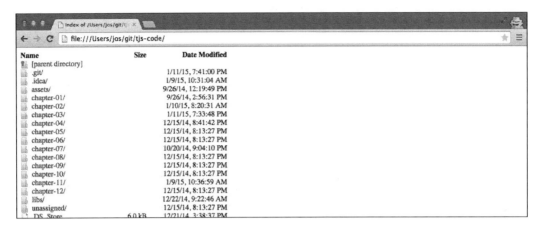

By just clicking on a chapter, we can show and access all the examples for that specific chapter. If I discuss an example in this book, I'll refer to the specific name and folder so that you can directly test and play around with the code.

Disabling security exceptions in Firefox and Chrome

If you use Chrome to run the examples, there is a way to disable some security settings so that you can use Chrome to view the examples without requiring a web server. To do this, you have to start Chrome in the following way:

- For Windows, you call the following:

```
chrome.exe --disable-web-security
```

- On Linux, do the following:

```
google-chrome --disable-web-security
```

- And on Mac OS, you disable the settings by starting Chrome like this:

```
open -a Google\ Chrome --args --disable-web-security
```

When you start Chrome this way, you can access all the examples directly from the local filesystem.

For Firefox users, we need to take a couple of different steps. Open Firefox and, in the URL bar, type about:config. This is what you'll see:

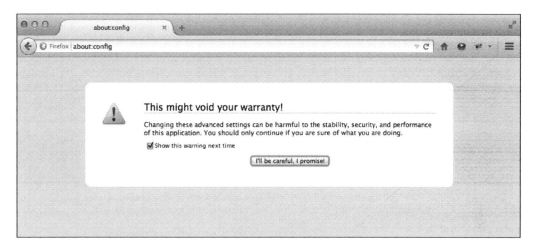

On this screen, click on the **I'll be careful, I promise!** button. This will show you all the available properties you can use to fine-tune Firefox. In the search box on this screen, type in security.fileuri.strict_origin_policy and change its value to false just as we did in the following screenshot:

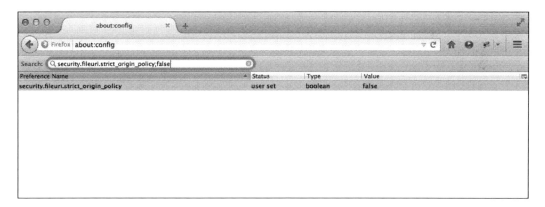

At this point, you can also use Firefox to directly run the examples provided in this book.

Now that you've either got a web server installed, or disabled the necessary security settings, it is time to start creating our first Three.js scene.

Creating the HTML skeleton

The first thing we need to do is create an empty skeleton page that we can use as the base for all our examples, as follows:

```html
<!DOCTYPE html>

<html>

  <head>
    <title>Example 01.01 - Basic skeleton</title>
    <script src="../libs/three.js"></script>
    <style>
      body{
        /* set margin to 0 and overflow to hidden, to use the
          complete page */

        margin: 0;
        overflow: hidden;
      }
    </style>
  </head>
  <body>

    <!-- Div which will hold the Output -->
    <div id="WebGL-output">
    </div>

    <!-- Javascript code that runs our Three.js examples -->
    <script>

      // once everything is loaded, we run our Three.js stuff.
      function init() {
        // here we'll put the Three.js stuff
      };
      window.onload = init;

    </script>
  </body>
</html>
```

As you can see from this listing, the skeleton is a very simple HTML page, with only
a couple of elements. In the <head> element, we load the external JavaScript libraries
that we'll use for the examples. For all the examples, we'll at least need to load the
Three.js library, three.js. In the <head> element, we also add a couple of lines of
CSS. These style elements remove any scrollbars when we create a full-page Three.
js scene. In the <body> element of this page, you can see a single <div> element.
When we write our Three.js code, we'll point the output of the Three.js renderer to
that element. At the bottom of this page, you can already see a bit of JavaScript. By
assigning the init function to the window.onload property, we make sure that this
function gets called when the HTML document has finished loading. In the init
function, we'll insert all the Three.js specific JavaScript.

Three.js comes in two versions:

- **Three.min.js**: This is the library you'd normally use when deploying Three.
  js sites on the Internet. This is a minified version of Three.js, created using
  UglifyJS, which is a quarter size of the normal Three.js library. All the
  examples and code used in this book are based on Three.js **r69**, which was
  released in October 2014.

- **Three.js**: This is the normal Three.js library. We use this library in our
  examples since it makes debugging much easier when you can read and
  understand the Three.js source code.

If we view this page in our browser, the results aren't very shocking. As you'd
expect, all you see is an empty page.

In the next section, you'll learn how to add the first couple of 3D objects and render
those to the <div> element we defined in our HTML skeleton.

Rendering and viewing a 3D object

In this step, you'll create your first scene and add a couple of objects and a camera. Our first example will contain the following objects:

Object	Description
Plane	This is a two-dimensional rectangle that serves as our ground area. In the second screenshot of this chapter, this is rendered as the gray rectangle in the middle of the scene.
Cube	This is a three-dimensional cube, which we'll render in red.
Sphere	This is a three-dimensional sphere, which we'll render in blue.
Camera	The camera determines what you'll see in the output.
Axes	These are the x, y, and z axes. This is a helpful debugging tool to see where the objects are rendered in 3D space. The x axis is colored red, the y axis is colored green, and the z axis is colored blue.

I'll first show you how this looks in code (the source with comments can be found in chapter-01/02-first-scene.html), and then I'll explain what's happening:

```
function init() {
  var scene = new THREE.Scene();
  var camera = new THREE.PerspectiveCamera(45, window.innerWidth
    /window.innerHeight, 0.1, 1000);

  var renderer = new THREE.WebGLRenderer();
  renderer.setClearColorHex(0xEEEEEE);
  renderer.setSize(window.innerWidth, window.innerHeight);

  var axes = new THREE.AxisHelper(20);
  scene.add(axes);

  var planeGeometry = new THREE.PlaneGeometry(60, 20, 1, 1);
  var planeMaterial = new THREE.MeshBasicMaterial({color:
    0xcccccc});
  var plane = new THREE.Mesh(planeGeometry, planeMaterial);

  plane.rotation.x = -0.5 * Math.PI;
  plane.position.x = 15;
  plane.position.y = 0;
  plane.position.z = 0
```

```
scene.add(plane);

var cubeGeometry = new THREE.BoxGeometry(4, 4, 4)
var cubeMaterial = new THREE.MeshBasicMaterial({color: 0xff0000,
  wireframe: true});
var cube = new THREE.Mesh(cubeGeometry, cubeMaterial);

cube.position.x = -4;
cube.position.y = 3;
cube.position.z = 0;

scene.add(cube);

var sphereGeometry = new THREE.SphereGeometry(4, 20, 20);
var sphereMaterial = new THREE.MeshBasicMaterial({color:
  0x7777ff, wireframe: true});
var sphere = new THREE.Mesh(sphereGeometry, sphereMaterial);

sphere.position.x = 20;
sphere.position.y = 4;
sphere.position.z = 2;

scene.add(sphere);

camera.position.x = -30;
camera.position.y = 40;
camera.position.z = 30;
camera.lookAt(scene.position);

document.getElementById("WebGL-output")
  .appendChild(renderer.domElement);
  renderer.render(scene, camera);
};
window.onload = init;
```

If we open this example in the browser, we see something that resembles what we're aiming at (see the screenshot at the beginning of this chapter), but it is still a long way off, as follows:

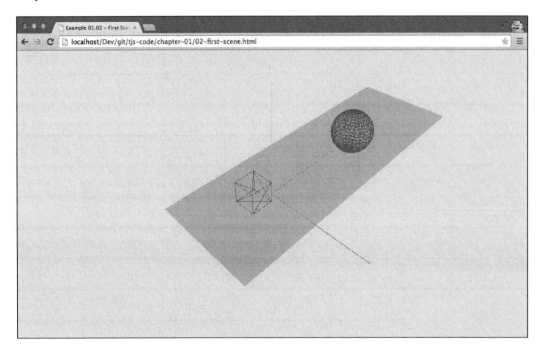

Before we start making this more beautiful, I'll first walk you through the code a step at a time so that you understand what the code does:

```
var scene = new THREE.Scene();
var camera = new THREE.PerspectiveCamera(45, window.innerWidth /
    window.innerHeight, 0.1, 1000);
var renderer = new THREE.WebGLRenderer();
renderer.setClearColorHex()
renderer.setClearColor(new THREE.Color(0xEEEEEE));
renderer.setSize(window.innerWidth, window.innerHeight);
```

At the top of the example, we define scene, camera, and renderer. The scene object is a container that is used to store and keep track of all the objects we want to render and all the lights we want to use. Without a THREE.Scene object, Three.js isn't able to render anything. More information on the THREE.Scene object can be found in the next chapter. The sphere and the cube we want to render will be added to scene later on in the example. In this first fragment, we also create a camera object. The camera object defines what we'll see when we render a scene. In *Chapter 2, Basic Components That Make Up a Three.js Scene*, you learn more about the arguments you can pass in to the camera object. Next we define renderer. The renderer object is responsible for calculating what the scene object will look like in the browser based on the camera object's angle. We create WebGLRenderer that uses your graphics card to render the scene in this example.

If you look through the source code and the documentation of Three.js (which you can find at http://threejs.org/), you'll notice that there are different renderers available besides the WebGL-based one. There is a canvas-based renderer and even an SVG-based one. Even though they work and can render simple scenes, I wouldn't recommend using them. They're very CPU-intensive and lack features such as good material support and shadows.

Here, we set the background color of renderer to almost white (new THREE.Color(0XEEEEEE)) with the setClearColor function and tell renderer how large the scene needs to be rendered using the setSize function.

So far, we've got a basic empty scene, a renderer, and a camera. There is, however, nothing yet to render. The following code adds the helper axes and the plane:

```
var axes = new THREE.AxisHelper( 20 );
scene.add(axes);

var planeGeometry = new THREE.PlaneGeometry(60,20);
var planeMaterial = new THREE.MeshBasicMaterial({color:
  0xcccccc});
var plane = new THREE.Mesh(planeGeometry,planeMaterial);

plane.rotation.x=-0.5*Math.PI;
plane.position.x=15
plane.position.y=0
plane.position.z=0
scene.add(plane);
```

As you can see, we create an `axes` object and use the `scene.add` function to add these axes to our scene. Next, we create the plane. This is done in two steps. First, we define what the plane looks like using the new `THREE.PlaneGeometry(60,20)` code. In this case, it has a width of `60` and a height of `20`. We also need to tell Three.js what this plane looks like (for example, its color and its transparency). In Three.js, we do this by creating a material object. For this first example, we'll create a basic material (`THREE.MeshBasicMaterial`) with the color `0xcccccc`. Next, we combine these two into a `Mesh` object with the name `plane`. Before we add `plane` to the scene, we need to put it in the correct position; we do this by first rotating it 90 degrees around the x axis, and next, we define its position in the scene using the position properties. If you're already interested in the details of this, look at the `06-mesh-properties.html` example from the code folder of *Chapter 2, Basic Components That Make Up a Three.js Scene*, which shows and explains rotation and positioning. We then need to do is add `plane` to `scene`, just like we did with `axes`.

The `cube` and `sphere` objects are added in the same manner, but with the `wireframe` property set to `true`, which tells Three.js to render a wireframe and not a solid object. Now, let's move on to the final part of this example:

```
camera.position.x = -30;
camera.position.y = 40;
camera.position.z = 30;
camera.lookAt(scene.position);

document.getElementById("WebGL-output")
  .appendChild(renderer.domElement);
  renderer.render(scene, camera);
```

At this point, all the elements we want to render are added to the scene at the correct positions. I've already mentioned that the camera defines what will be rendered. In this piece of code, we position the camera using the x, y, and z position attributes to hover above our scene. To make sure the camera is looking at our objects, we use the `lookAt` function to point it at the center of our scene, which is located at position (0, 0, 0) by default. All that is left to do is append the output from the renderer to the `<div>` element of our HTML skeleton. We use standard JavaScript to select the correct output element and append it to our `div` element with the `appendChild` function. Finally, we tell `renderer` to render `scene` using the `camera` object provided.

In the next couple of sections, we'll make this scene more pretty by adding lights, shadows, more materials, and even animations.

Adding materials, lights, and shadows

Adding new materials and lights in Three.js is very simple and is done in pretty much the same way as we explained in the previous section. We start by adding a light source to the scene (for the complete source look at `03-materials-light.html`), as follows:

```
var spotLight = new THREE.SpotLight( 0xffffff );
spotLight.position.set( -40, 60, -10 );
scene.add( spotLight );
```

`THREE.SpotLight` illuminates our scene from its position (`spotLight.position.set( -40, 60, -10 )`). If we render the scene this time, however, you won't see any difference from the previous one. The reason is that different materials respond differently to light. The basic material we used in the previous example (`THREE.MeshBasicMaterial`) doesn't do anything with the light sources in the scene. They just render the object in the specified color. So, we have to change the materials for `plane`, `sphere`, and `cube` to the following:

```
var planeGeometry = new THREE.PlaneGeometry(60,20);
var planeMaterial = new THREE.MeshLambertMaterial({color:
  0xffffff});
var plane = new THREE.Mesh(planeGeometry, planeMaterial);
...
var cubeGeometry = new THREE.BoxGeometry(4,4,4);
var cubeMaterial = new THREE.MeshLambertMaterial({color:
  0xff0000});
var cube = new THREE.Mesh(cubeGeometry, cubeMaterial);
...
var sphereGeometry = new THREE.SphereGeometry(4,20,20);
var sphereMaterial = new THREE.MeshLambertMaterial({color:
  0x7777ff});
var sphere = new THREE.Mesh(sphereGeometry, sphereMaterial);
```

In this piece of code, we changed the materials for our objects to `MeshLambertMaterial`. This material and `MeshPhongMaterial` are the materials Three.js provides that take light sources into account when rendered.

The result, shown in the following screenshot, however, still isn't what we're looking for:

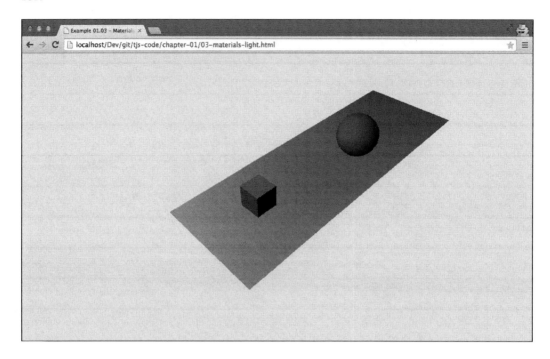

We're getting there, and cube and sphere are looking a lot better. What is still missing, though, are the shadows.

Rendering shadows takes a lot of computing power, and for that reason, shadows are disabled by default in Three.js. Enabling them, though, is very easy. For shadows, we have to change the source in a couple of places, as follows:

```
renderer.setClearColor(new THREE.Color(0xEEEEEE, 1.0));
renderer.setSize(window.innerWidth, window.innerHeight);
renderer.shadowMapEnabled = true;
```

The first change we need to make is tell `renderer` that we want shadows. You do this by setting the `shadowMapEnabled` property to `true`. If you look at the result from this change, you won't notice anything different yet. That is because we need to explicitly define which objects cast shadows and which objects receive shadows. In our example, we want the sphere and the cube to cast shadows on the ground plane. You do this by setting the corresponding properties on those objects:

```
plane.receiveShadow = true;
...
cube.castShadow = true;
...
sphere.castShadow = true;
```

Now, there is just one more thing to do to get the shadows. We need to define which light sources in our scene will cause shadows. Not all the lights can cast shadows, and you'll learn more about that in the next chapter, but THREE.SpotLight, which we used in this example, can. We only need to set the correct property, as shown in the following line of code, and the shadows will finally be rendered:

```
spotLight.castShadow = true;
```

And with this, we get a scene complete with shadows from our light source, as follows:

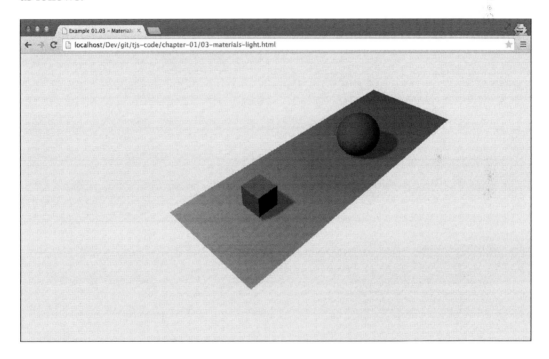

The last feature that we'll add to this first scene is some simple animation. In *Chapter 9, Animations and Moving the Camera*, you'll learn more advanced animation options.

Expanding your first scene with animations

If we want to animate the scene, the first thing that we need to do is find some way to re-render the scene at a specific interval. Before HTML5 and the related JavaScript APIs came along, the way to do this was using the `setInterval(function, interval)` function. With `setInterval`, we could specify a function that, for instance, would be called every 100 milliseconds. The problem with this function is that it doesn't take into account what is happening in the browser. If you were browsing another tab, this function would still be fired every couple of milliseconds. Besides that, `setInterval` isn't synchronized with the redrawing of the screen. This can lead to higher CPU usage and bad performance.

Introducing requestAnimationFrame

Modern browsers luckily have a solution for that with the `requestAnimationFrame` function. With `requestAnimationFrame`, you can specify a function that is called at an interval defined by the browser. You do any drawing you need to do in the supplied function, and the browser will make sure it is painted as smoothly and efficiently as possible. Using this is really simple (the complete source can be found in the `04-materials-light-animation.html` file), you just create a function that handles the rendering:

```
function renderScene() {
  requestAnimationFrame(renderScene);
  renderer.render(scene, camera);
}
```

In this `renderScene` function, we call `requestAnimationFrame` again, to keep the animation going. The only thing we need to change in the code is that instead of calling `renderer.render` after we've created the complete scene, we call the `renderScene` function once to kick off the animation:

```
...
document.getElementById("WebGL-output")
  .appendChild(renderer.domElement);
renderScene();
```

If you run this, you won't see any changes yet compared to the previous example because we haven't animated anything yet. Before we add the animation, though, I want to introduce a small helper library that gives us information about the frame rate the animation is running at. This library, from the same author as Three.js, renders a small graph that shows us the frames per second we're getting for this animation.

To add these statistics, we first need to include the library in the `<head>` element of the HTML, as follows:

```
<script src="../libs/stats.js"></script>
```

And we add a `<div>` element that will be used as output for the statistics graph, as follows:

```
<div id="Stats-output"></div>
```

The only thing left to do is initialize the statistics and add them to this `<div>` element, as follows:

```
function initStats() {
  var stats = new Stats();
  stats.setMode(0);
  stats.domElement.style.position = 'absolute';
  stats.domElement.style.left = '0px';
  stats.domElement.style.top = '0px';
  document.getElementById("Stats-output")
    .appendChild( stats.domElement );
      return stats;
}
```

This function initializes the statistics. The interesting part is the `setMode` function. If we set it to `0`, we'll measure frames per second (fps), and if we set this to `1`, we can measure rendering time. For this example, we're interested in fps, so `0` it is. At the beginning of our `init()` function, we'll call this function, and we've got `stats` enabled, as follows:

```
function init(){

  var stats = initStats();
  ...
}
```

The only thing left to do is tell the `stats` object when we're in a new rendering cycle. We do this by adding a call to the `stats.update` function in our `renderScene` function, as follows.

```
function renderScene() {
  stats.update();
  ...
  requestAnimationFrame(renderScene);
  renderer.render(scene, camera);
}
```

If you run the code with these additions, you'll see the statistics in the upper-left corner, as shown in the following screenshot:

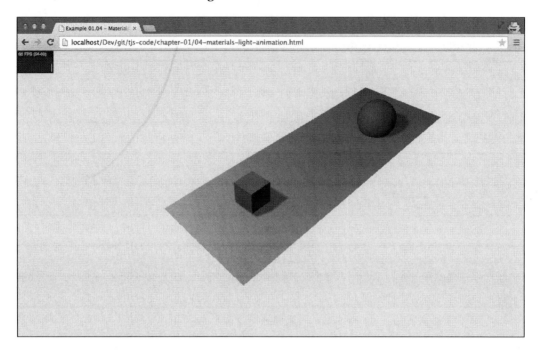

Animating the cube

With `requestAnimationFrame` and the statistics configured, we've got a place to put our animation code. In this section, we'll expand the `renderScene` function with code that will rotate our red cube around all of its axes. Let's start by showing you the code:

```
function renderScene() {
  ...
  cube.rotation.x += 0.02;
  cube.rotation.y += 0.02;
  cube.rotation.z += 0.02;
  ...
  requestAnimationFrame(renderScene);
  renderer.render(scene, camera);
}
```

That looks simple, right? What we do is that we increase the `rotation` property of each of the axes with 0.02 every time the `renderScene` function is called, which shows up as a cube smoothly rotating around all if its axes. Bouncing the blue ball isn't much harder.

Bouncing the ball

To bounce the ball, we once again add a couple of lines of code to our `renderScene` function, as follows:

```
var step=0;
function renderScene() {
  ...
  step+=0.04;
  sphere.position.x = 20+( 10*(Math.cos(step)));
  sphere.position.y = 2 +( 10*Math.abs(Math.sin(step)));
  ...
  requestAnimationFrame(renderScene);
  renderer.render(scene, camera);
}
```

With the cube, we changed the `rotation` property; for the sphere, we're going to change its `position` property in the scene. We want the sphere to bounce from one point in the scene to another with a nice, smooth curve. This is shown in the following figure:

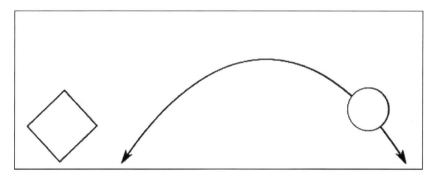

For this, we need to change its position on the *x* axis and its position on the *y* axis. The `Math.cos` and `Math.sin` functions help us in creating a smooth trajectory using the step variable. I won't go into the details of how this works here. For now, all you need to know is that `step+=0.04` defines the speed of the bouncing sphere. In *Chapter 8, Creating and Loading Advanced Meshes and Geometries*, we'll look in much more detail how these functions can be used for animation, and I'll explain everything. Here's how the ball looks in the middle of a bounce:

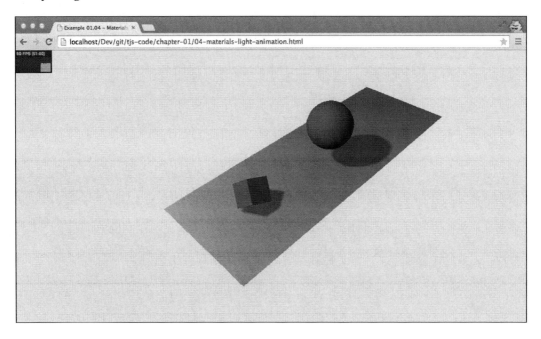

Before wrapping up this chapter, I want to add one more element to our basic scene. When working with 3D scenes, animations, colors, and properties like that, it often requires a bit of experimenting to get the correct color or speed. It would be very easy if you could just have a simple GUI that allows you to change these kinds of properties on the fly. Luckily, there is!

Using dat.GUI to make experimenting easier

A couple of employees from Google created a library called **dat.GUI** (you can find the documentation online at `http://code.google.com/p/dat-gui/`), which allows you to very easily create a simple user interface component that can change variables in your code. In this last part of this chapter, we'll use dat.GUI to add a user interface to our example that allows us to change the following:

- Control the speed of the bouncing ball
- Control the rotation of the cube

Just like we had to do for the statistics, we first add this library to the `<head>` element of our HTML page, as follows:

```
<script src="../libs/dat.gui.js"></script>
```

The next thing we need to configure is a JavaScript object that will hold the properties we want to change using dat.GUI. In the main part of our JavaScript code, we add the following JavaScript object, as follows:

```
var controls = new function() {
  this.rotationSpeed = 0.02;
  this.bouncingSpeed = 0.03;
}
```

In this JavaScript object, we define two properties—`this.rotationSpeed` and `this.bouncingSpeed`—and their default values. Next, we pass this object into a new dat. GUI object and define the range for these two properties, as follows:

```
var gui = new dat.GUI();
gui.add(controls, 'rotationSpeed', 0, 0.5);
gui.add(controls, 'bouncingSpeed', 0, 0.5);
```

The `rotationSpeed` and `bouncingSpeed` properties are both set to a range of `0` to `0.5`. All we need to do now is make sure that in our `renderScene` loop, we reference these two properties directly so that when we make changes through the dat.GUI user interface, it immediately affects the rotation and bounce speed of our objects, as follows:

```
function renderScene() {
  ...
  cube.rotation.x += controls.rotationSpeed;
  cube.rotation.y += controls.rotationSpeed;
  cube.rotation.z += controls.rotationSpeed;
  step += controls.bouncingSpeed;
  sphere.position.x = 20 +(10 * (Math.cos(step)));
  sphere.position.y = 2 +(10 * Math.abs(Math.sin(step)));
  ...
}
```

Now, when you run this example (`05-control-gui.html`), you'll see a simple user interface that you can use to control the bouncing and rotation speeds. A screenshot of the bouncing ball and the rotating cube is shown here:

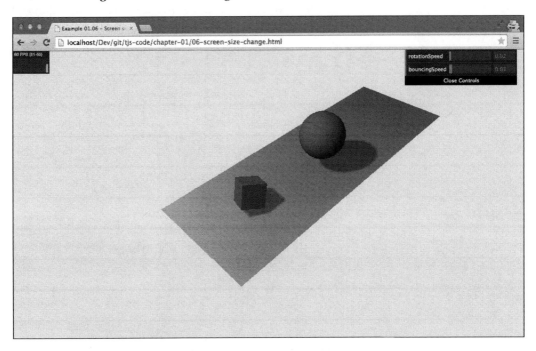

If you've looked at the examples in your browser, you might have noticed that when you change the size of your browser, the scene doesn't automatically scale. In the next section, we'll add this as a final feature for this chapter.

Automatically resize the output when browser size changes

Changing the camera when the browser is resized can be done pretty simply. The first thing we need to do is register an event listener like this:

```
window.addEventListener('resize', onResize, false);
```

Now, whenever the browser window is resized, the `onResize` function, which we'll specify next, is called. In this `onResize` function, we need to update the camera and renderer, as follows:

```
function onResize() {
    camera.aspect = window.innerWidth / window.innerHeight;
```

```
    camera.updateProjectionMatrix();
    renderer.setSize(window.innerWidth, window.innerHeight);
}
```

For the camera, we need to update the `aspect` property, which holds the aspect ratio of the screen, and for the `renderer`, we need to change its size. The final step is to move the variable definitions for `camera`, `renderer`, and `scene` outside of the `init()` function so that we can access them from different functions (like the `onResize` function), as follows:

```
var camera;
var scene;
var renderer;

function init() {
  ...
  scene = new THREE.Scene();
  camera = new THREE.PerspectiveCamera(45, window.innerWidth /
    window.innerHeight, 0.1, 1000);
  renderer = new THREE.WebGLRenderer();
  ...
}
```

To see this effect in action, open the `06-screen-size-change.html` example and resize your browser window.

Summary

That's it for the first chapter. In this chapter, we showed you how to set up your development environment, how to get the code, and how to get started with the examples provided with this book. You further learned that to render a scene with Three.js, you first have to create a `THREE.Scene` object, add a camera, a light, and the objects that you want to render. We also showed you how you can expand this basic scene by adding shadows and animations. Lastly, we added a couple of helper libraries. We used dat.GUI, which allows you to quickly create control user interfaces, and we added `stats.js`, which provided feedback on the frame rate at which your scene is rendered.

In the next chapter, we'll expand on the example we created here. You'll learn more about the most important building blocks that you can use in Three.js.

2
Basic Components That Make Up a Three.js Scene

In the previous chapter, you learned the basics of Three.js. We showed a couple of examples, and you created your first complete Three.js scene. In this chapter, we'll dive a bit deeper into Three.js and explain the basic components that make up a Three.js scene. In this chapter, you'll explore the following topics:

- The components that are used in a Three.js scene
- What you can do with the THREE.Scene object
- How geometries and meshes are related
- The difference between the orthographic and perspective cameras

We start with looking at how you can create a scene and add objects.

Creating a scene

In the previous chapter, you created THREE.Scene, so you already know the basics of Three.js. We saw that for a scene to show anything, we need three types of components:

Component	Description
Camera	This determines what is rendered on the screen.
Lights	These have an effect on how materials are shown and used when creating shadow effects (discussed in detail in *Chapter 3, Working with the Different Light Sources Available in Three.js*).
Objects	These are the main objects that are rendered from the perspective of the camera: cubes, spheres, and the like.

THREE.Scene serves as the container for all these different objects. This object itself doesn't have that many options and functions.

> THREE.Scene is a structure that is sometimes also called a scene graph. A scene graph is a structure that can hold all necessary information of a graphical scene. In Three.js, this means that THREE.Scene contains all the objects, lights, and other objects necessary for rendering. What is interesting to note is that a scene graph, as the name implies, isn't just an array of objects; a scene graph consists of a set of nodes in a tree structure. Each object you can add to the scene in Three.js, and even THREE.Scene itself, extends from a base object named THREE.Object3D. A THREE.Object3D object can also have its own children, which you can use to create a tree of objects that Three.js will interpret and render.

Basic functionality of a scene

The best way to explore the functionality of a scene is by looking at an example. In the source code for this chapter, you can find the 01-basic-scene.html example. I'll use this example to explain the various functions and options a scene has. When we open this example in the browser, the output will look somewhat like what's shown in the next screenshot:

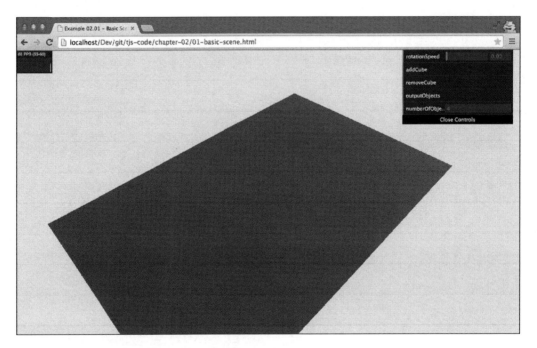

This looks pretty much like the examples we saw in the previous chapter. Even though the scene looks pretty empty, it already contains a couple of objects. Looking at the following source, we can see that we used the `scene.add(object)` function from the `THREE.Scene` object to add `THREE.Mesh` (the ground plane you see), `THREE.SpotLight`, and `THREE.AmbientLight`. The `THREE.Camera` object is added automatically by Three.js when you render the scene, but it is good practice to add it to the scene manually, especially when you're working with multiple cameras. Take a look at the following source code for this scene:

```
var scene = new THREE.Scene();
var camera = new THREE.PerspectiveCamera(45, window.innerWidth
  / window.innerHeight, 0.1, 1000);
scene.add(camera);
...
var planeGeometry = new THREE.PlaneGeometry(60,40,1,1);
var planeMaterial = new THREE.MeshLambertMaterial({color:
  0xffffff});
var plane = new THREE.Mesh(planeGeometry,planeMaterial);
...
scene.add(plane);
var ambientLight = new THREE.AmbientLight(0x0c0c0c);
scene.add(ambientLight);
...
var spotLight = new THREE.SpotLight( 0xffffff );
...
scene.add( spotLight );
```

Before we look deeper into the THREE.Scene object, I'll first explain what you can do in the demo, and after that, we'll look at some code. Open the 01-basic-scene.html example in your browser and look at the controls in the upper-right corner, as you can see in the following screenshot:

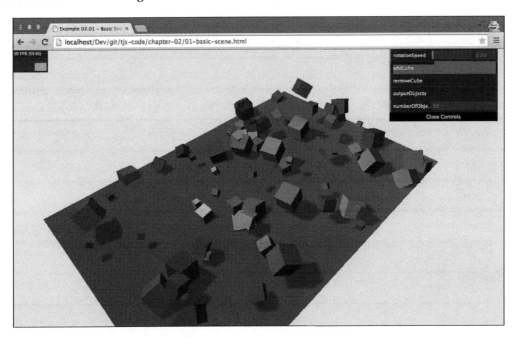

With these controls, you can add a cube to the scene, remove the cube that was last added to the scene, and show all the current objects that the scene contains in the console of your browser. The last entry in the controls section shows the current number of objects in the scene. What you'll probably notice when you start up the scene is that there are already four objects in the scene. These are the ground plane, the ambient light, and the spotlight, as well as the camera we mentioned earlier. We'll look at each of the functions in the control section and start with the easiest one, addCube, as follows:

```
this.addCube = function() {
  var cubeSize = Math.ceil((Math.random() * 3));
  var cubeGeometry = new THREE.BoxGeometry
    (cubeSize,cubeSize,cubeSize);
  var cubeMaterial = new THREE.MeshLambertMaterial({color:
    Math.random() * 0xffffff });
  var cube = new THREE.Mesh(cubeGeometry, cubeMaterial);
  cube.castShadow = true;
  cube.name = "cube-" + scene.children.length;
  cube.position.x=-30 + Math.round(Math.random() *
    planeGeometry.width));
```

```
cube.position.y= Math.round((Math.random() * 5));
cube.position.z=-20 + Math.round((Math.random() *
  planeGeometry.height));

scene.add(cube);
this.numberOfObjects = scene.children.length;
};
```

This piece of code should already be pretty easy to read by now. Not many new concepts are introduced here. When you hit the **addCube** button, a new THREE. BoxGeometry object is created whose width, height, and depth are set to a random value between 1 and 3. Besides a random size, the cube also gets a random color and a random position.

 A new element that we introduce here is that we also give the cube a name using its name attribute. Its name is set to cube-, appended with the number of objects currently in the scene (scene.children. length). A name is very useful for debugging purposes but can also be used to directly access an object from your scene. If you use the THREE. Scene.getObjectByName(name) function, you can directly retrieve a specific object and, for instance, change its location without having to make the JavaScript object a global variable. You might wonder what the last line does. The numberOfObjects variable is used by our control GUI to list the number of objects in the scene. So, whenever we add or remove an object, we set this variable to the updated count.

The next function we can call from the control GUI is removeCube. As the name implies, clicking on the **removeCube** button removes the last added cube from the scene. In code, it looks like this:

```
this.removeCube = function() {
  var allChildren = scene.children;
  var lastObject = allChildren[allChildren.length-1];
  if (lastObject instanceof THREE.Mesh) {
    scene.remove(lastObject);
    this.numberOfObjects = scene.children.length;
  }
}
```

To add an object to the scene, we use the add function. To remove an object from the scene, we use, not very surprisingly, the remove function. Since Three.js stores its children as a list (new ones are added at the end), we can use the children property, which contains an array of all the objects in the scene, from the THREE.Scene object to get the last object that was added. We also need to check whether that object is a THREE.Mesh object to avoid removing the camera and the lights. After we've removed the object, we once again update the GUI property, numberOfObjects, that holds the number of objects in the scene.

The final button on our GUI is labeled **outputObjects**. You probably already clicked on this and nothing seemed to happen. This button prints out all the objects that are currently in our scene to the web browser console, as shown in the following screenshot:

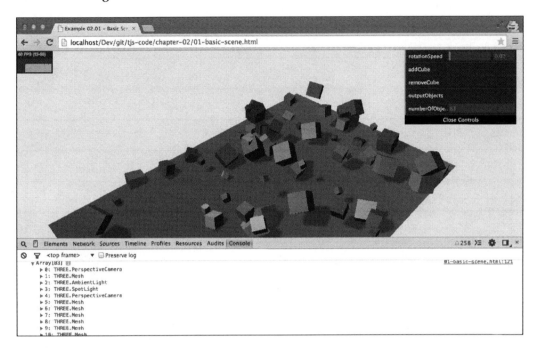

The code to output information to the console log makes use of the built-in console object:

```
this.outputObjects = function() {
  console.log(scene.children);
}
```

This is great for debugging purposes, and especially when you name your objects, it's very useful to find issues and problems with a specific object in your scene. For instance, the properties of cube-17 look like this (if you already know the name beforehand, you could also use console.log(scene.getObjectByName("cube-17") to output only that single object):

```
__webglActive: true
__webglInit: true
_listeners: Object
_modelViewMatrix: THREE.Matrix4
```

```
_normalMatrix: THREE.Matrix3
castShadow: true
children: Array[0]
eulerOrder: (...)
frustumCulled: true
geometry: THREE.BoxGeometryid: 8
material: THREE.MeshLambertMaterial
matrix: THREE.Matrix4
matrixAutoUpdate: true
matrixWorld: THREE.Matrix4
matrixWorld
NeedsUpdate: false
name: "cube-17"
parent: THREE.Scene
position: THREE.Vector3
quaternion: THREE.Quaternion
receiveShadow: false
renderDepth: null
rotation: THREE.Euler
rotationAutoUpdate: true
scale: THREE.Vector3
type: "Mesh"
up: THREE.Vector3
useQuaternion: (...)
userData: Object
uuid: "DCDC0FD2-6968-44FD-8009-20E9747B8A73"
visible: true
```

Until now, we've seen the following scene-related functionality:

- `THREE.Scene.Add`: This adds an object to the scene
- `THREE.Scene.Remove`: This removes an object from the scene
- `THREE.Scene.children`: This gets a list of all the children in the scene
- `THREE.Scene.getObjectByName`: This gets a specific object, by name, from the scene

These are the most important scene-related functions, and most often, you won't need any more than this. There are, however, a couple of helper functions that could come in handy, and I'd like to show them based on the code that handles the cube rotation.

As you saw in the previous chapter, we used a *render loop* to render the scene. Let's look at that loop for this example:

```
function render() {
  stats.update();
  scene.traverse(function(obj) {
    if (obj instanceof THREE.Mesh && obj != plane ) {
      obj.rotation.x+=controls.rotationSpeed;
      obj.rotation.y+=controls.rotationSpeed;
      obj.rotation.z+=controls.rotationSpeed;
    }
  });

  requestAnimationFrame(render);
  renderer.render(scene, camera);
}
```

Here, we see the THREE.Scene.traverse() function being used. We can pass a function to the traverse() function that will be called for each child of the scene. If a child itself has children, remember that a THREE.Scene object can contain a tree of objects. The traverse() function will also be called for all the children of that object. You traverse through the complete scene graph.

We use the render() function to update the rotation for each of the cubes (note that we explicitly ignore the ground plane). We could also have done this by iterating ourselves over the children property array using a for loop since we've only added objects to THREE.Scene and haven't created a nested structure.

Before we dive into the details of THREE.Mesh and THREE.Geometry, I'd like to show two interesting properties that you can set on the THREE.Scene object: fog and overrideMaterial.

Adding fog to the scene

The **fog** property lets you add a fog effect to the complete scene; the farther off an object is, the more it will be hidden from sight, as shown in the following screenshot:

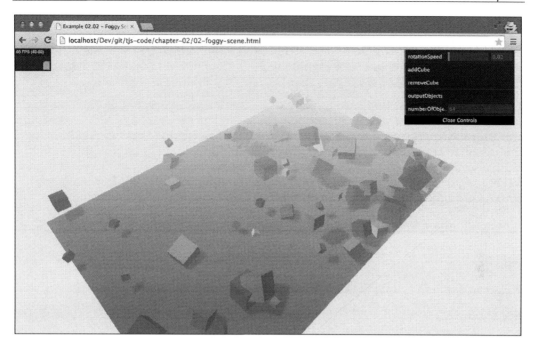

Enabling fog is really easy in Three.js. Just add the following line of code after you've defined your scene:

```
scene.fog=new THREE.Fog( 0xffffff, 0.015, 100 );
```

Here, we define a white fog (0xffffff). The preceding two properties can be used to tune how the mist appears. The 0.015 value sets the near property, and the 100 value sets the far property. With these properties, you can determine where the mist starts and how fast it gets denser. With the THREE.Fog object, the fog increases linearly. There is also a different way to set the mist for the scene; for this, use the following definition:

```
scene.fog=new THREE.FogExp2( 0xffffff, 0.01 );
```

This time, we don't specify near and far, but just the color (0xffffff) and the mist's density (0.01). It's best to experiment a bit with these properties to get the effect you want. Note that with THREE.FogExp2, the fog doesn't increase linearly but grows exponentially denser with the distance.

Using the overrideMaterial property

The last property we discuss for the scene is **overrideMaterial**. When you use this property, all the objects in the scene will use the material that is set to the overrideMaterial property and ignore the material that is set on the object itself.

Use it like this:

```
scene.overrideMaterial = new THREE.MeshLambertMaterial({color:
  0xffffff});
```

Upon using the overrideMaterial property as shown in the preceding code, the scene will be rendered as shown in the following screenshot:

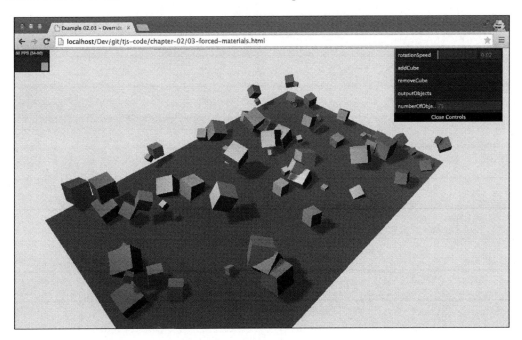

In the preceding figure, you can see that all the cubes are rendered using the same material and the same color. In this example, we used a THREE. MeshLambertMaterial object as the material. With this material type, we can create non-shiny-looking objects that respond to the lights that are present in the scene. In *Chapter 4*, *Working with Three.js Materials*, you'll learn more about this material.

In this section, we looked at the first of the core concepts of Three.js: THREE.Scene. The most important thing to remember about the scene is that it is basically a container for all the objects, lights, and cameras you want to use when rendering. The following table summarizes the most important functions and attributes of the THREE.Scene object:

Function/Property	Description
`add(object)`	This is used to add an object to the scene. You can also use this function, as we'll see later on, to create groups of objects.
`children`	This returns a list of all the objects that have been added to the scene, including the camera and lights.
`getObjectByName(name, recursive)`	When you create an object, you can give it a distinct name. The scene object has a function that you can use to directly return an object with a specific name. If you set the recursive argument to `true`, Three.js will also search through the complete tree of objects to find the object with the specified name.
`remove(object)`	If you have a reference to an object in the scene, you can also remove it from the scene using this function.
`traverse(function)`	The children property returns a list of all the children in the scene. With the traverse function, we can also access these children. With traverse, all the children are passed in to the supplied function one by one.
`fog`	This property allows you to set the fog for the scene. The fog will render a haze that hides faraway objects.
`overrideMaterial`	With this property, you can force all the objects in the scene to use the same material.

In the next section, we'll take a closer look at the objects that you can add to the scene.

Geometries and meshes

In each of the examples until now, you've seen geometries and meshes being used. For instance, to add a sphere to the scene, we did the following:

```
var sphereGeometry = new THREE.SphereGeometry(4,20,20);
var sphereMaterial = new THREE.MeshBasicMaterial({color:
  0x7777ff);
var sphere = new THREE.Mesh(sphereGeometry,sphereMaterial);
```

We defined the shape of the object and its geometry (`THREE.SphereGeometry`), we defined what this object looks like (`THREE.MeshBasicMaterial`) and its material, and we combined these two in a mesh (`THREE.Mesh`) that can be added to a scene. In this section, we'll take a closer look at what a geometry is and what a mesh is. We'll start with the geometry.

The properties and functions of a geometry

Three.js comes with a large set of geometries out of the box that you can use in your 3D scene. Just add a material, create a mesh, and you're pretty much done. The following screenshot, from example `04-geometries`, shows a couple of the standard geometries available in Three.js:

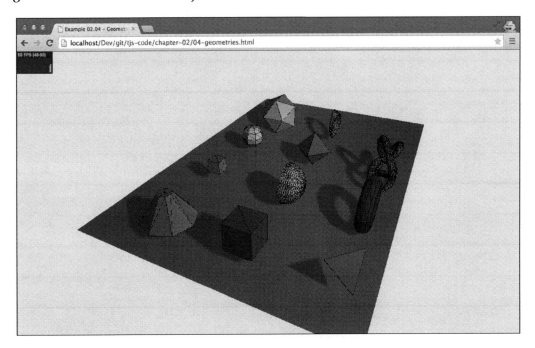

In *Chapter 5, Learning to Work with Geometries,* and *Chapter 6, Advanced Geometries and Binary Operations,* we'll explore all the basic and advanced geometries that Three.js has to offer. For now, we'll look in greater detail at what a geometry actually is.

A geometry in Three.js, and in most other 3D libraries, is basically a collection of points in a 3D space, also called vertices, and a number of faces connecting those points together. Take, for example, a cube:

- A cube has eight corners. Each of these corners can be defined as an *x*, *y*, and *z* coordinate. So each cube has eight points in a 3D space. In Three.js, these points are called vertices, and a single one is called a vertex.

- A cube has six sides, with a vertex at each corner. In Three.js, a face always consists of three vertices that make a triangle. So, in the case of a cube, each side consists of two triangles to make the complete side.

When you use one of the geometries provided by Three.js, you don't have to define all the vertices and faces yourself. For a cube, you only need to define the width, height, and depth. Three.js uses that information and creates a geometry with eight vertices at the correct position and the correct number of faces (12 in the case of a cube). Even though you'd normally use the geometries provided by Three.js or generate them automatically, you can still create geometries completely by hand using vertices and faces. This is shown in the following lines of code:

```
var vertices = [
  new THREE.Vector3(1,3,1),
  new THREE.Vector3(1,3,-1),
  new THREE.Vector3(1,-1,1),
  new THREE.Vector3(1,-1,-1),
  new THREE.Vector3(-1,3,-1),
  new THREE.Vector3(-1,3,1),
  new THREE.Vector3(-1,-1,-1),
  new THREE.Vector3(-1,-1,1)
];

var faces = [
  new THREE.Face3(0,2,1),
  new THREE.Face3(2,3,1),
  new THREE.Face3(4,6,5),
  new THREE.Face3(6,7,5),
  new THREE.Face3(4,5,1),
  new THREE.Face3(5,0,1),
  new THREE.Face3(7,6,2),
  new THREE.Face3(6,3,2),
  new THREE.Face3(5,7,0),
  new THREE.Face3(7,2,0),
  new THREE.Face3(1,3,4),
  new THREE.Face3(3,6,4),
];

var geom = new THREE.Geometry();
geom.vertices = vertices;
geom.faces = faces;
geom.computeFaceNormals();
```

This code shows how to create a simple cube. We define the points that make up this cube in the `vertices` array. These points are connected to create triangular faces and are stored in the `faces` array. For instance, `new THREE.Face3(0,2,1)` creates a triangular face using the points `0`, `2`, and `1` from the `vertices` array. Note that you have to take care of the sequence of the vertices used to create `THREE.Face`. The order in which they are defined determines whether Three.js thinks it is a front-facing face (a face facing the camera) or a back-facing face. If you create the faces, you should use a clockwise sequence for front-facing faces and a counterclockwise sequence if you want to create a back-facing face.

In this example, we used a `THREE.Face3` element to define the six sides of the cube, with two triangles for each face. In previous versions of Three.js, you could also use a quad instead of a triangle. A quad uses four vertices instead of three to define the face. Whether using quads or triangles is better is a heated debate raging in the 3D modeling world. Basically though, using quads is often preferred during modeling since they can be more easily enhanced and smoothed than triangles. For render and game engines though, working with triangles is often easier since every shape can be rendered very efficiently as a triangle.

Using these vertices and faces, we can now create a new instance of `THREE.Geometry` and assign the vertices to the `vertices` attribute and the faces to the `faces` attribute. The last step that we need to take is call `computeFaceNormals()` on the geometry we created. When we call this function, Three.js determines the *normal* vector for each of the faces. This is the information Three.js uses to determine how to color the faces based on the various lights in the scene.

With this geometry, we can now create a mesh just as we saw earlier. I've created an example that you can use to play around with the position of the vertices, and which also shows the individual faces. In example `05-custom-geometry`, you can change the position of all the vertices of a cube and see how the faces react. This is shown in the following screenshot (should the control GUI be in the way, you can hide it by pressing *H*):

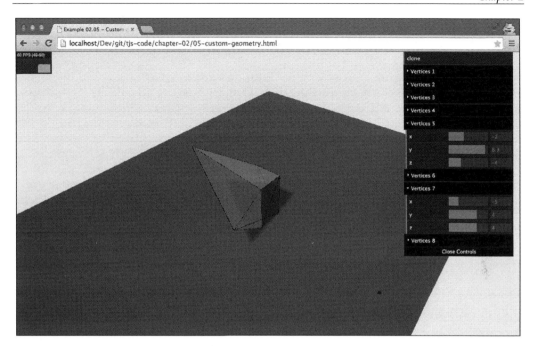

This example, which uses the same setup as all our other examples, has a render loop. Whenever you change one of the properties in the drop-down control box, the cube is rendered based on the changed position of one of the vertices. This isn't something that works out of the box. For performance reasons, Three.js assumes that the geometry of a mesh won't change during its lifetime. For most geometries and use cases, this is a very valid assumption. To get our example to work, however, we need to make sure the following is added to the code in the render loop:

```
mesh.children.forEach(function(e) {
    e.geometry.vertices=vertices;
    e.geometry.verticesNeedUpdate=true;
    e.geometry.computeFaceNormals();
});
```

In the first line, we point the vertices of the mesh you see on screen to an array of updated vertices. We don't need to reconfigure the faces since they are still connected to the same points as they were before. After we've set the updated vertices, we need to tell the geometry that the vertices need to be updated. We do this by setting the `verticesNeedUpdate` property of the geometry to `true`. Finally, we do a recalculation of the faces to update the complete model using the `computeFaceNormals` function.

The last geometry functionality we'll look at is the `clone()` function. We mentioned that the geometry defines the form and shape of an object, and combined with a material, we create an object that can be added to the scene to be rendered by Three. js. With the `clone()` function, as the name implies, we can make a copy of the geometry, and for instance, use it to create a different mesh with a different material. In the same example, `05-custom-geometry`, you can see a **clone** button at the top of the control GUI, as can be seen in the following screenshot:

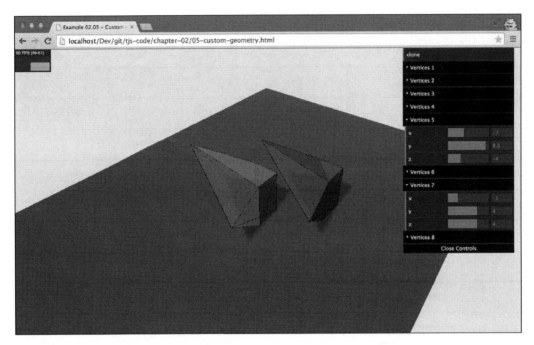

If you click on this button, a clone (a copy) will be made of the geometry as it currently is, a new object is created with a different material, and it is added to the scene. The code for this is rather simple but is made a bit more complex because of the materials I used. Let's take a step back and first look at how the green material for the cube was created, as shown in the following code:

```
var materials = [
  new THREE.MeshLambertMaterial( { opacity:0.6, color: 0x44ff44,
    transparent:true } ),
  new THREE.MeshBasicMaterial( { color: 0x000000, wireframe: true
    } )
];
```

As you can see, I didn't use a single material, but I used an array of two materials. The reason is that besides showing a transparent green cube, I also wanted to show you the wireframe since that shows up very clearly where the vertices and faces are located.

Three.js, of course, supports using multiple materials when creating a mesh. You can use the `SceneUtils.createMultiMaterialObject` function for this, as shown in the following code:

```
var mesh = THREE.SceneUtils.createMultiMaterialObject( geom,
    materials);
```

What Three.js does in this function is that it doesn't create one `THREE.Mesh` object, but it creates one for each material you specified and puts these meshes in a group (a `THREE.Object3D` object). This group can be used in the same manner as you've used the scene object. You can add meshes, get objects by name, and so on. For instance, to make sure all the children of the group cast shadows, you do the following:

```
mesh.children.forEach(function(e) {e.castShadow=true});
```

Now, let's get back to the `clone()` function we were discussing:

```
this.clone = function() {

  var clonedGeom = mesh.children[0].geometry.clone();
  var materials = [
    new THREE.MeshLambertMaterial( { opacity:0.6, color: 0xff44ff,
      transparent:true } ),
    new THREE.MeshBasicMaterial({ color: 0x000000, wireframe: true
      } )
  ];

  var mesh2 = THREE.SceneUtils.createMultiMaterialObject
    (clonedGeom, materials);
  mesh2.children.forEach(function(e) {e.castShadow=true});
  mesh2.translateX(5);
  mesh2.translateZ(5);
  mesh2.name="clone";
  scene.remove(scene.getObjectByName("clone"));
  scene.add(mesh2);
}
```

This piece of JavaScript is called when the **clone** button is clicked on. Here, we clone the geometry of the first child of our cube. Remember, the mesh variable contains two children; it contains two meshes, one for each material we specified. Based on this cloned geometry, we create a new mesh, aptly named mesh2. We move this new mesh using translate functions (more on this in *Chapter 5, Learning to Work with Geometries*), remove the previous clone (if present), and add the clone to the scene.

In the previous section, we used createMultiMaterialObject from the THREE.SceneUtils object to add a wireframe to the geometry we created. Three.js also provides an alternative way of adding a wireframe using THREE.WireFrameHelper. To use this helper, first instantiate the helper like this:

var helper = new THREE.WireframeHelper(mesh, 0x000000);

You provide the mesh you want to show the wireframe for and the color of the wireframe. Three.js will now create a helper object that you can add to the scene, scene.add(helper). Since this helper internally is just a THREE.Line object, you can style how the wireframe appears. For instance, to set the width of the wireframe lines, use helper.material. linewidth = 2;.

That's enough on geometries for now.

Functions and attributes for meshes

We've already learned that to create a mesh, we need a geometry and one or more materials. Once we have a mesh, we add it to the scene and it's rendered. There are a couple of properties that you can use to change where and how this mesh appears on the scene. In this first example, we'll look at the following set of properties and functions:

Function/Property	Description
position	This determines the position of this object relative to the position of its parent. Most often, the parent of an object is a THREE.Scene object or a THREE.Object3D object.
rotation	With this property, you can set the rotation of an object around any of its axes. Three.js also provides specific functions for rotations around an axis: rotateX(), rotateY(), and rotateZ().
scale	This property allows you to scale the object around its *x, y,* and *z* axes.
translateX(amount)	This property moves the object the specified amount over the *x* axis.

Function/Property	Description
`translateY(amount)`	This property moves the object the specified amount over the *y* axis.
`translateZ(amount)`	This property moves the object the specified amount over the *z* axis. For the translate functions, you could also use the `translateOnAxis(axis, distance)` function, which allows you to translate the mesh a distance along a specific axis.
`visible`	If you set this property to `false`, `THREE.Mesh` won't be rendered by Three.js.

As always, we have an example ready for you that will allow you to play around with these properties. If you open up `06-mesh-properties.html` in your browser, you get a drop-down menu where you can alter all these properties and directly see the result, as shown in the following screenshot:

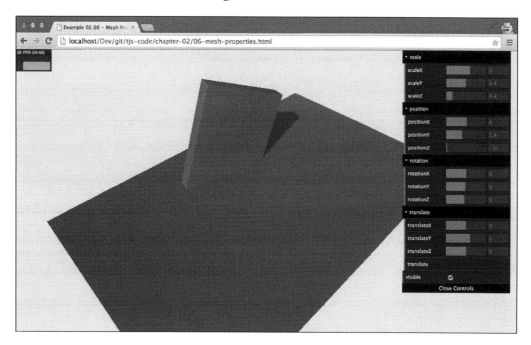

Let me walk you through them, and I'll start with the position property. We've already seen this property a couple of times, so let's quickly address this. With this property, you set the *x*, *y*, and *z* coordinates of the object. This position is relative to its parent object, which is normally the scene you add the object to, but could also be a THREE. Object3D object or another THREE.Mesh object. We'll get back to this in *Chapter 5, Learning to Work with Geometries*, when we look at grouping objects. We can set an object's position property in three different ways. We can set each coordinate directly:

```
cube.position.x=10;
cube.position.y=3;
cube.position.z=1;
```

However, we can also set all of them at once, as follows:

```
cube.position.set(10,3,1);
```

There is also a third option. The position property is a THREE.Vector3 object. That means, we can also do the following to set this object:

```
cube.postion=new THREE.Vector3(10,3,1)
```

I want to make a quick sidestep before looking at the other properties of this mesh. I mentioned that this position is set relative to the position of its parent. In the previous section on THREE.Geometry, we used THREE.SceneUtils. createMultiMaterialObject to create a multi-material object. I explained that this doesn't really return a single mesh but a group that contains a mesh based on the same geometry for each material; in our case, it's a group that contains two meshes. If we change the position of one of these meshes that is created, you can clearly see that it really is two distinct THREE.Mesh objects. However, if we now move the group around, the offset will remain the same, as shown in the following screenshot. In *Chapter 5, Learning to Work with Geometries*, we look deeper into parent-child relations and how grouping affects transformation, such as scaling, rotation, and translation.

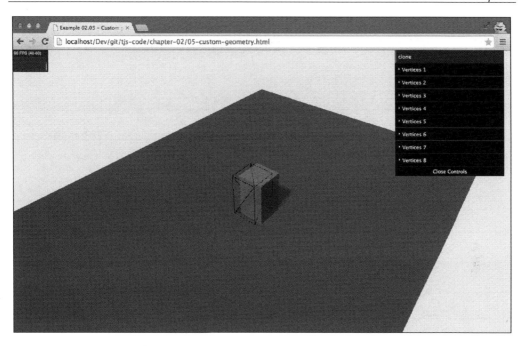

OK, next on the list is the `rotation` property. You've already seen this property being used a couple of times in this chapter and the previous chapter. With this property, you set the rotation of the object around one of its axes. You can set this value in the same manner as we did the position. A complete rotation, as you might remember from math class, is $2 \times \pi$. You can configure this in Three.js in a couple of different ways:

```
cube.rotation.x = 0.5*Math.PI;
cube.rotation.set(0.5*Math.PI, 0, 0);
cube.rotation = new THREE.Vector3(0.5*Math.PI,0,0);
```

If you want to use degrees (from 0 to 360) instead, we'll have to convert those to radians. This can be easily done like this:

```
Var degrees = 45;
Var inRadians = degrees * (Math.PI / 180);
```

You can play around with this property using the `06-mesh-properties.html` example.

The next property on our list is one we haven't talked about: `scale`. The name pretty much sums up what you can do with this property. You can scale the object along a specific axis. If you set the scale to values smaller than one, the object will shrink, as shown in the following screenshot:

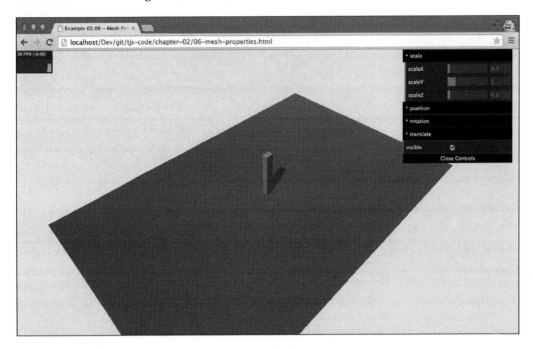

When you use values larger than one, the object will become larger, as shown in the following screenshot:

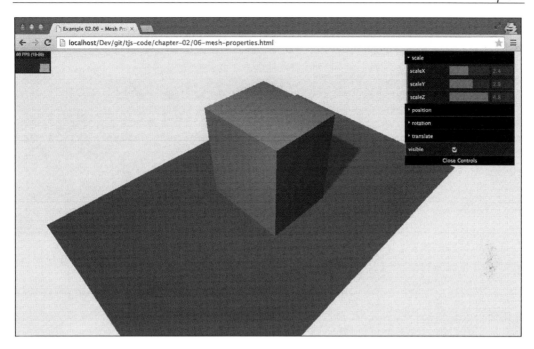

The next part of the mesh that we'll look at in this chapter is the **translate** functionality. With translate, you can also change the position of an object, but instead of defining the absolute position where you want the object to be, you define where the object should move to, relative to its current position. For instance, we have a sphere that is added to a scene, and its position has been set to (1,2,3). Next, we translate the object along its *x* axis: translateX(4). Its position will now be (5,2,3). If we want to restore the object to its original position, we do this: translateX(-4). In the 06-mesh-properties.html example, there is a menu tab called **translate**. From there, you can experiment with this functionality. Just set the translate values for *x*, *y*, and *z* and hit the **translate** button. You'll see the object being moved to a new position based on these three values.

The last property you can use from the menu in the top-right corner is the **visible** property. If you click on the **visible** menu item, you'll see that the cube becomes invisible, as follows:

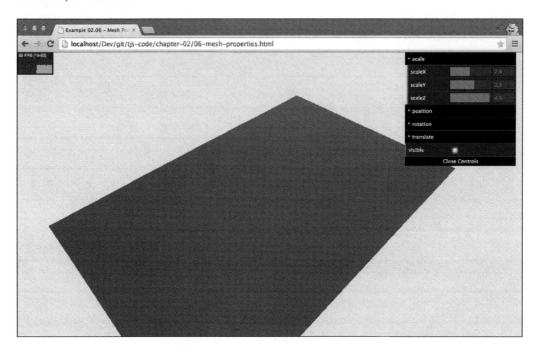

When you click on it another time, the cube becomes visible again. For more information on meshes, geometries, and what you can do with these objects, look at *Chapter 5, Learning to Work with Geometries*, and *Chapter 7, Particles, Sprites, and the Point Cloud*.

Different cameras for different uses

There are two different camera types in Three.js: the orthographic camera and the perspective camera. In *Chapter 3, Working with the Different Light Sources Available in Thrree.js*, we'll have a much more detailed look at how to work with these cameras, so in this chapter, I'll stick to the basics. The best way to explain the differences between these cameras is by looking at a couple of examples.

Orthographic camera versus perspective camera

In the examples for this chapter, you can find a demo called `07-both-cameras.html`. When you open this example, you'll see something like this:

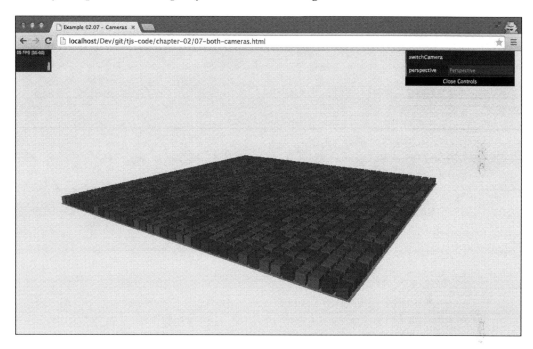

This is called a perspective view and is the most natural view. As you can see from this figure, the farther away the cubes are from the camera, the smaller they are rendered.

If we change the camera to the other type supported by Three.js, the orthographic camera, you'll see the following view of the same scene:

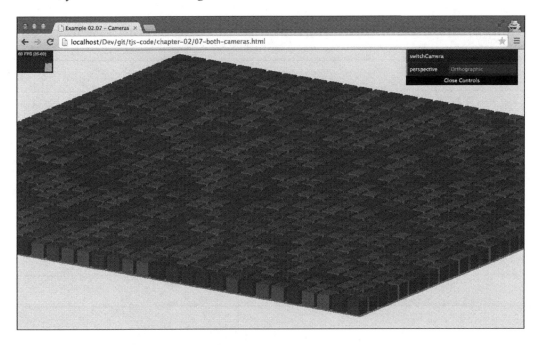

With the orthographic camera, all the cubes are rendered the same size; the distance between an object and the camera doesn't matter. This is often used in 2D games such as *SimCity 4* and old versions of *Civilization*.

In our examples, we'll use the perspective camera the most since it best resembles the real world. Switching cameras is really very easy. The following piece of code is called whenever you hit the switch camera button on the 07-both-cameras example:

```
this.switchCamera = function() {
  if (camera instanceof THREE.PerspectiveCamera) {
    camera = new THREE.OrthographicCamera( window.innerWidth / -
      16, window.innerWidth / 16, window.innerHeight / 16,
      window.innerHeight / - 16, -200, 500 );
    camera.position.x = 120;
    camera.position.y = 60;
    camera.position.z = 180;
    camera.lookAt(scene.position);
    this.perspective = "Orthographic";
  } else {
    camera = new THREE.PerspectiveCamera(45, window.innerWidth /
      window.innerHeight, 0.1, 1000);

    camera.position.x = 120;
    camera.position.y = 60;
    camera.position.z = 180;

    camera.lookAt(scene.position);
    this.perspective = "Perspective";
  }
};
```

In this table, you can see that there is a difference in the way we create the camera. Let's look at THREE.PerspectiveCamera first. This camera takes the following arguments:

Argument	Description
fov	**FOV** stands for **Field Of View**. This is the part of the scene that can be seen from the position of the camera. Humans, for instance, have an almost 180-degree FOV, while some birds might even have a complete 360-degree FOV. But since a normal computer screen doesn't completely fill our vision, normally a smaller value is chosen. Most often, for games, a FOV between 60 and 90 degrees is chosen. *Good default: 50*

Argument	Description
aspect	This is the aspect ratio between the horizontal and vertical sizes of the area where we're to render the output. In our case, since we use the entire window, we just use that ratio. The aspect ratio determines the difference between the horizontal FOV and the vertical FOV, as you can see in the following image. *Good default: window.innerWidth / window.innerHeight*
near	The `near` property defines from how close to the camera Three.js should render the scene. Normally, we set this to a very small value to directly render everything from the position of the camera. *Good default: 0.1*
far	The `far` property defines how far the camera can see from the position of the camera. If we set this too low, a part of our scene might not be rendered, and if we set it too high, in some cases, it might affect the rendering performance. *Good default: 1000*
zoom	The `zoom` property allows you to zoom in and out of the scene. When you use a number lower than 1, you zoom out of the scene, and if you use a number higher than 1, you zoom in. Note that if you specify a negative value, the scene will be rendered upside down. *Good default value: 1*

The following image gives a good overview of how these properties work together to determine what you see:

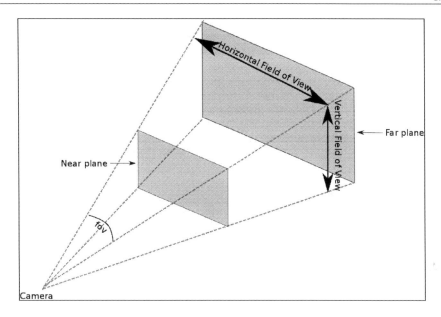

The `fov` property of the camera determines the horizontal FOV. Based on the `aspect` property, the vertical FOV is determined. The `near` property is used to determine the position of the near plane, and the `far` property determines the position of the far plane. The area between the near plane and the far plane will be rendered.

To configure the orthographic camera, we need to use other properties. The orthographic projection isn't interested either in the aspect ratio to use or with what FOV we look at the scene since all the objects are rendered at the same size. What you do when you define an orthographic camera is define the cuboid area that needs to be rendered. The properties for the orthographic camera reflect this, as follows:

Argument	Description
left	This is described in the Three.js documentation as *Camera frustum left plane*. You should see this as what is the left-hand border of what will be rendered. If you set this value to `-100`, you won't see any objects that are farther to the left-hand side.
right	The `right` property works in a way similar to the `left` property, but this time, to the other side of the screen. Anything farther to the right won't be rendered.
top	This is the top position to be rendered.
bottom	This is the bottom position to be rendered.

Argument	Description
near	From this point, based on the position of the camera, the scene will be rendered.
far	To this point, based on the position of the camera, the scene will be rendered.
zoom	This allows you to zoom in and out of the scene. When you use a number lower than 1, you'll zoom out of the scene; if you use a number higher than 1, you'll zoom in. Note that if you specify a negative value, the scene will be rendered upside down. The default value is 1.

All these properties can be summarized in the following figure:

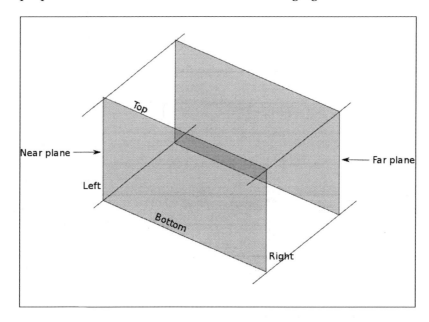

Looking at specific points

Until now, you've seen how to create a camera and what the various arguments mean. In the previous chapter, you also saw that you need to position your camera somewhere in the scene, and that the view from that camera is rendered. Normally, the camera is pointed to the center of the scene: position (0,0,0). We can, however, easily change what the camera is looking at, as follows:

```
camera.lookAt(new THREE.Vector3(x,y,z));
```

I've added an example where the camera moves, and the point it is looking at is marked with a red dot, as follows:

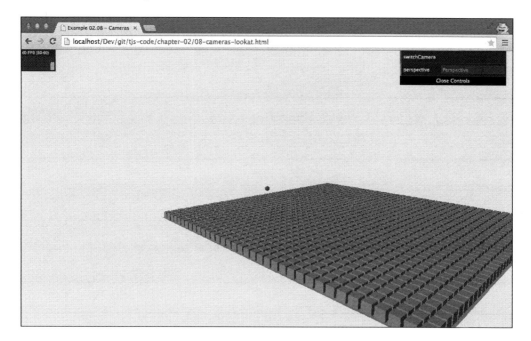

If you open the `08-cameras-lookat` example, you'll see the scene moving from left to right. The scene isn't really moving. The camera is looking at different points (see the red dot in the center), which gives the effect that the scene is moving from left to right. In this example, you can also switch cameras to the orthographic one. There, you see that changing the point the camera looks at has pretty much the same effect as with `THREE.PerspectiveCamera`. The interesting part to notice, though, is that with `THREE.OrthographicCamera`, you can clearly see that the sizes of all the cubes stay the same regardless of where the camera is looking.

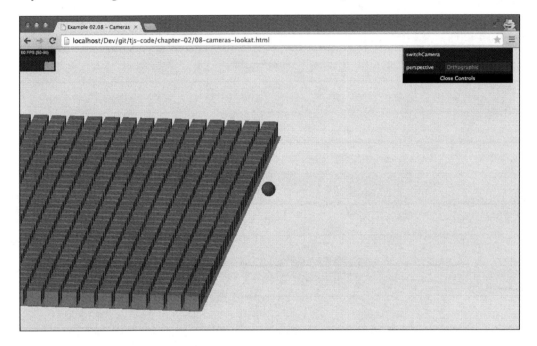

 When you use the `lookAt` function, you point the camera at a specific position. You can also use this to make the camera follow an object around the scene. Since every `THREE.Mesh` object has a position that is a `THREE.Vector3` object, you can use the `lookAt` function to point to a specific mesh in the scene. All you need to do is this: `camera.lookAt(mesh.position)`. If you call this in the render loop, you'll make the camera follow an object as it moves through the scene.

Summary

We discussed a lot of items in this second introduction chapter. We showed all the functions and properties of THREE.Scene and explained how you can use these properties to configure your main scene. We also showed you how you can create geometries. You can either create them from scratch using a THREE.Geometry object or use any of the built-in geometries Three.js provides. Finally, we showed you how you can configure the two cameras Three.js provides. THREE.PerspectiveCamera renders a scene using a real-world perspective, and THREE.OrthographicCamera provides a fake 3D effect also often seen in games. We've also introduced how geometries work in Three.js. You can now easily create your own geometries.

In the next chapter, we'll look at the various light sources that are available in Three.js. You'll learn how the various light sources behave, how to create and configure them, and how they affect specific materials.

3

Working with the Different Light Sources Available in Three.js

In the first chapter, you learned about the basics of Three.js, and in the previous chapter, we looked a bit deeper at the most important parts of the scene: the geometries, meshes, and cameras. You might have noticed that we skipped lights in that chapter even though they make up an important part of every Three.js scene. Without lights, we won't see anything rendered. Since Three.js contains a large number of lights, each of which has a specific use, we'll use this whole chapter to explain the various details of the lights and prepare you for the next chapter on material usage.

 WebGL itself doesn't have inherent support for lighting. Without Three.js, you would have to write specific WebGL shader programs to simulate these kinds of lights. A good introduction on simulating lighting in WebGL from scratch can be found at `https://developer.mozilla.org/en-US/docs/Web/WebGL/Lighting_in_WebGL`.

In this chapter, you'll learn about the following subjects:

- The light sources that are available in Three.js
- When a specific light source should be used
- How you can tune and configure the behavior of all these light sources
- As a bonus, we'll also quickly look at how you can create lens flares

As with all the chapters, we have a lot of examples that you can use to experiment with the lights' behavior. The examples shown in this chapter can be found in the `chapter-03` folder of the supplied sources.

Different kinds of lighting provided by Three.js

There are a number of different lights available in Three.js that all have specific behavior and usages. In this chapter, we'll discuss the following set of lights:

Name	Description
THREE.AmbientLight	This is a basic light, the color of which is added to the current color of the objects in the scene.
THREE.PointLight	This is a single point in space from which light spreads in all directions. This light can't be used to create shadows.
THREE.SpotLight	This light source has a cone-like effect like that of a desk lamp, a spot in the ceiling, or a torch. This light can cast shadows.
THREE.DirectionalLight	This is also called infinite light. The light rays from this light can be seen as parallel, like, for instance, the light from the sun. This light can also be used to create shadows.
THREE.HemisphereLight	This is a special light and can be used to create more natural-looking outdoors lighting by simulating a reflective surface and a faintly illuminating sky. This light also doesn't provide any shadow-related functionality.
THREE.AreaLight	With this light source, instead of a single point in space, you can specify an area from which light emanates. THREE.AreaLight doesn't cast any shadows.
THREE.LensFlare	This is not a light source, but with THREE.LensFlare, you can add a lens flare effect to the lights in your scene.

This chapter is divided into two main parts. First, we'll look at the basic lights: THREE.AmbientLight, THREE.PointLight, THREE.SpotLight, and THREE.DirectionalLight. All these lights extend the base THREE.Light object, which provides shared functionality. The lights mentioned here are simple lights that require little setting up and can be used to recreate most of the required lighting scenarios. In the second part, we will look at a couple of special-purpose lights and effects: THREE.HemisphereLight, THREE.AreaLight, and THREE.LensFlare. You'll probably only need these lights in very specific cases.

Basic lights

We'll start with the most basic of the lights: THREE.AmbientLight.

THREE.AmbientLight

When you create `THREE.AmbientLight`, the color is applied globally. There isn't a specific direction this light comes from, and `THREE.AmbientLight` doesn't contribute to any shadows. You would normally not use `THREE.AmbientLight` as the single source of light in a scene since it colors all the objects in the same color, regardless of shape. You use it together with other lighting sources, such as `THREE.SpotLight` or `THREE.DirectionalLight` to soften the shadows or add some additional color to the scene. The easiest way to understand this is by looking at the `01-ambient-light.html` example in the `chapter-03` folder. With this example, you get a simple user interface that can be used to modify `THREE.AmbientLight` that is available in this scene. Note that in this scene, we also have `THREE.SpotLight`, which adds additional lighting and provides shadows.

In the following screenshot, you can see that we used the scene from the first chapter and made the color of `THREE.AmbientLight` configurable. In this example, you can also turn off the spotlight to see what the effect of `THREE.AmbientLight` is on its own:

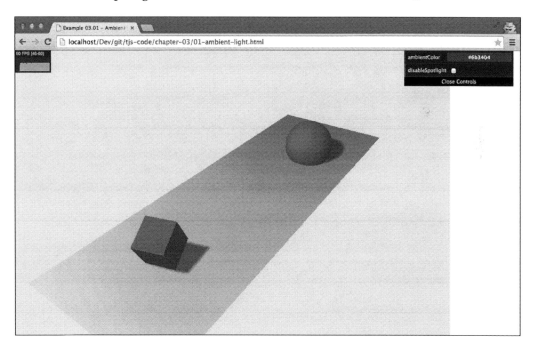

The standard color we use in this scene is `#0c0c0c`. This is a hexadecimal representation of a color. The first two values specify the red part of the color, the next two values specify the green part, and the last two values specify the blue part.

In this example, we use a very dimmed light-gray color that we mainly use to smoothen the hard shadows our meshes cast to the ground plane. You can change the color to a more prominent yellow/orange color (#523318) with the menu in the top-right corner, and then the objects will have a sun-like glow over them. This is shown in the following screenshot:

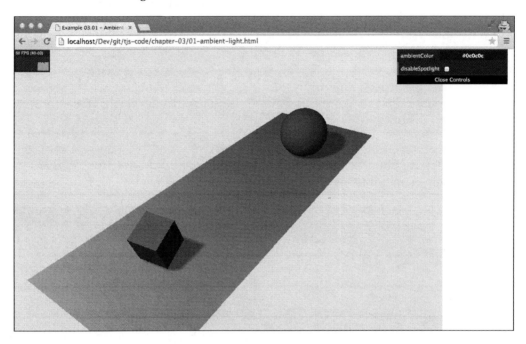

As the preceding image shows, the yellow/orange color is applied to all the objects and casts a green glow over the complete scene. What you should remember when working with this light is that you should be very conservative with the color you specify. If the color you specify is too bright, you'll quickly get a completely oversaturated image.

Now that we've seen what it does, let's look at how you can create and use THREE. AmbientLight. The next couple of lines of code show you how to create THREE. AmbientLight and also show how to connect this to the GUI control menu, which we will introduce in *Chapter 11, Custom Shaders and Render Post Processing*:

```
var ambiColor = "#0c0c0c";
var ambientLight = new THREE.AmbientLight(ambiColor);
scene.add(ambientLight);

...

var controls = new function() {
  this.ambientColor = ambiColor  ;
```

```
}

var gui = new dat.GUI();
gui.addColor(controls, 'ambientColor').onChange(function(e) {
  ambientLight.color = new THREE.Color(e);
});
```

Creating THREE.AmbientLight is very simple and only takes a couple of steps. THREE.AmbientLight doesn't have a position and is applied globally, so we only need to specify the color (in hex), new THREE.AmbientLight(ambiColor), and add this light to the scene, scene.add(ambientLight). In the example, we bind the color of THREE.AmbientLight to the control menu. To do this, you can use the same kind of configuration we used in the previous two chapters. The only change is that instead of using the gui.add(...) function, we use the gui.addColor(...) function. This creates an option in the control menu, with which we can directly change the color of the passed-in variable. In the code, you can see that we use the onChange feature of dat.GUI: gui.addColor(...).onChange(function(e){...}). With this function, we tell dat.GUI to call the passed-in function each time the color changes. In this specific case, we set the color of THREE.AmbientLight to a new value.

Using the THREE.Color object

Before we move on to the next light, here's a quick note on using the THREE.Color object. In Three.js, when you construct an object, you can (usually) specify the color as either a hex string ("#0c0c0c") or a hex value (0x0c0c0c), which is the preferred way of doing it, or by specifying the individual RGB values (0.3, 0.5, 0.6) on a scale of 0 to 1. If you want to change the color after construction, you'll have to create a new THREE.Color object or modify the internal properties of the current THREE.Color object. The THREE.Color object comes with the following functions to set and get information about the current object:

Name	Description
set(value)	Set the value of this color to the supplied hex value. This hex value may be a string, a number, or an existing THREE.Color instance.
setHex(value)	Set the value of this color to the supplied numeric hex value.
setRGB(r,g,b)	Set the value of this color based on the supplied RGB values. The values range from 0 to 1.

Name	Description
setHSL(h,s,l)	Set the value of this color on the supplied HSL values. The values range from 0 to 1. A good explanation of how HSL works for configuring colors can be found at http://en.wikibooks.org/wiki/Color_ Models:_RGB,_HSV,_HSL.
setStyle(style)	Set the value of this color based on the CSS way of specifying colors. For instance, you could use "rgb(255,0,0)", "#ff0000", "#f00", or even "red".
copy(color)	Copy the color values from the THREE.Color instance provided to this color.
copyGammaToLinear(color)	This is mostly used internally. Set the color of this object based on the THREE.Color instance supplied. The color is first converted from the gamma color space to the linear color space. The gamma color space also uses RGB values, but uses an exponential scale instead of a linear one.
copyLinearToGamma(color)	This is mostly used internally. Set the color of this object based on the THREE.Color instance supplied. The color is first converted from the linear color space to the gamma color space.
convertGammaToLinear()	This converts the current color from the gamma color space to the linear color space.
convertLinearToGamma()	This converts the current color from the linear color space to the gamma color space.
getHex()	Return the value from this color object as a number: 435241.
getHexString()	Return the value from this color object as a hex string: "0c0c0c".
getStyle()	Return the value from this color object as a CSS-based value: "rgb(112,0,0)".
getHSL(optionalTarget)	Return the value from this color object as a HSL value. If you provide the optionalTarget object, Three.js will set the h, s, and l properties on that object.
offsetHSL(h, s, l)	Add the h, s, and l values provided to the h, s, and l values of the current color.
add(color)	This adds the r, g, and b values of the color supplied to the current color.

Name	Description
addColors(color1, color2)	This is mostly used internally. Add color1 and color2, and set the value of the current color to the result.
addScalar(s)	This is mostly used internally. Add a value to the RGB components of the current color. Bear in mind that the internal values use a range from 0 to 1.
multiply(color)	This is mostly used internally. Multiply the current RGB values with the RGB values from THREE.Color.
multiplyScalar(s)	This is mostly used internally. This multiplies the current RGB values with the value supplied. Bear in mind that the internal values use a range from 0 to 1.
lerp(color, alpha)	This is mostly used internally. This finds the color that is between the color of this object and the color supplied. The alpha property defines how far between the current color and the supplied color you want the result to be.
equals(color)	This returns true if the RGB values of the THREE.Color instance supplied match the values of the current color.
fromArray(array)	This has the same functionality as setRGB, but now the RGB values can be provided as an array of numbers.
toArray	This returns an array with three elements, [r, g, b].
clone()	This creates an exact copy of this color.

In this table, you can see that there are many ways in which you can change the current color. A lot of these functions are used internally by Three.js, but they also provide a good way to easily change the color of lights and materials.

Before we move on to the discussion on THREE.PointLight, THREE.SpotLight, and THREE.DirectionalLight, let's first highlight their main difference, that is, how they emit light. The following diagram shows how these three light sources emit light:

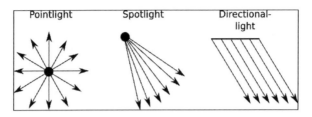

You can see the following from this diagram:

- THREE.PointLight emits light from a specific point in all directions
- THREE.SpotLight emits light from a specific point in a cone-like shape
- THREE.DirectionalLight doesn't emit light from a single point, but emits light rays from a 2D plane, where the rays are parallel to each other

We'll look at these light sources in more detail in the next couple of paragraphs; let's start with THREE.Pointlight.

THREE.PointLight

THREE.PointLight in Three.js is a light source that shines light in all directions emanating from a single point. A good example of a point light is a signal flare fired in the night sky. Just as with all the lights, we have a specific example you can use to play around with THREE.PointLight. If you look at 02-point-light.html in the chapter-03 folder, you can find an example where a THREE.PointLight light is moving around a simple Three.js scene. The following screenshot shows an example of this:

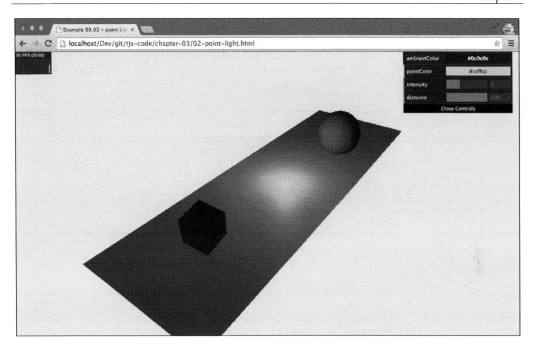

In this example, THREE.PointLight moves around the scene we already saw in *Chapter 1, Create Your First 3D Scene with Three.js*. To make it more clear where THREE.PointLight is, we move a small orange sphere along the same path. As this light moves around, you'll see the red cube and blue sphere being illuminated by this light on different sides.

> You might notice that we don't see any shadows in this example. In Three.js, THREE.PointLight doesn't cast shadows. Since THREE.PointLight emits light in all directions, calculating shadows is a very heavy process for the GPU.

With the THREE.AmbientLight we saw earlier, all you had to do was provide THREE.Color and add the light to the scene. With THREE.PointLight, however, we have a couple of additional configuration options:

Property	Description
color	This is the color of the light.
distance	This is the distance for which the light shines. The default value is 0, which means that the light's intensity doesn't decrease based on distance.
intensity	This is the intensity the light shines with. This defaults to 1.

Property	Description
position	This is the position of the light in THREE.Scene.
visible	If this property is set to true (the default), this light is turned on, and if set it to false, the light is turned off.

In the next couple of examples and screenshots, we'll explain these properties. First, let's look at how you can create THREE.PointLight:

```
var pointColor = "#ccffcc";
var pointLight = new THREE.PointLight(pointColor);
pointLight.position.set(10,10,10);
scene.add(pointLight);
```

We create a light with a specific color property (here we use a string value; we could have also used a number or THREE.Color), set its position property, and add it to the scene.

The first property we'll look at is intensity. With this property, you can set how brightly the light shines. If you set this to 0, you won't see anything; set it to 1, and you've got the default brightness; set it to 2, and you get a light that shines twice as bright; and so on. In the following screenshot, for instance, we set the intensity of the light to 2.4:

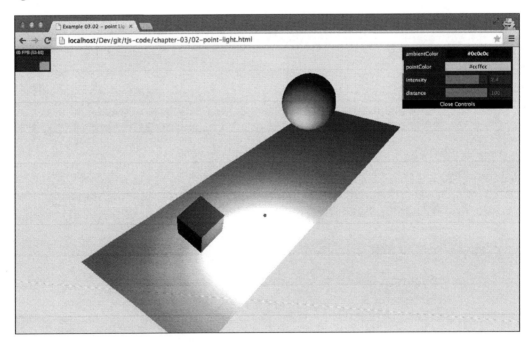

All you have to do to change the intensity of the light is use the intensity property of THREE.PointLight, as follows:

```
pointLight.intensity = 2.4;
```

Or you can use the dat.GUI listener, like this:

```
var controls = new function() {
  this.intensity = 1;
}
var gui = new dat.GUI();
  gui.add(controls, 'intensity', 0, 3).onChange(function (e) {
    pointLight.intensity = e;
  });
```

The distance property of PointLight is a very interesting one and is best explained with an example. In the following screenshot, you see the same scene again, but this time with a very high intensity property (we have a very bright light), but with a small distance:

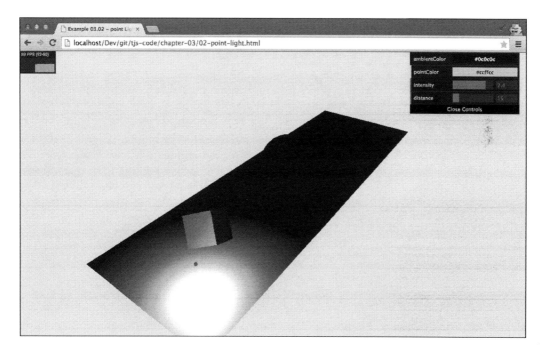

The `distance` property of `SpotLight` determines how far the light travels from the source before its intensity property is 0. You can set this property like this: `pointLight.distance = 14`. In the preceding screenshot, the light's brightness slowly decreases to 0 at a distance of 14. That's why, in the example, you can still see a brightly lit cube, but the light won't reach the blue sphere. The default value for the `distance` property is 0, which means that the light won't decay over a distance.

THREE.SpotLight

`THREE.SpotLight` is one of the lights you'll use most often (especially if you want to use shadows). `THREE.SpotLight` is a light source that has a cone-like effect. You can compare this with a flashlight or a lantern. This light has a direction and an angle at which it produces light. The following table lists all the properties that apply to `THREE.SpotLight`:

Property	Description
angle	This determines how wide the beam emerging from this light is. This is measured in radians and defaults to `Math.PI/3`.
castShadow	If set to `true`, this light will cast shadows.
color	This is the color of the light.
distance	This is the distance up to which the light shines. The default value is 0, which means that the light's intensity doesn't decrease based on distance.
exponent	With `THREE.SpotLight`, the emitted light's intensity decreases the further away you are from the source. The `exponent` property determines how quickly this intensity decreases. With a low value, the light emitted from this source will reach faraway objects, while with a high value, it will only reach objects that are very near to `THREE.SpotLight`.
intensity	This is the intensity the light shines with. This defaults to 1.
onlyShadow	If this property is set to `true`, this light will only cast a shadow and won't add any light to the scene.
position	This is the position of the light in `THREE.Scene`.
shadowBias	The shadow bias moves the cast shadow away or towards the object casting the shadow. You can use this to solve some strange effects when you work with very thin objects (a good example can be found at `http://www.3dbuzz.com/training/view/unity-fundamentals/lights/8-shadows-bias`). If you see strange shadow effects, small values (for example, `0.01`) for this property can often resolve the issue. The default value for this property is 0.

Property	Description
shadowCameraFar	This determines what distance from the light shadows should be created. The default value is 5,000.
shadowCameraFov	This determines how large the field of view used to create shadows is (see the *Different cameras for different uses* section in *Chapter 2, Basic Components That Make Up a Three.js Scene*). The default value is 50.
shadowCameraNear	This determines what distance from the light shadows should be created. The default value is 50.
shadowCameraVisible	If this is set to true, you can see how and where this light source casts a shadow (see the example in the next section). The default value is false.
shadowDarkness	This defines how dark the shadow is rendered. This can't be changed after the scene is rendered. The default value is 0.5.
shadowMapWidth and shadowMapHeight	This determines how many pixels are used to create the shadow. Increase this when the shadow has jagged edges or doesn't look smooth. This can't be changed after the scene is rendered. The default value for both is 512.
target	With THREE.SpotLight, the direction it is pointed in is important. With the target property, you can point THREE.SpotLight to look at a specific object or position in the scene. Note that this property requires a THREE.Object3D object (like THREE.Mesh). This is in contrast to the cameras we saw in the previous chapter that use THREE.Vector3 in their lookAt function.
visible	If this is set to true (the default), this light is turned on, and if this is set to false, the light is turned off.

Creating THREE.SpotLight is very easy. Just specify the color, set the properties you want, and add it to the scene, as follows:

```
var pointColor = "#ffffff";
var spotLight = new THREE.SpotLight(pointColor);
spotLight.position.set(-40, 60, -10);
spotLight.castShadow = true;
spotLight.target = plane;
scene.add(spotLight);
```

THREE.SpotLight is not very different from THREE.PointLight. The only difference is that we set the castShadow property to true because we want shadows, and we need to set the target property for this SpotLight. The target property determines where the light is aimed at. In this case, we point it at the object named plane. When you run the example (03-spot-light.html), you'll see a scene like the following screenshot:

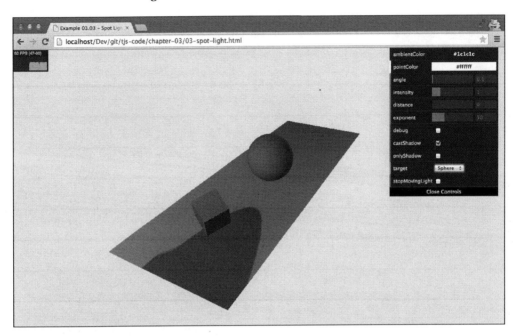

In this example, you can set a number of properties specific to THREE.SpotLight. One of them is the target property. If we set this property to the blue sphere, the light will focus at the center of the sphere even if it moves around the scene. When we created the light, we aimed it at the ground plane, and in our example, we can also aim it at the other two objects. But what if you don't want to aim the light at a specific object, but rather at an arbitrary point in space? You can do that by creating a THREE.Object3D() object like this:

```
var target = new THREE.Object3D();
target.position = new THREE.Vector3(5, 0, 0);
```

Then, set the target property of THREE.SpotLight:

```
spotlight.target = target
```

In the table at the beginning of this section, we showed a couple of properties that can be used to control how the light emanates from THREE.SpotLight. The distance and angle properties define the shape of the cone of light. The angle property defines the width of the cone, and with the distance property, we set the length of the cone. The following figure explains how these two values together define the area that will receive light from THREE.SpotLight:

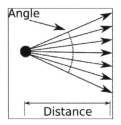

Usually, you won't really need to set these values since they come with reasonable defaults, but you can use these properties, for instance, to create a THREE.SpotLight that has a very narrow beam or quickly decreases in light intensity. The last property you can use to change the way THREE.SpotLight produces light is the exponent property. With this property, you set how fast the light intensity decreases from the center of the light cone towards the edges of the cone. In the following image, you can see the result of the exponent property in action. We have a very bright light (high intensity) that rapidly decreases in intensity (high exponent) as it moves from the center towards the sides of the cone:

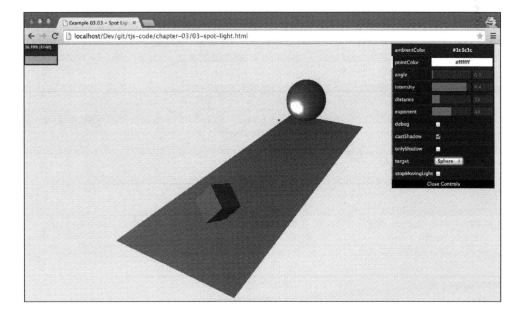

You could use this to highlight a specific object or simulate a small flashlight. We could also have created the same focused beam effect using a small `exponent` value and `angle`. On a cautionary note on this second approach, remember that a very small angle can quickly lead to all kinds of rendering artifacts (an artifact is a term used in graphics for unwanted distortions and strangely rendered parts of the screen).

Before moving on to the next light, we'll quickly look at the shadow-related properties available to `THREE.SpotLight`. You've already learned that we can get shadows by setting the `castShadow` property of `THREE.SpotLight` to `true` (and, of course, making sure that we set the `castShadow` property for objects that should cast shadows, and that we cast the `receiveShadow` property, for objects that should show a shadow, on the `THREE.Mesh` objects in our scene). Three.js also allows you very fine-grained control on how the shadow is rendered. This is done by a couple of properties we explained in the table at the beginning of the section. With `shadowCameraNear`, `shadowCameraFar`, and `shadowCameraFov`, you can control how and where this light casts a shadow. This works in the same way as the perspective camera's field of view we explained in the preceding chapter. The easiest way to see this in action is by setting `shadowCameraVisible` to `true`; you can do this by checking the menu's debug checkbox. This shows, as you can see in the following screenshot, the area that is used to determine the shadows for this light:

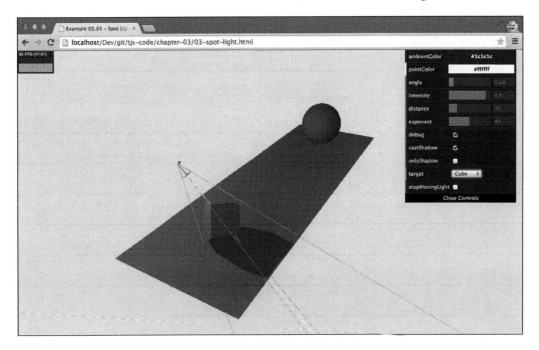

I'll end this section with a couple of pointers, just in case you run into issues with shadows:

- Enable the `shadowCameraVisible` property. This shows the area that is affected by this light for shadow purposes.

- If the shadow looks blocky, you can either increase the `shadowMapWidth` and `shadowMapHeight` properties or make sure the area that is used to calculate the shadow tightly wraps your object. You can use the `shadowCameraNear`, `shadowCameraFar`, and `shadowCameraFov` properties to configure this area.

- Remember that you not only have to tell the light to cast shadows, but also have to tell each geometry whether it will receive and/or cast shadows by setting the `castShadow` and `receiveShadow` properties.

- If you use thin objects in your scene, you might see strange artifacts when you render shadows. You can use the `shadowBias` property to slightly offset the shadows, which will often fix these kinds of issues.

- You can change the darkness of the shadow cast by setting the `shadowDarkness` property. If your shadows are too dark or not dark enough, changing this property allows you to fine-tune how the shadows are rendered.

- If you want to have softer shadows, you can set a different `shadowMapType` value on `THREE.WebGLRenderer`. By default, this property is set to `THREE.PCFShadowMap`; if you set this property to `PCFSoftShadowMap`, you get softer shadows.

THREE.DirectionalLight

The last of the basic lights we will look at is `THREE.DirectionalLight`. This type of light can be considered as a light that is very far away. All the light rays it sends out are parallel to each other. A good example of this is the sun. The sun is so far away that the light rays we receive on earth are (almost) parallel to each other. The main difference between `THREE.DirectionalLight` and `THREE.SpotLight` (which we saw in the previous section) is that this light won't diminish the farther it gets from the target of `THREE.DirectionalLight` as it does with `THREE.SpotLight` (you can fine-tune this with the `distance` and `exponent` parameters). The complete area that is lit by `THREE.DirectionalLight` receives the same intensity of light.

To see this in action, look at the `04-directional-light` example, which is shown here:

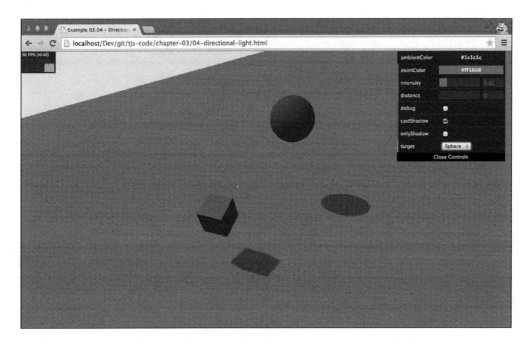

As you can see in the preceding image, there isn't a cone of light that is applied to the scene. Everything receives the same amount of light. Only the direction, the color, and the intensity of the light is used to calculate the colors and shadows.

Just as with `THREE.SpotLight`, there are a couple of properties you can set that control the intensity of the light and the way it casts shadows. `THREE.DirectionalLight` has a lot of properties that are the same as those of `THREE.SpotLight`: position, target, intensity, distance, castShadow, onlyShadow, shadowCameraNear, shadowCameraFar, shadowDarkness, shadowCameraVisible, shadowMapWidth, shadowMapHeight, and shadowBias. For information on those properties, you can look at the preceding section on `THREE.SpotLight`. The few additional properties are discussed in the next couple of paragraphs.

If you look back at the THREE.SpotLight examples, you can see that we had to define the cone of light where shadows were applied. Since, for THREE.DirectionalLight, all the rays are parallel to each other, we don't have a cone of light, instead, we have a cuboid area, as you can see in the following screenshot (if you want to see this for yourself, move the camera further away from the scene):

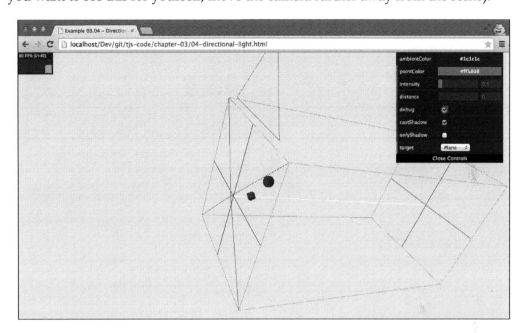

Everything that falls within this cube can cast and receive shadows from the light. Just as for THREE.SpotLight, the tighter you define this area around the objects, the better your shadows will look. Define this cube using the following properties:

```
directionalLight.shadowCameraNear = 2;
directionalLight.shadowCameraFar = 200;
directionalLight.shadowCameraLeft = -50;
directionalLight.shadowCameraRight = 50;
directionalLight.shadowCameraTop = 50;
directionalLight.shadowCameraBottom = -50;
```

You can compare this with the way we configured the orthographic camera in the section on cameras in *Chapter 2, Basic Components That Make Up a Three.js Scene*.

There is one property that is available to THREE.DirectionalLight that we haven't addressed yet: shadowCascade. This property can be used to create better shadows when you want to use shadows on a large area with THREE.DirectionalLight. If you set the property to true, Three.js will use an alternative approach to generate the shadows. It splits the shadow generation up to the value specified by shadowCascadeCount. This will result in more detailed shadows close to the viewpoint of the camera and less detailed shadows far away. To use this, you'll have to experiment with the settings for shadowCascadeCount, shadowCascadeBias, shadowCascadeWidth, shadowCascadeHeight, shadowCascadeNearZ, and shadowCascadeFarZ. You can find an example where this setup is used at http://alteredqualia.com/three/examples/webgl_road.html.

Special lights

In this section on special lights, we'll discuss two additional lights provided by Three.js. First, we'll discuss THREE.HemisphereLight, which helps in creating more natural lighting for outdoor scenes, then we'll look at THREE.AreaLight, which emits lights from a large area instead of a single point, and finally, we'll show you how you can add a lens flare effect to your scene.

THREE.HemisphereLight

The first special light we're going to look at is THREE.HemisphereLight. With THREE.HemisphereLight, we can create more natural-looking outdoor lighting. Without this light, we could simulate the outdoors by creating THREE.DirectionalLight, which emulates the sun, and maybe add additional THREE.AmbientLight to provide some general color to the scene. This, however, won't look really natural. When you're outdoors, not all the light comes directly from above: much is diffused by the atmosphere and reflected by the ground and other objects. THREE.HemisphereLight in Three.js is created for this scenario. This is an easy way to get more natural-looking outdoor lighting. To see an example, look at 05-hemisphere-light.html:

 Note that this is the first example that loads additional resources and can't run directly from your local filesystem. So if you haven't done so, look at *Chapter 1, Create Your First 3D Scene with Three.js*, to find out how to set up a local web server or disable the security settings in your browser to make loading external resources work.

In this example, you can turn THREE.HemisphereLight on and off and set the colors and intensity. Creating a hemisphere light is just as easy as creating any of the other lights:

```
var hemiLight = new THREE.HemisphereLight(0x0000ff, 0x00ff00,
  0.6);
hemiLight.position.set(0, 500, 0);
scene.add(hemiLight);
```

You just specify the color that is received from the sky, the color received from the ground, and the intensity of these lights. If you want to change these values later on, you can access them through the following properties:

Property	Description
groundColor	This is the color that is emitted from the ground
color	This is the color that is emitted from the sky
intensity	This is the intensity with which the light shines

THREE.AreaLight

The last real light source we'll look at is THREE.AreaLight. With THREE.AreaLight, we can define a rectangular area that emits light. THREE.AreaLight isn't included in the standard Three.js library, but in its extensions, so we have to take a couple of additional steps before we can use this light source. Before we look at the details, let's first look at the result we're aiming for (06-area-light.html opens this example); the following screenshot encapsulates the result we want to see:

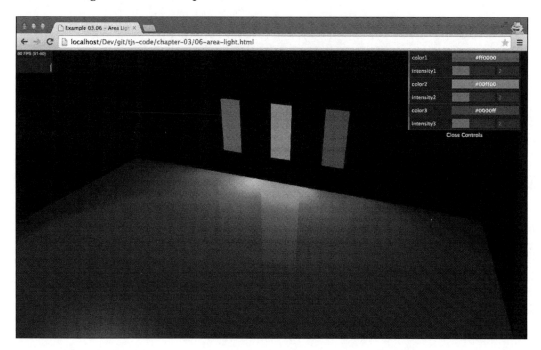

What you see in this screenshot is that we've defined three THREE.AreaLight objects, each with their own color. You can also see how these lights affect the whole area.

When we want to use THREE.AreaLight, we can't use THREE.WebGLRenderer, which we used in our examples until now. The reason is that THREE.AreaLight is a very complex light source that would cause a very serious performance penalty in the normal THREE.WebGLRenderer object. It uses a different approach when rendering a scene (it breaks it up into multiple steps) and can handle complex lights (or a very high number of light sources for that matter) much better than the standard THREE.WebGLRenderer object.

To use `THREE.WebGLDeferredRenderer`, we have to include a couple of additional JavaScript sources provided by Three.js. In the head of your HTML skeleton, make sure you have the following set of `<script>` sources defined:

```
<head>
  <script type="text/javascript" src="../libs/three.js"></script>
  <script type="text/javascript" src="../libs/stats.js"></script>
  <script type="text/javascript" src="../libs/dat.gui.js">
    </script>

  <script type="text/javascript" src="../libs/
    WebGLDeferredRenderer.js"></script>
  <script type="text/javascript" src="../libs/ShaderDeferred.js">
    </script>
  <script type="text/javascript" src="../libs/RenderPass.js">
    </script>
  <script type="text/javascript" src="../libs/EffectComposer.js">
    </script>
  <script type="text/javascript" src="../libs/CopyShader.js">
    </script>
  <script type="text/javascript" src="../libs/ShaderPass.js">
    </script>
  <script type="text/javascript" src="../libs/FXAAShader.js">
    </script>
  <script type="text/javascript" src="../libs/MaskPass.js">
    </script>
</head>
```

With these libraries included, we can use `THREE.WebGLDeferredRenderer`. We can use this renderer in pretty much the same way as the one we discussed in the other examples. It just takes a couple of extra arguments:

```
var renderer = new THREE.WebGLDeferredRenderer({width:
  window.innerWidth,height: window.innerHeight,scale: 1,
  antialias: true,tonemapping: THREE.FilmicOperator, brightness:
  2.5 });
```

Don't worry too much about what all these properties mean at the moment. In *Chapter 10, Loading and Working with Textures*, we'll dive deeper into `THREE.WebGLDeferredRenderer` and explain them to you. With the correct JavaScript libraries and a different renderer, we can start adding `Three.AreaLight`.

We do this in pretty much the same way as all the other lights:

```
var areaLight1 = new THREE.AreaLight(0xff0000, 3);
areaLight1.position.set(-10, 10, -35);
areaLight1.rotation.set(-Math.PI / 2, 0, 0);
areaLight1.width = 4;
areaLight1.height = 9.9;
scene.add(areaLight1);
```

In this example, we create a new THREE.AreaLight. This light has a color value of 0xff0000 and an intensity value of 3. Just like the other lights, we can use the position attribute to set its location in the scene. When you create THREE.AreaLight, it will be created as a horizontal plane. In our example, we created three THREE.AreaLight objects that are positioned vertically, so we need to rotate our lights -Math.PI/2 around their *x* axis. Finally, we set the size of THREE.AreaLight using the width and height properties and add them to the scene. If you try this yourself for the first time, you might wonder why you don't see anything where you positioned your light. This is because you can't see the light source itself, only the light it emits, which you only see when it touches an object. If you want to recreate what I've shown in the example, you can add THREE.PlaneGeometry or THREE.BoxGeometry at the same position (areaLight1.position) to simulate the area emitting light, as follows:

```
var planeGeometry1 = new THREE.BoxGeometry(4, 10, 0);
var planeGeometry1Mat = new THREE.MeshBasicMaterial({color:
  0xff0000})
var plane = new THREE.Mesh(planeGeometry1, planeGeometry1Mat);
plane.position = areaLight1.position;
scene.add(plane);
```

You can create really beautiful effects with THREE.AreaLight, but you'll probably have to experiment a bit to get the desired effect. If you pull down the control panel from the top-right corner, you've got some controls you can play around with to set the color and intensity of the three lights from this scene and immediately see the effect, as follows:

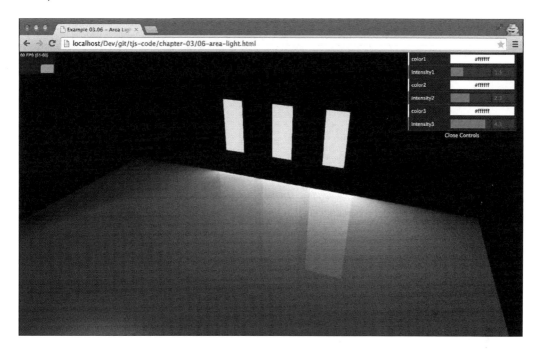

LensFlare

The last subject we'll explore in this chapter is **lens flares**. You are probably already familiar with lens flares. For instance, they appear when you take a photograph directly into the sun or another bright light source. In most cases, you want to avoid this, but for games and 3D-generated images, it provides a nice effect that makes scenes look a bit more realistic.

Three.js also has support for lens flares and makes it very easy to add them to your scene. In this last section, we're going to add a lens flare to a scene and create the output as you can see in the following screenshot; you can see this for yourself by opening `07-lensflares.html`:

We can create a lens flare by instantiating the `THREE.LensFlare` object. The first thing we need to do is create this object. `THREE.LensFlare` takes the following arguments:

```
flare = new THREE.LensFlare(texture, size, distance, blending,
    color, opacity);
```

These arguments are explained in the following table:

Argument	Description
texture	A texture is an image that determines the shape of the flare.
size	We can specify how large the flare should be. This is the size in pixels. If you specify -1, the size of the texture itself is used.
distance	This is the distance from the light source (0) to the camera (1). Use this to position the lens flare in the right position.

Argument	Description
blending	We can specify multiple textures for the flares. The blending mode determines how these are blended together. The default to use with LensFlare is THREE.AdditiveBlending. There's more on blending in the next chapter.
color	This is the color of the flare.

Let's look at the code used to create this object (see 07-lensflares.html):

```
var textureFlare0 = THREE.ImageUtils.loadTexture
        ("../assets/textures/lensflare/lensflare0.png");

var flareColor = new THREE.Color(0xffaacc);
var lensFlare = new THREE.LensFlare(textureFlare0, 350, 0.0,
    THREE.AdditiveBlending, flareColor);

lensFlare.position = spotLight.position;
scene.add(lensFlare);
```

We first load a texture. For this example, I've used the lens flare texture provided by the Three.js examples, as follows:

If you compare this image with the screenshot at the beginning of this section, you can see that it defines what the lens flare looks like. Next, we define the color of the lens flare using new THREE.Color(0xffaacc);, which gives the lens flare a red glow. With these two objects, we can create the THREE.LensFlare object. For this example, we've set the size of the flare to 350 and the distance to 0.0 (directly at the light source).

After we've created the `LensFlare` object, we position it at the location of our light and add it to the scene, which can be seen in the following screenshot:

It already looks nice, but if you compare this with the image from the beginning of this chapter you'll notice that we're missing the small round artifacts in the middle of the page. We create these in pretty much the same way as we did the main flare, as follows:

```
var textureFlare3 = THREE.ImageUtils.loadTexture
    ("../assets/textures/lensflare/lensflare3.png");

lensFlare.add(textureFlare3, 60, 0.6, THREE.AdditiveBlending);
lensFlare.add(textureFlare3, 70, 0.7, THREE.AdditiveBlending);
lensFlare.add(textureFlare3, 120, 0.9, THREE.AdditiveBlending);
lensFlare.add(textureFlare3, 70, 1.0, THREE.AdditiveBlending);
```

This time, though, we don't create a new `THREE.LensFlare`, but use the add function provided by the `LensFlare` we just created. In this method, we need to specify the texture, size, distance, and blending mode, and that's it. Note that the add function can take two additional parameters. You can also set the `color` and the `opacity` properties of the new flare to add. The texture we use for these new flares is a very light circle, as shown in the following screenshot:

If you look at the scene again, you'll see the artifacts appearing at the positions you've specified with the `distance` argument.

Summary

In this chapter, we covered a lot of information about the different kinds of lights that are available in Three.js. In this chapter, you learned that configuring lights, colors, and shadows is not an exact science. To get to the correct result, you should experiment with the different settings and use a dat.GUI control to fine-tune your configuration. The different lights behave in different manners. A `THREE.AmbientLight` color is added to each and every color in the scene and is often used to smooth hard colors and shadows. `THREE.PointLight` emits light in all directions but can't be used to create shadows. `THREE.SpotLight` is a light that resembles a flashlight. It has a conical shape, can be configured to fade over distance, and is able to cast shadows. We also looked at `THREE.DirectionalLight`. This light can be compared with a faraway light, such as the sun, whose light rays travel parallel to each other, the intensity of which doesn't decrease the farther away it gets from the configured target. Besides the standard lights, we also looked at a couple of more specialized lights. For a more natural outdoor effect, you can use `THREE.HemisphereLight`, which takes into account ground and sky reflections; `THREE.AreaLight` doesn't shine from a single point, but emits light from a large area. We showed you how to add a photographic lens flare with the `THREE.LenseFlare` object.

In the chapters so far, we already introduced a couple of different materials, and in this chapter, you saw that not all materials respond in the same manner to the available lights. In the next chapter, we'll give an overview of the materials that are available in Three.js.

4
Working with Three.js Materials

In the previous chapters, we talked a bit about materials. You learned that a material, together with `THREE.Geometry`, forms `THREE.Mesh`. The material is like the skin of the object that defines what the outside of a geometry looks like. For example, a skin defines whether a geometry is metallic-looking, transparent, or shown as a wireframe. The resulting `THREE.Mesh` object can then be added to the scene to be rendered by Three.js. Until now, we haven't really looked at materials in much detail. In this chapter, we'll dive into all the materials Three.js has to offer, and you'll learn how you can use these materials to create good-looking 3D objects. The materials we'll explore in this chapter are shown in the following table:

Name	Description
MeshBasicMaterial	This is a basic material that you can use to give your geometries a simple color or show the wireframe of your geometries.
MeshDepthMaterial	This is a material that uses the distance from the camera to determine how to color your mesh.
MeshNormalMaterial	This is a simple material that bases the color of a face on its normal vector.
MeshFacematerial	This is a container that allows you to specify a unique material for each face of the geometry.
MeshLambertMaterial	This is a material that takes lighting into account and is used to create *dull* non-shiny-looking objects.
MeshPhongMaterial	This is a material that also takes lighting into account and can be used to create shiny objects.

Name	Description
ShaderMaterial	This material allows you to specify your own shader programs to directly control how vertices are positioned and pixels are colored.
LineBasicMaterial	This is a material that can be used on the THREE.Line geometry to create colored lines.
LineDashMaterial	This is the same as LineBasicMaterial, but this material also allows you to create a dashed effect.

If you look through the source code of Three.js, you might run into THREE.RawShaderMaterial. This is a specialized material that can only be used together with THREE.BufferedGeometry. This geometry is a specialized form that is optimized for static geometries (for instance, vertices and faces don't change). We won't explore this material in this chapter, but we will use it in *Chapter 11, Custom Shaders and Render Postprocessing*, when we talk about creating custom shaders. In the code, you can also find THREE.SpriteCanvasMaterial, THREE.SpriteMaterial, and THREE.PointCloudMaterial. These are materials you use when styling individual points. We won't discuss those in this chapter, but we'll explore them in *Chapter 7, Particles, Sprites, and the Point Cloud*.

Materials have a number of common properties, so before we look at the first material, MeshBasicMaterial, we'll look at the properties shared by all the materials.

Understanding common material properties

You can quickly see for yourself which properties are shared between all the materials. Three.js provides a material base class, THREE.Material, that lists all the common properties. We've divided these common material properties into the following three categories:

- **Basic properties**: These are the properties you'll use most often. With these properties, you can, for instance, control the opacity of the object, whether it is visible, and how it is referenced (by ID or custom name).

- **Blending properties**: Every object has a set of blending properties. These properties define how the object is combined with its background.

- **Advanced properties**: There are a number of advanced properties that control how the low-level WebGL context renders objects. In most cases, you won't need to mess with these properties.

Note that in this chapter, we skip any properties related to textures and maps. Most materials allow you to use images as textures (for instance, a wood-like or stone-like texture). In *Chapter 10, Loading and Working with Textures*, we will dive into the various texture and mapping options that are available. Some materials also have specific properties related to animation (skinning and `morphTargets`); we'll also skip those properties. These will be addressed in *Chapter 9, Animations and Moving the Camera*.

We start with the first one from the list: the basic properties.

Basic properties

The basic properties of the `THREE.Material` object are listed in the following table (you can see these properties in action in the section on `THREE.BasicMeshMaterial`):

Property	Description
id	This is used to identify a material and is assigned when you create a material. This starts at 0 for the first material and is increased by 1 for each additional material that is created.
uuid	This is a uniquely generated ID and is used internally.
name	You can assign a name to a material with this property. This can be used for debugging purposes.
opacity	This defines how transparent an object is. Use this together with the transparent property. The range of this property is from 0 to 1.
transparent	If this is set to true, Three.js will render this object with the set opacity. If this is set to false, the object won't be transparent—just more lightly colored. This property should also be set to true if you use a texture that uses an alpha (transparency) channel.
overdraw	When you use THREE.CanvasRenderer, the polygons will be rendered a bit bigger. Set this to true when you see gaps when using this renderer.
visible	This defines whether this material is visible. If you set this to false, you won't see the object in the scene.
Side	With this property, you can define to which side of the geometry a material is applied. The default is THREE.Frontside, which applies the material to the front (outside) of an object. You can also set this to THREE.BackSide, which applies is to the back (inside), or THREE.DoubleSide, which applies it to both sides.
needsUpdate	For some updates to the material, you need to tell Three.js that the material has been changed. If this property is set to true, Three.js will update its cache with the new material properties.

For each material, you can also set a number of blending properties.

Blending properties

Materials have a couple of generic blending-related properties. Blending determines how the colors we render interact with the colors that are behind them. We'll touch upon this subject a little bit when we talk about combining materials. The blending properties are listed in the following table:

Name	Description
blending	This determines how the material on this object blends with the background. The normal mode is THREE.NormalBlending, which only shows the top layer.
blendsrc	Besides using the standard blending modes, you can also create custom blend modes by setting blendsrc, blenddst, and blendequation. This property defines how this object (the source) is blended into the background (the destination). The default THREE.SrcAlphaFactor setting uses the alpha (transparency) channel for blending.
blenddst	This property defines how the background (the destination) is used in blending and defaults to THREE.OneMinusSrcAlphaFactor, which means this property too uses the alpha channel of the source for blending but uses 1 (alpha channel of the source) as the value.
blendequation	This defines how the blendsrc and blenddst values are used. The default is to add them (AddEquation). With these three properties, you can create your own custom blend modes.

The last set of properties is mostly used internally and controls the specifics of how WebGL is used to render the scene.

Advanced properties

We won't go into the details of these properties. These are related to how WebGL works internally. If you do want to know more about these properties, the OpenGL specification is a good starting point. You can find this specification at http://www.khronos.org/registry/gles/specs/2.0/es_full_spec_2.0.25.pdf. The following table provides a brief description of these advanced properties:

Name	Description
depthTest	This is an advanced WebGL property. With this property, you can enable or disable the GL_DEPTH_TEST parameter. This parameter controls whether the *depth* of a pixel is used to determine a new pixel's value. Normally, you wouldn't need to change this. More information can be found in the OpenGL specifications we mentioned earlier.

Name	Description
depthWrite	This is another internal property. This property can be used to determine whether this material affects the WebGL depth buffer. If you use an object for a 2D overlay (for example, a hub), you should set this property to false. Usually, though, you shouldn't need to change this property.
polygonOffset, polygonOffsetFactor, and polygonOffsetUnits	With these properties, you can control the POLYGON_ OFFSET_FILL WebGL feature. These are normally not needed. For an explanation of what they do in detail, you can look at the OpenGL specifications.
alphatest	This value can be set to a specific value (0 to 1). Whenever a pixel has an alpha value smaller than this value, it won't be drawn. You can use this property to remove some transparency-related artifacts.

Now, let's look at all the available materials so that you can see the effect these properties have on the rendered output.

Starting with a simple mesh

In this section, we'll look at a few simple materials: MeshBasicMaterial, MeshDepthMaterial, MeshNormalMaterial, and MeshFaceMaterial. We start with MeshBasicMaterial.

Before we look into the properties of these materials, here's a quick note on how you can pass in properties to configure the materials. There are two options:

- You can pass in the arguments in the constructor as a parameters object, like this:

```
var material = new THREE.MeshBasicMaterial(
{
  color: 0xff0000, name: 'material-1', opacity: 0.5,
    transparency: true, ...
});
```

- Alternatively, you can also create an instance and set the properties individually, like this:

```
var material = new THREE.MeshBasicMaterial();
material.color = new THREE.Color(0xff0000);
material.name = 'material-1';
material.opacity = 0.5;
material.transparency = true;
```

Usually, the best way is to use the constructor if we know all the properties' values while creating the material. The arguments used in both these styles use the same format. The only exception to this rule is the `color` property. In the first style, we can just pass in the hex value, and Three.js will create a `THREE.Color` object itself. In the second style, we have to explicitly create a `THREE.Color` object. In this book, we'll use both of these styles.

THREE.MeshBasicMaterial

`MeshBasicMaterial` is a very simple material that doesn't take into account the lights that are available in the scene. Meshes with this material will be rendered as simple, flat polygons, and you also have the option to show the geometry's wireframe. Besides the common properties we saw in the earlier section on this material, we can set the following properties:

Name	Description
color	This property allows you to set the color of the material.
wireframe	This allows you to render the material as a wireframe. This is great for debugging purposes.
Wireframelinewidth	If you enable the wireframe, this property defines the width of the wires from the wireframe.
Wireframelinecap	This property defines how the ends of lines look in wireframe mode. The possible values are butt, round, and square. The default value is round. In practice, the results from changing this property are very difficult to see. This property isn't supported on WebGLRenderer.
wireframeLinejoin	This defines how the line joints are visualized. The possible values are round, bevel, and miter. The default value is round. If you look very closely, you can see this in the example using low opacity and a very large wireframeLinewidth value. This property isn't supported on WebGLRenderer.

Name	Description
Shading	This defines how shading is applied. The possible values are THREE.SmoothShading, THREE.NoShading, and THREE.FlatShading. The default value is THREE.SmoothShading, which results in a smooth object where you won't see the individual faces. This property isn't enabled in the example for this material. For an example, look at the section on MeshNormalMaterial.
vertexColors	You can define individual colors to be applied to each vertex with this property. The default value is THREE.NoColors. If you set this value to THREE.VertexColors, the renderer will take the colors set on the colors property of THREE.Geometry into account. This property doesn't work on CanvasRenderer but does work on WebGLRenderer. Look at the LineBasicMaterial example, where we use this property to color the various parts of a line. You can also use this property to create a gradient effect for this material type.
fog	This property determines whether this material is affected by global fog settings. This is not shown in action, but if this is set to false, the global fog we saw in *Chapter 2, Basic Components That Make Up a Three.js Scene*, doesn't affect how this object is rendered.

In the previous chapters, we saw how to create materials and assign them to objects. For THREE.MeshBasicMaterial, we do it like this:

```
var meshMaterial = new THREE.MeshBasicMaterial({color: 0x7777ff});
```

This creates a new THREE.MeshBasicMaterial and initializes the color property to 0x7777ff (which is purple).

I've added an example that you can use to play around with the THREE. MeshBasicMaterial properties and the basic properties we discussed in the previous section. If you open up the 01-basic-mesh-material.html example in the chapter-04 folder, you'll see a rotating cube like the one shown in the following screenshot:

This is a very simple object. With the menu in the upper-right corner, you can play around with the properties and select different meshes (you can also change the renderer). For instance, a sphere with opacity of 0.2, transparent set to true, wireframe set to true, wireframeLinewidth of 9, and using CanvasRenderer is rendered like this:

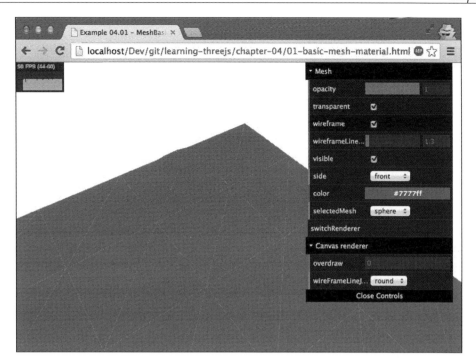

One of the properties you can set in this example is the `side` property. With this property, you define to which side of THREE.Geometry the material is applied. You can test how this property works when you select the plane mesh. Since normally a material is only applied to the front side of a material, the rotating plane will be invisible half the time (when it shows it's back to you). If you set the `side` property to `double`, the plane will be visible the whole time, since the material is applied to both sides of the geometry. Note, though, that the renderer will need to do more work when the `side` property is set to `double`, so this could have an impact on the performance of your scene.

THREE.MeshDepthMaterial

The next material on the list is THREE.MeshDepthMaterial. With this material, the way an object looks isn't defined by lights or by a specific material property; it is defined by the distance from the object to the camera. You can combine this with other materials to easily create fading effects. The only relevant properties this material has are the following two that control whether you want to show a wireframe:

Name	Description
wireframe	This determines whether or not to show the wireframe.
wireframeLineWidth	This determines the width of the wireframe.

To demonstrate this, we modified the cubes example from *Chapter 2, Basic Components That Make Up a Three.js Scene* (02-depth-material from the chapter-04 folder). Remember that you have to click on the **addCube** button to populate the scene. The following screenshot shows the modified example:

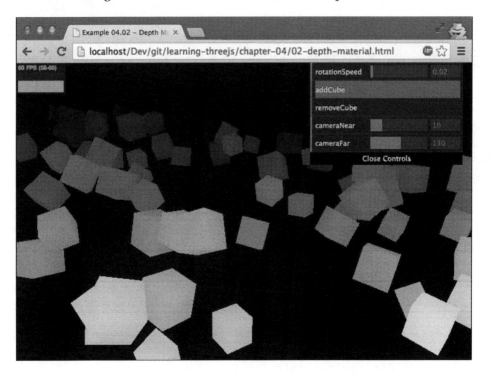

Even though the material doesn't have many additional properties to control how an object is rendered, we can still control how fast the object's color fades out. In this example, we exposed the near and far properties of the camera. As you probably remember from *Chapter 2, Basic Components That Make Up a Three.js Scene*, with these two properties, we set the visible area for the camera. Any objects that are nearer to the camera than the near property aren't shown, and any objects further away than the far property also fall outside the camera's visible area.

The distance between the near and far properties of the camera defines the brightness and the rate at which objects fade out. If the distance is very large, objects will only fade out a little as they move away from the camera. If the distance is small, the fadeout will be much more notable (as you can see in the following screenshot):

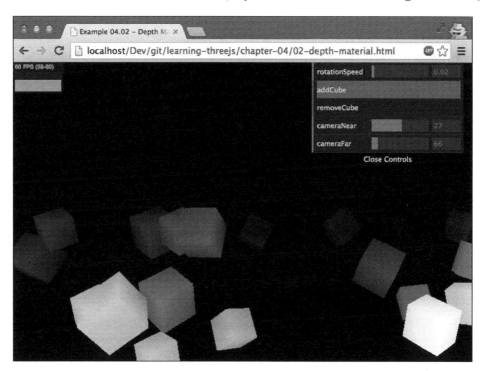

Creating THREE.MeshDepthMaterial is very easy and the object doesn't require any arguments. For this example, we've used the scene.overrideMaterial property to make sure all the objects in the scene use this material without having to explicitly specify it for each THREE.Mesh object:

```
var scene = new THREE.Scene();
scene.overrideMaterial = new THREE.MeshDepthMaterial();
```

The next part in this chapter isn't really about a specific material, but shows a way in which you can combine multiple materials together.

Combining materials

If you look back at the properties of THREE.MeshDepthMaterial, you can see that there isn't an option to set the color of the cubes. Everything was decided for you by the default properties of the material. Three.js, however, has the option to combine materials together to create new effects (this is also where blending comes into play). The following code shows how we can combine materials together:

```
var cubeMaterial = new THREE.MeshDepthMaterial();
var colorMaterial = new THREE.MeshBasicMaterial({color: 0x00ff00,
    transparent: true, blending: THREE.MultiplyBlending})
var cube = new THREE.SceneUtils.createMultiMaterialObject
    (cubeGeometry, [colorMaterial, cubeMaterial]);
cube.children[1].scale.set(0.99, 0.99, 0.99);
```

We get the following green-colored cubes that use the brightness from THREE. MeshDepthMaterial and the color from THREE.MeshBasicMaterial (open 03-combined-material.html for this example). The following screenshot shows the example:

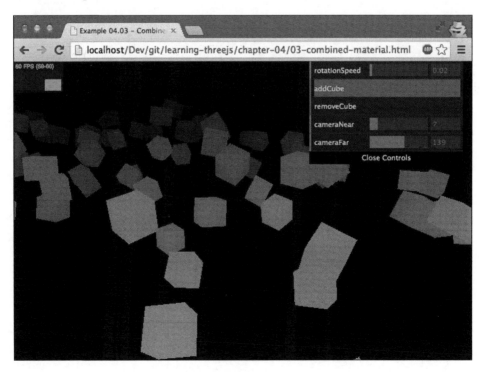

Let's look at the steps you need to take to get this specific result.

First, we need to create our two materials. For THREE.MeshDepthMaterial, we don't do anything special; for THREE.MeshBasicMaterial, however, we set transparent to true and define a blending mode. If we don't set the transparent property to true, we'll just have solid, green objects since Three.js won't know to take the already-rendered colors into account. With transparent set to true, Three.js will check the blending property to see how the green THREE.MeshBasicMaterial object should interact with the background. The background in this case is the cube rendered with THREE.MeshDepthMaterial. In *Chapter 9, Animations and Moving the Camera*, we'll discuss in greater detail the various blend modes that are available.

For this example, though, we used THREE.MultiplyBlending. This blend mode multiplies the foreground color with the background color and gives you the desired effect. The last line in this code fragment is also an important one. What happens when we create a mesh with the THREE.SceneUtils.createMultiMaterialObject() function is that the geometry gets copied and two exactly the same meshes are returned in a group. If we render these without the last line, you should see a flickering effect. This can happen sometimes when objects are rendered one on top of the other and one of them is transparent. By scaling down the mesh created with THREE.MeshDepthMaterial, we can avoid this. To do so, use the following code:

```
cube.children[1].scale.set(0.99, 0.99, 0.99);
```

The next material is also one where we won't have any influence on the colors used in rendering.

THREE.MeshNormalMaterial

The easiest way to understand how this material is rendered is by first looking at an example. Open up the `04-mesh-normal-material.html` example from the `chapter-04` folder. If you select the sphere as the mesh, you'll see something like this:

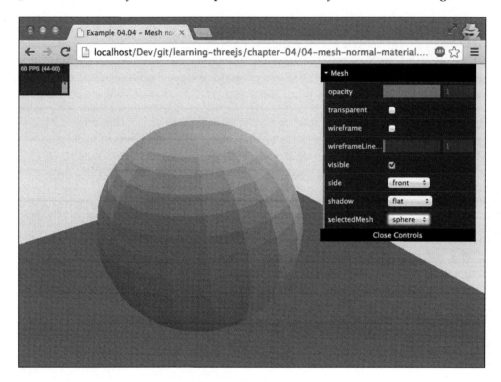

As you can see, each face of the mesh is rendered in a slightly different color, and even though the sphere rotates, the colors stay pretty much at the same place. This happens because the color of each face is based on the *normal* pointing out from the face. This normal is the vector perpendicular to the face. The normal vector is used in many different parts of Three.js. It is used to determine light reflections, helps in mapping textures to 3D models, and gives information on how to light, shade, and color pixels on a surface. Luckily, though, Three.js handles the computation of these vectors and uses them internally, so you don't have to calculate them yourselves. The following screenshot shows all the normal vectors of `THREE.SphereGeometry`:

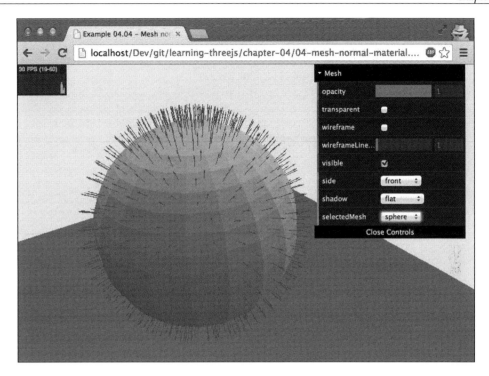

The direction this normal points in determines the color a face gets when you use THREE.MeshNormalMaterial. Since all normals for the faces of a sphere point in a different direction, we get the colorful sphere you can see in the examples. As a quick side note, to add these normal arrows, you can use THREE.ArrowHelper like this:

```
for (var f = 0, fl = sphere.geometry.faces.length; f < fl; f++) {
  var face = sphere.geometry.faces[ f ];
  var centroid = new THREE.Vector3(0, 0, 0);
  centroid.add(sphere.geometry.vertices[face.a]);
  centroid.add(sphere.geometry.vertices[face.b]);
  centroid.add(sphere.geometry.vertices[face.c]);
  centroid.divideScalar(3);

  var arrow = new THREE.ArrowHelper(face.normal, centroid, 2,
    0x3333FF, 0.5, 0.5);
  sphere.add(arrow);
}
```

In this code snippet, we iterate through all the faces of THREE.SphereGeometry. For each of these THREE.Face3 objects, we calculate the center (the centroid) by adding the vertices that make up this face and dividing the result by 3. We use this centroid, together with the normal vector of the face, to draw an arrow. The THREE.ArrowHelper takes the following arguments: direction, origin, length, color, headLength, and headWidth.

There are a couple of other properties that you can set on THREE.MeshNormalMaterial:

Name	Description
wireframe	This determines whether or not to show the wireframe.
wireframeLineWidth	This determines the width of the wireframe.
shading	This configures shading in the form of flat shading with THREE.FlatShading and smooth shading with THREE.SmoothShading.

We've already seen wireframe and wireframeLinewidth but skipped the shading property in our THREE.MeshBasicMaterial example. With the shading property, we can tell Three.js how to render our objects. If you use THREE.FlatShading, each face will be rendered as is (as you can see in the previous couple of screenshots), or you can use THREE.SmoothShading, which smoothens out the faces of our object. For instance, if we render the sphere using THREE.SmoothShading, the result looks like this:

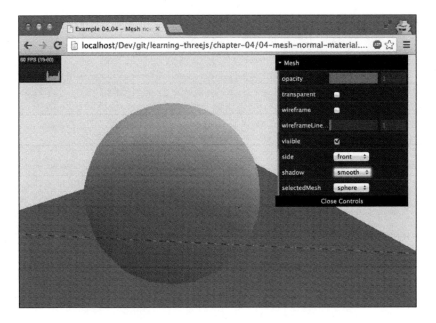

We're almost done with the simple materials. The last one is THREE. MeshFaceMaterial.

THREE.MeshFaceMaterial

The last of the basic materials isn't really a material but much more a container of other materials. THREE.MeshFaceMaterial allows you to assign a different material to each face of your geometry. For instance, if you have a cube, which has 12 faces (remember, Three.js only works with triangles), you can use this material to assign a different material (for example, with a different color) to each side of the cube. Using this material is really simple, as you can see from the following piece of code:

```
var matArray = [];
matArray.push(new THREE.MeshBasicMaterial( { color: 0x009e60 }));
matArray.push(new THREE.MeshBasicMaterial( { color: 0x009e60 }));
matArray.push(new THREE.MeshBasicMaterial( { color: 0x0051ba }));
matArray.push(new THREE.MeshBasicMaterial( { color: 0x0051ba }));
matArray.push(new THREE.MeshBasicMaterial( { color: 0xffd500 }));
matArray.push(new THREE.MeshBasicMaterial( { color: 0xffd500 }));
matArray.push(new THREE.MeshBasicMaterial( { color: 0xff5800 }));
matArray.push(new THREE.MeshBasicMaterial( { color: 0xff5800 }));
matArray.push(new THREE.MeshBasicMaterial( { color: 0xC41E3A }));
matArray.push(new THREE.MeshBasicMaterial( { color: 0xC41E3A }));
matArray.push(new THREE.MeshBasicMaterial( { color: 0xffffff }));
matArray.push(new THREE.MeshBasicMaterial( { color: 0xffffff }));

var faceMaterial = new THREE.MeshFaceMaterial(matArray);

var cubeGeom = new THREE.BoxGeometry(3,3,3);
var cube = new THREE.Mesh(cubeGeom, faceMaterial);
```

We first create an array, named `matArray`, to hold all the materials. Next, we create a new material, `THREE.MeshBasicMaterial` in this example, with a different color for each face. With this array, we instantiate `THREE.MeshFaceMaterial` and use it together with the cube geometry to create the mesh. Let's dive a bit deeper into the code and see what you need to do to recreate the following example: a simple 3D Rubik's cube. You can find this example in `05-mesh-face-material.html`. The following screenshot shows this example:

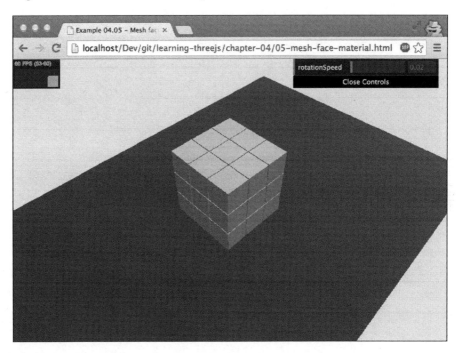

This Rubik's cube consists of a number of smaller cubes: three cubes along the *x* axis, three along the *y* axis, and three along the *z* axis. Here's how this is done:

```
var group = new THREE.Mesh();
// add all the rubik cube elements
var mats = [];
mats.push(new THREE.MeshBasicMaterial({ color: 0x009e60 }));
mats.push(new THREE.MeshBasicMaterial({ color: 0x009e60 }));
mats.push(new THREE.MeshBasicMaterial({ color: 0x0051ba }));
mats.push(new THREE.MeshBasicMaterial({ color: 0x0051ba }));
mats.push(new THREE.MeshBasicMaterial({ color: 0xffd500 }));
mats.push(new THREE.MeshBasicMaterial({ color: 0xffd500 }));
```

```
mats.push(new THREE.MeshBasicMaterial({ color: 0xff5800 }));
mats.push(new THREE.MeshBasicMaterial({ color: 0xff5800 }));
mats.push(new THREE.MeshBasicMaterial({ color: 0xC41E3A }));
mats.push(new THREE.MeshBasicMaterial({ color: 0xC41E3A }));
mats.push(new THREE.MeshBasicMaterial({ color: 0xffffff }));
mats.push(new THREE.MeshBasicMaterial({ color: 0xffffff }));

var faceMaterial = new THREE.MeshFaceMaterial(mats);

for (var x = 0; x < 3; x++) {
  for (var y = 0; y < 3; y++) {
    for (var z = 0; z < 3; z++) {
      var cubeGeom = new THREE.BoxGeometry(2.9, 2.9, 2.9);
      var cube = new THREE.Mesh(cubeGeom, faceMaterial);
      cube.position.set(x * 3 - 3, y * 3, z * 3 - 3);

      group.add(cube);
    }
  }
}
```

In this piece of code, we first create THREE.Mesh, which will hold all the individual cubes (group); next, we create the materials for each face and push them to the mats array. Remember, each side of the cube consists of two faces, so we need 12 materials. From these materials, we create THREE.MeshFaceMaterial. Then, we create three loops to make sure we create the right number of cubes. In this loop, we create each of the individual cubes, assign the material, position them, and add them to the group. What you should remember is that the position of the cubes is relative to the position of this group. If we move or rotate the group, all the cubes will move and rotate with it. For more information on how to work with groups, look at *Chapter 8, Creating and Loading Advanced Meshes and Geometries*.

If you've opened the example in your browser, you can see that the complete Rubik's cube rotates, and not the individual cubes. This happens because we use the following in our rendering loop:

```
group.rotation.y=step+=0.01;
```

This causes the complete group to rotate around its center (0,0,0). When we positioned the individual cubes, we made sure they were positioned around this center point. That's why you see the -3 offset in the cube.position.set(x * 3 - 3, y * 3, z * 3 - 3); line of the preceding code.

If you look at this code, you might wonder how Three.js determines which material to use for a specific face. For this, Three.js uses the `materialIndex` property, which you can set on each individual face of the `geometry.faces` array. The property points to the array index of the materials we add in the constructor of the `THREE.FaceMaterial` object. When you create a geometry using one of the standard Three.js geometries, Three.js provides sensible defaults. If you want other behavior, you can just set the `materialIndex` property yourself for each face to point at one of the provided materials.

`THREE.MeshFaceMaterial` was the last of our basic materials. In the next section, we'll look at some of the more advanced materials available in Three.js.

Advanced materials

In this section, we'll look at the more advanced materials Three.js has to offer. We'll first look at `THREE.MeshPhongMaterial` and `THREE.MeshLambertMaterial`. These two materials react to light sources and can be used to create shiny and dull-looking materials, respectively. In this section, we'll also look at one of the most versatile, but most difficult to use, materials: `THREE.ShaderMaterial`. With `THREE.ShaderMaterial`, you can create your own shader programs that define how the material and object should be shown.

THREE.MeshLambertMaterial

This material can be used to create dull-looking, non-shiny surfaces. This is a very easy-to-use material that responds to the lighting sources in the scene. This material can be configured with a number of properties we've seen before: `color`, `opacity`, `shading`, `blending`, `depthTest`, `depthWrite`, `wireframe`, `wireframeLinewidth`, `wireframeLinecap`, `wireframeLineJoin`, `vertexColors`, and `fog`. We won't go into the details of those properties, but will focus on the ones specific to this material. That just leaves us with the following four properties:

Name	Description
ambient	This is the *ambient* color of the material. This works together with the ambient light we saw in the previous chapter. This color is multiplied with the color provided by the ambient light. This defaults to white.
emissive	This is the color this material emits. It doesn't really act as a light source, but this is a solid color that is unaffected by other lighting. This defaults to black.

Name	Description
wrapAround	If this property is set to `true`, you enable the half-lambert lighting technique. With half-lambert lighting, the drop-off of light is more subtle. If you have a mesh with harsh, dark areas, enabling this property will soften the shadows and more evenly distribute the light.
wrapRGB	When `wrapAround` is set to true, you can use `THREE.Vector3` to control how fast the light is dropped off.

This material is created just like all the other ones. Here's how it's done:

```
var meshMaterial = new THREE.MeshLambertMaterial({color:
    0x7777ff});
```

For an example of this material, look at `06-mesh-lambert-material.html`. The following screenshot shows this example:

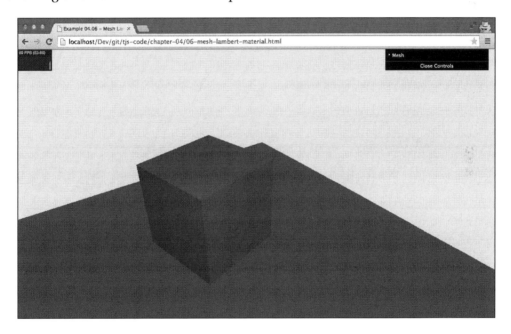

As you can see in the preceding screenshot, the material looks rather dull. There is another material we can use to create shiny surfaces.

THREE.MeshPhongMaterial

With THREE.MeshPhongMaterial, we can create a material that is shiny. The properties you can use for that are pretty much the same as for a non-shiny THREE. MeshLambertMaterial object. We'll once again skip the basic properties and those already discussed: color, opacity, shading, blending, depthTest, depthWrite, wireframe, wireframeLinewidth, wireframeLinecap, wireframelineJoin, and vertexColors.

The interesting properties for this material are shown in the following table:

Name	Description
ambient	This is the *ambient* color of the material. This works together with the ambient light we saw in the previous chapter. This color is multiplied with the color provided by the ambient light. This defaults to white.
emissive	This is the color this material emits. It doesn't really act as a light source, but this is a solid color that is unaffected by other lighting. This defaults to black.
specular	This property defines how shiny the materials are and with what color it shines. If this is set to the same color as the color property, you get a more metallic-looking material. If this is set to grey, it results in a more plastic-looking material.
shininess	This property defines how shiny the specular highlight is. The default value for the shininess is 30.
metal	When this property is set to true, Three.js uses a slightly different way of calculating the color of a pixel to make the object look more like a metal. Note that the effect is very minimal.
wrapAround	If this property is set to true, you enable the half-lambert lighting technique. With half-lambert lighting, the drop-off of light is more subtle. If you have a mesh with harsh, dark areas, enabling this property will soften the shadows and more evenly distribute the light.
wrapRGB	When wrapAround is set to true, you can use THREE.Vector3 to control how fast the light is dropped off.

Initializing a THREE.MeshPhongMaterial object is done in the same way as we've already seen for all the other materials and is shown in the following line of code:

```
var meshMaterial = new THREE.MeshPhongMaterial({color: 0x7777ff});
```

To give you the best comparison, we've created the same example for this material as we did for THREE.MeshLambertMaterial. You can use the control GUI to play around with this material. For instance, the following settings create a plastic-looking material. You can find this example in 07-mesh-phong-material.html. The following screenshot shows this example:

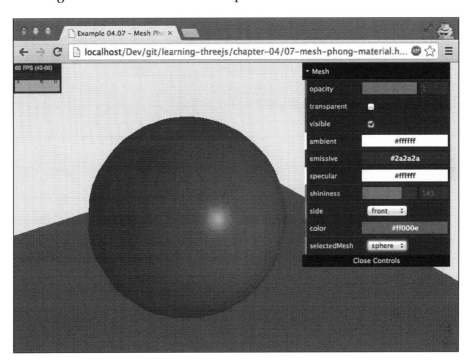

The last one of the advanced materials we'll explore is THREE.ShaderMaterial.

Creating your own shaders with THREE. ShaderMaterial

THREE.ShaderMaterial is one of the most versatile and complex materials available in Three.js. With this material, you can pass in your own custom shaders that are directly run in the WebGL context. A shader converts Three.js JavaScript meshes to pixels on screen. With these custom shaders, you can define exactly how your object should be rendered and how to override or alter the defaults from Three.js. In this section, we won't go into the details yet of how to write custom shaders. For more information on that, see *Chapter 11, Custom Shaders and Render Postprocessing*. For now, we'll just look at a very basic example that shows how you can configure this material.

THREE.ShaderMaterial has a number of properties you can set that we've already seen. With THREE.ShaderMaterial, Three.js passes in all the information regarding these properties, but you still have to process the information in your own shader programs. The following are the properties of THREE.ShaderMaterial that we have already seen:

Name	Description
wireframe	This renders the material as a wireframe. This is great for debugging purposes.
Wireframelinewidth	If you enable the wireframe, this property defines the width of the wires from the wireframe.
linewidth	This defines the width of the line to be drawn.
Shading	This defines how shading is applied. The possible values are THREE.SmoothShading and THREE.FlatShading. This property isn't enabled in the example for this material. For example, look at the section on MeshNormalMaterial.
vertexColors	You can define individual colors to be applied to each vertex with this property. This property doesn't work on CanvasRenderer but does work on WebGLRenderer. Look at the LineBasicMaterial example, where we use this property to color the various parts of a line.
fog	This determines whether this material is affected by global fog settings. This is not shown in action. If this is set to false, the global fog we saw in *Chapter 2, Basic Components That Make Up a Three.js Scene*, doesn't affect how this object is rendered.

Besides these properties that are passed into the shader, THREE.ShaderMaterial also provides a number of specific properties you can use to pass in additional information into your custom shader (they might seem a bit obscure at the moment; for more details, see *Chapter 11, Custom Shaders and Render Postprocessing*), which are as follows:

Name	Description
fragmentShader	This shader defines the color of each pixel that is passed in. Here, you need to pass in the string value of your fragment shader program.
vertexShader	This shader allows you to change the position of each vertex that is passed in. Here, you need to pass in the string value of your vertex shader program.
uniforms	This allows you to send information to your shader. The same information is sent to each vertex and fragment.

Name	Description
defines	Converts to #define code fragments. With these fragments, you can set some additional global variables in the shader programs.
attributes	These can change between each vertex and fragment. They are usually used to pass positional and normal-related data. If you want to use this, you need to provide information for all the vertices of the geometry.
lights	This determines whether light data should be passed into the shaders. This defaults to `false`.

Before we look at an example, we'll give a quick explanation about the most important parts of ShaderMaterial. To work with this material, we have to pass in two different shaders:

- vertexShader: This is run on each vertex of the geometry. You can use this shader to transform the geometry by moving the position of the vertices around.

- fragmentShader: This is run on each fragment of the geometry. In vertexShader, we return the color that should be shown for this specific fragment.

For all the materials we've discussed until now in this chapter, Three.js provides fragmentShader and vertexShader, so you don't have to worry about those.

For this section, we'll look at a simple example that uses a very simple vertexShader program that changes the *x*, *y*, and *z* coordinates of the vertices of a cube and a fragmentShader program that uses shaders from http://glslsandbox.com/ to create an animating material.

Up next, you can see the complete code for vertexShader that we'll use. Note that writing shaders isn't done in JavaScript. You write shaders in a C-like language called **GLSL** (WebGL supports OpenGL ES Shading Language 1.0—for more information on GLSL, see https://www.khronos.org/webgl/), as follows:

```
<script id="vertex-shader" type="x-shader/x-vertex">
  uniform float time;

  void main()
  {
    vec3 posChanged = position;
    posChanged.x = posChanged.x*(abs(sin(time*1.0)));
    posChanged.y = posChanged.y*(abs(cos(time*1.0)));
```

```
    posChanged.z = posChanged.z*(abs(sin(time*1.0)));

    gl_Position = projectionMatrix * modelViewMatrix *
      vec4(posChanged,1.0);
  }
</script>
```

We won't go into too much detail here and just focus on the most important parts of this code. To communicate with the shaders from JavaScript, we use something called uniforms. In this example, we use the uniform float time; statement to pass in an external value. Based on this value, we change the *x*, *y*, and *z* coordinates of the passed-in vertex (which is passed in as the position variable):

```
vec3 posChanged = position;
posChanged.x = posChanged.x*(abs(sin(time*1.0)));
posChanged.y = posChanged.y*(abs(cos(time*1.0)));
posChanged.z = posChanged.z*(abs(sin(time*1.0)));
```

The posChanged vector now contains the new coordinate for this vertex based on the passed-in time variable. The last step we need to perform is pass this new position back to Three.js, which is always done like this:

```
gl_Position = projectionMatrix * modelViewMatrix *
  vec4(posChanged,1.0);
```

The gl_Position variable is a special variable that is used to return the final position. Next, we need to create shaderMaterial and pass in vertexShader. For this, we've created a simple helper function, which we use like this: var meshMaterial1 = createMaterial("vertex-shader","fragment-shader-1"); in the following code:

```
function createMaterial(vertexShader, fragmentShader) {
  var vertShader = document.getElementById
    (vertexShader).innerHTML;
  var fragShader = document.getElementById
    (fragmentShader).innerHTML;

  var attributes = {};
  var uniforms = {
    time: {type: 'f', value: 0.2},
    scale: {type: 'f', value: 0.2},
    alpha: {type: 'f', valuc: 0.6},
    resolution: { type: "v2", value: new THREE.Vector2() }
  };
```

```
uniforms.resolution.value.x = window.innerWidth;
uniforms.resolution.value.y = window.innerHeight;

var meshMaterial = new THREE.ShaderMaterial({
  uniforms: uniforms,
  attributes: attributes,
  vertexShader: vertShader,
  fragmentShader: fragShader,
  transparent: true

});
  return meshMaterial;
}
```

The arguments point to the ID of the `script` element in the HTML page. Here, you can also see that we set up a uniforms variable. This variable is used to pass information from our renderer into our shader. Our complete render loop for this example is shown in the following code snippet:

```
function render() {
  stats.update();

  cube.rotation.y = step += 0.01;
  cube.rotation.x = step;
  cube.rotation.z = step;

  cube.material.materials.forEach(function (e) {
    e.uniforms.time.value += 0.01;
  });

  // render using requestAnimationFrame
  requestAnimationFrame(render);
  renderer.render(scene, camera);
}
```

You can see that we increase the time variable by 0.01 each time the render loop is run. This information is passed into `vertexShader` and used to calculate the new position of the vertices of our cube. Now open up the `08-shader-material.html` example, and you'll see that the cube shrinks and grows around its axis. The following screenshot gives a still image of this example:

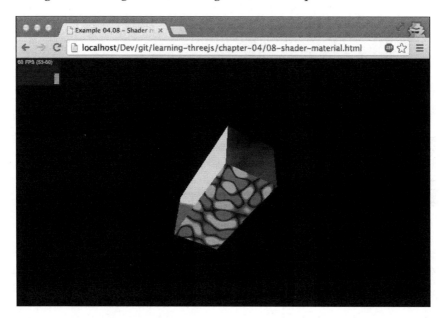

In this example, you can see that each of the cube's faces has an animating pattern. The fragment shader that is assigned to each face of the cube creates these patterns. As you might have guessed, we've used `THREE.MeshFaceMaterial` (and the `createMaterial` function we explained earlier) for this:

```
var cubeGeometry = new THREE.CubeGeometry(20, 20, 20);

var meshMaterial1 = createMaterial("vertex-shader", "fragment-
    shader-1");
var meshMaterial2 = createMaterial("vertex-shader", "fragment-
    shader-2");
var meshMaterial3 = createMaterial("vertex-shader", "fragment-
    shader-3");
var meshMaterial4 = createMaterial("vertex-shader", "fragment-
    shader-4");
var meshMaterial5 = createMaterial("vertex-shader", "fragment-
    shader-5");
var meshMaterial6 = createMaterial("vertex-shader", "fragment-
    shader-6");
```

```
var material = new THREE.MeshFaceMaterial([meshMaterial1,
  meshMaterial2, meshMaterial3, meshMaterial4, meshMaterial5,
  meshMaterial6]);

var cube = new THREE.Mesh(cubeGeometry, material);
```

The only part we haven't explained yet is about `fragmentShader`. For this example, all the `fragmentShader` objects were copied from `http://glslsandbox.com/`. This site provides an experimental playground where you can write and share `fragmentShader` objects. I won't go into the details here, but `fragment-shader-6` used in this example looks like this:

```
<script id="fragment-shader-6" type="x-shader/x-fragment">
  #ifdef GL_ES
  precision mediump float;
  #endif

  uniform float time;
  uniform vec2 resolution;


  void main( void )
  {

    vec2 uPos = ( gl_FragCoord.xy / resolution.xy );

    uPos.x -= 1.0;
    uPos.y -= 0.5;

    vec3 color = vec3(0.0);
    float vertColor = 2.0;
    for( float i = 0.0; i < 15.0; ++i ) {
      float t = time * (0.9);

      uPos.y += sin( uPos.x*i + t+i/2.0 ) * 0.1;
      float fTemp = abs(1.0 / uPos.y / 100.0);
      vertColor += fTemp;
      color += vec3( fTemp*(10.0-i)/10.0, fTemp*i/10.0,
        pow(fTemp,1.5)*1.5 );
    }

    vec4 color_final = vec4(color, 1.0);
    gl_FragColor = color_final;
  }
</script>
```

The color that finally gets passed back to Three.js is the one set with `gl_FragColor = color_final`. A good way to get a bit more of a feeling for `fragmentShader` is to explore what's available at `http://glslsandbox.com/` and to use the code for your own objects. Before we move to the next set of materials, here is one more example of what is possible with a custom `vertexShader` program (`https://www.shadertoy.com/view/4dXGR4`):

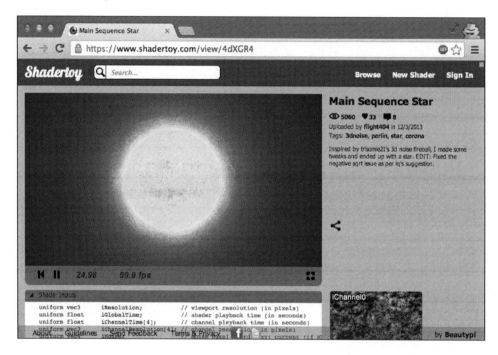

Much more on the subject of fragment and vertex shaders can be found in *Chapter 11, Custom Shaders and Render Postprocessing*.

Materials you can use for a line geometry

The last couple of materials we're going to look at can only be used on one specific geometry: `THREE.Line`. As the name implies, this is just a single line that only consists of vertices and doesn't contain any faces. Three.js provides two different materials you can use on a line, which are as follows:

- `THREE.LineBasicMaterial`: The basic material for a line allows you to set the `colors`, `linewidth`, `linecap`, and `linejoin` properties

- `THREE.LineDashedMaterial`: This has the same properties as `THREE.LineBasicMaterial` but allows you to create a *dash* effect by specifying dash and spacing sizes

We'll start with the basic variant and after that look at the dashed variant.

THREE.LineBasicMaterial

The materials available for the THREE.Line geometry are very simple. The following table shows the properties available to this material:

Name	Description
color	This determines the color of the line. If you specify vertexColors, this property is ignored.
linewidth	This determines the width of the line.
linecap	This property defines how the ends of lines look in the wireframe mode. The possible values are butt, round, and square. The default is round. In practice, the results from changing this property are very difficult to see. This property isn't supported on WebGLRenderer.
linejoin	Define how the line joints are visualized. The possible values are round, bevel, and miter. The default value is round. If you look very closely, you can see this in the example using low opacity and a very large wireframeLinewidth. This property isn't supported on WebGLRenderer.
vertexColors	You can supply a specific color for each vertex by setting this property to the THREE.VertexColors value.
fog	This determines whether this object is affected by the global fog property.

Before we look at an example of LineBasicMaterial, let's first have a quick look at how we can create a THREE.Line mesh from a set of vertices and combine that with LineMaterial to create the mesh, as shown in the following code:

```
var points = gosper(4, 60);
var lines = new THREE.Geometry();
var colors = [];
var i = 0;
points.forEach(function (e) {
  lines.vertices.push(new THREE.Vector3(e.x, e.z, e.y));
  colors[ i ] = new THREE.Color(0xffffff);
  colors[ i ].setHSL(e.x / 100 + 0.5, ( e.y * 20 ) / 300, 0.8);
  i++;
});

lines.colors = colors;
var material = new THREE.LineBasicMaterial({
  opacity: 1.0,
```

```
    linewidth: 1,
    vertexColors: THREE.VertexColors });

  var line = new THREE.Line(lines, material);
```

The first part of this code fragment, `var points = gosper(4, 60);`, is used as an example to get a set of *x* and *y* coordinates. This function returns a gosper curve (for more information, check out `http://en.wikipedia.org/wiki/Gosper_curve`), which is a simple algorithm that fills a 2D space. What we do next is we create a `THREE.Geometry` instance, and for each coordinate, we create a new vertex, which we push into the lines property of this instance. For each coordinate, we also calculate a color value that we use to set the `colors` property.

> In this example, we've set the color using the `setHSL()` method. Instead of providing values for red, green, and blue, with HSL, we provide the hue, saturation, and lightness. Using HSL is much more intuitive than RGB, and it is much easier to create sets of matching colors. A very good explanation of HSL can be found in the CSS specification: `http://www.w3.org/TR/2003/CR-css3-color-20030514/#hsl-color`.

Now that we have our geometry, we can create `THREE.LineBasicMaterial` and use this together with the geometry to create a `THREE.Line` mesh. You can see the result in the `09-line-material.html` example. The following screenshot shows this example:

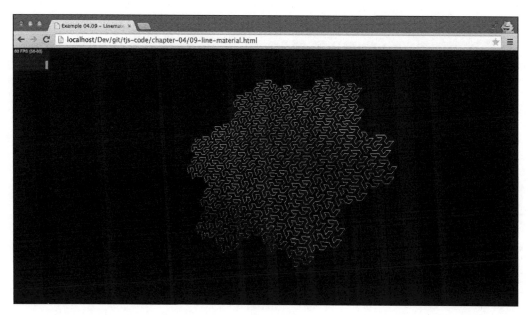

The next and last material we'll discuss in this chapter is only slightly different from
THREE.LineBasicMaterial. With THREE.LineDashedMaterial, not only can we
color lines, but we can also add a *dash* effect.

THREE.LineDashedMaterial

This material has the same properties as THREE.LineBasicMaterial and two
additional ones you can use to define the dash width and the width of the gaps
between the dashes, which are as follows:

Name	Description
scale	This scales dashSize and gapSize. If the scale is smaller than 1, dashSize and gapSize increase, and if the scale is larger than 1, dashSize and gapSize decrease.
dashSize	This is the size of the dash.
gapSize	This is the size of the gap.

This material works almost exactly like THREE.LineBasicMaterial. Here's how
it works:

```
lines.computeLineDistances();
var material = new THREE.LineDashedMaterial({ vertexColors: true,
  color: 0xffffff, dashSize: 10, gapSize: 1, scale: 0.1 });
```

The only difference is that you have to call computeLineDistances() (which is used
to determine the distance between the vertices that make up a line). If you don't do
this, the gaps won't be shown correctly. An example of this material can be found in
10-line-material-dashed.html and looks like the following screenshot:

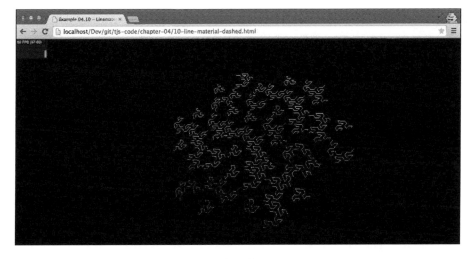

Summary

Three.js gives you a lot of materials you can use to skin your geometries. The materials range from the very simple (THREE.MeshBasicMaterial) to the complex (THREE.ShaderMaterial), where you can provide your own vertexShader and fragmentShader programs. Materials share a lot of basic properties. If you know how to use a single material, you'll probably also know how to use the other materials. Note that not all materials respond to the lights in your scene. If you want a material that takes lighting into effect, use THREE.MeshPhongMaterial or THREE.MeshLamberMaterial. Determining the effect of certain material properties just from code is very hard. Often, a good idea is to use a dat.GUI approach to experiment with these properties.

Also, remember that most of the properties of a material can be modified at runtime. Some though (for example, side) can't be modified at runtime. If you change such a value, you need to set the needsUpdate property to true. For a complete overview of what can and cannot be changed at runtime, see the following page: https://github.com/mrdoob/three.js/wiki/Updates.

In this and the previous chapters, we talked about geometries. We used these in our examples and explored a couple of them. In the next chapter, you'll learn everything about geometries and how you can work with them.

5
Learning to Work with Geometries

In the previous chapters, you learned a lot about how to work with Three.js. You know how to create a basic scene, add lighting, and configure the material for your meshes. In *Chapter 2, Basic Components That Make Up a Three.js Scene*, we touched upon, but didn't really go into the details of, the available geometries that Three.js provides and that you can use to create your 3D objects. In this and the next chapter, we'll walk you through all the geometries (except `THREE.Line`, which we discussed in the previous chapter) Three.js provides out of the box. In this chapter, we'll look at the following geometries:

- `THREE.CircleGeometry`
- `THREE.RingGeometry`
- `THREE.PlaneGeometry`
- `THREE.ShapeGeometry`
- `THREE.BoxGeometry`
- `THREE.SphereGeometry`
- `THREE.CylinderGeometry`
- `THREE.TorusGeometry`
- `THREE.TorusKnotGeometry`
- `THREE.PolyhedronGeometry`
- `THREE.IcosahedronGeometry`
- `THREE.OctahedronGeometry`
- `THREE.TetraHedronGeometry`
- `THREE.DodecahedronGeometry`

And in the next chapter, we'll have a look at the following complex geometries:

- `THREE.ConvexGeometry`

- `THREE.LatheGeometry`

- `THREE.ExtrudeGeometry`

- `THREE.TubeGeometry`

- `THREE.ParametricGeometry`

- `THREE.TextGeometry`

So let's look at all the basic geometries that Three.js has to offer.

The basic geometries provided by Three.js

In Three.js, we have a couple of geometries that result in a two-dimensional mesh and a larger number of geometries that create a three-dimensional mesh. In this section, we'll first look at the 2D geometries: `THREE.CircleGeometry`, `THREE.RingGeometry`, `THREE.PlaneGeometry`, and `THREE.ShapeGeometry`. After that, we'll explore all the basic 3D geometries that are available.

Two-dimensional geometries

Two-dimensional objects look like flat objects and, as the name implies, only have two dimensions. The first two-dimensional geometry on the list is `THREE.PlaneGeometry`.

THREE.PlaneGeometry

A `PlaneGeometry` object can be used to create a very simple two-dimensional rectangle. For an example of this geometry, look at the `01-basic-2d-geometries-plane.html` example in the sources for this chapter. A rectangle created using `PlaneGeometry` is shown in the following screenshot:

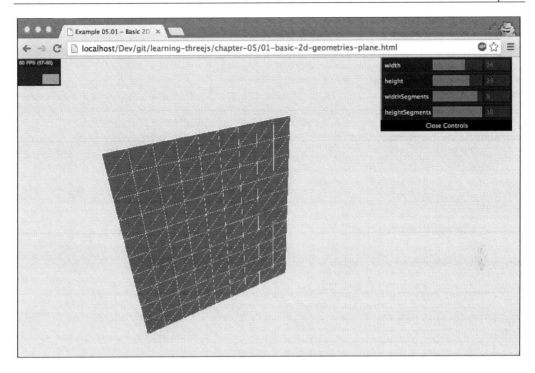

Creating this geometry is very simple, as follows:

```
new THREE.PlaneGeometry(width, height,widthSegments,
    heightSegments);
```

In this example for THREE.PlaneGeometry, you can change these properties and directly see the effect it has on the resulting 3D object. An explanation of these properties is shown in the following table:

Property	Mandatory	Description
width	Yes	This is the width of the rectangle.
height	Yes	This is the height of the rectangle.
widthSegments	No	This is the number of segments the width should be divided into. This defaults to 1.
heightSegments	No	This is the number of segments the height should be divided into. This defaults to 1.

As you can see, this is not a very complex geometry. You just specify the size, and you're done. If you want to create more faces (for example, when you want to create a checkered pattern), you can use the widthSegments and heightSegments properties to divide the geometry into smaller faces.

Before we move on to the next geometry, here's a quick note on the material that is used for this example, and which we also use for most of the other examples in this chapter. We use the following method to create a mesh based on the geometry:

```
function createMesh(geometry) {

  // assign two materials
  var meshMaterial = new THREE.MeshNormalMaterial();
  meshMaterial.side = THREE.DoubleSide;
  var wireframeMaterial = new THREE.MeshBasicMaterial();
  wireFrameMaterial.wireframe = true;

  // create a multimaterial
  var mesh = THREE.SceneUtils.createMultiMaterialObject(
    geometry, [meshMaterial,wireframeMaterial]);
  return mesh;
}
```

In this function, we create a multimaterial mesh based on the mesh provided. The first material used is `THREE.MeshNormalMaterial`. As you learned in the previous chapter, `THREE.MeshNormalMaterial` creates colored faces based on its normal vector (the orientation of the face). We also set this material to be double-sided (`THREE.DoubleSide`). If we don't do this, we won't see this object when its back is turned to the camera. Besides `THREE.MeshNormalMaterial`, we also add `THREE.MeshBasicMaterial`, on which we enable the wireframe property. This way, we can nicely see the 3D shape of the object and the faces that are created for a specific geometry.

> If you want to access the properties of a geometry after it has been created, you can't just say `plane.width`. To access the properties of a geometry, you have to use the `parameters` property of the object. So, to get the `width` property of the `plane` object we created in this section, you'd have to use `plane.parameters.width`.

THREE.CircleGeometry

You can probably already guess what `THREE.CircleGeometry` creates. With this geometry, you can create a very simple two-dimensional circle (or partial circle). Let's first look at the example for this geometry, `02-basic-2d-geometries-circle. html`. In the following screenshot, you can find an example where we created `THREE. CircleGeometry` with a `thetaLength` value that is smaller than `2 * PI`:

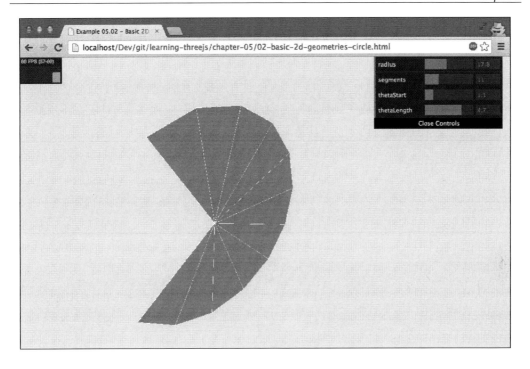

Note that 2 * PI represents a complete circle in radians. If you'd rather work with degrees than radians, converting between them is very easy. The following two functions can help you to convert between radians and degrees, as follows:

```
function deg2rad(degrees) {
    return degrees * Math.PI / 180;
}

function rad2deg(radians) {
    return radians * 180 / Math.PI;
}
```

In this example, you can see and control a mesh created using `THREE.CircleGeometry`. When you create `THREE.CircleGeometry`, you can specify a few properties that define what the circle looks like, as follows:

Property	Mandatory	Description
radius	No	The radius of a circle defines its size. The radius is the distance from the center of the circle to its side. The default value is 50.
segments	No	This property defines the number of faces that are used to create the circle. The minimum number is 3, and if not specified, this number defaults to 8. A higher value means a smoother circle.
thetaStart	No	This property defines the position from which to start drawing the circle. This value can range from 0 to 2 * PI, and the default value is 0.
thetaLength	No	This property defines to what extent the circle is completed. This defaults to 2 * PI (a full circle) when not specified. For instance, if you specify 0.5 * PI for this value, you'll get a quarter circle. Use this property together with the thetaStart property to define the shape of the circle.

You can create a full circle using the following snippet of code:

```
new THREE.CircleGeometry(3, 12);
```

If you wanted to create half a circle from this geometry, you'd use something like this:

```
new THREE.CircleGeometry(3, 12, 0, Math.PI);
```

Before moving on to the next geometry, a quick note on the orientation that Three.js uses when creating these two-dimensional shapes (`THREE.PlaneGeometry`, `THREE.CircleGeometry`, and `THREE.ShapeGeometry`): Three.js creates these objects *standing up*, so they lie along the *x-y* plane. This is very logical since they are two-dimensional shapes. However, often, especially with `THREE.PlaneGeometry`, you want to have the mesh lying down on the ground (the x-z plane)—some sort of ground area on which you can position the rest of your objects. The easiest way to create a two-dimensional object that is horizontally orientated instead of vertically is by rotating the mesh a quarter rotation backwards (-PI/2) around its *x* axis, as follows:

```
mesh.rotation.x =- Math.PI/2;
```

That's all for `THREE.CircleGeometry`. The next geometry, `THREE.RingGeometry`, looks a lot like `THREE.CircleGeometry`.

THREE.RingGeometry

With THREE.RingGeometry, you can create a 2D object that not only closely resembles THREE.CircleGeometry, but also allows you to define a hole in the center (see 03-basic-3d-geometries-ring.html):

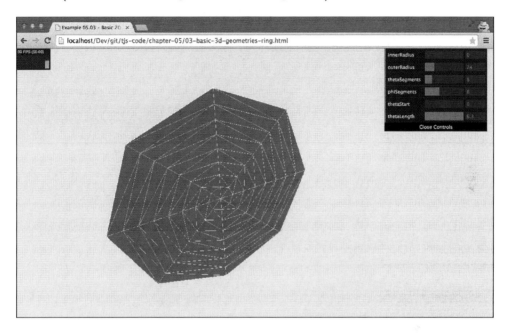

THREE.RingGeometry doesn't have any required properties (see the next table for the default values), so to create this geometry, you only have to specify the following:

```
Var ring = new THREE.RingGeometry();
```

You can further customize the appearance of the ring geometry by passing the following arguments into the constructor:

Property	Mandatory	Description
innerRadius	No	The inner radius of a circle defines the size of the center hole. If this property is set to 0, no hole will be shown. The default value is 0.
outerRadius	No	The outer radius of a circle defines its size. The radius is the distance from the center of the circle to its side. The default value is 50.
thetaSegments	No	This is the number of diagonal segments that will be used to create the circle. A higher value means a smoother ring. The default value is 8.

Property	Mandatory	Description
phiSegments	No	This is the number of segments required to be used along the length of the ring. The default value is 8. This doesn't really affect the smoothness of the circle but increases the number of faces.
thetaStart	No	This defines the position from which to start drawing the circle. This value can range from 0 to 2 * PI, and the default value is 0.
thetaLength	No	This defines the extent to which the circle is completed. This defaults to 2 * PI (a full circle) when not specified. For instance, if you specify 0.5 * PI for this value, you'll get a quarter circle. Use this property together with the thetaStart property to define the shape of the circle.

In the next section, we'll look at the last of the two-dimensional shapes: THREE.ShapeGeometry.

THREE.ShapeGeometry

THREE.PlaneGeometry and THREE.CircleGeometry have limited ways of customizing their appearance. If you want to create custom two-dimensional shapes, you can use THREE.ShapeGeometry. With THREE.ShapeGeometry, you have a couple of functions you can call to create your own shapes. You can compare this functionality with the <path> element functionality that is also available to the HTML canvas element and SVG. Let's start with an example, and after that, we'll show you how you can use the various functions to draw your own shape. The 04-basic-2d-geometries-shape.html example can be found in the sources of this chapter. The following screenshot shows this example:

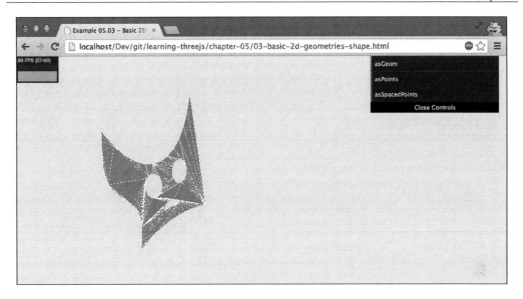

In this example, you can see a custom-created two-dimensional shape. Before going into a description of the properties, first let's look at the code that is used to create this shape. Before we create `THREE.ShapeGeometry`, we first have to create `THREE.Shape`. You can trace these steps by looking at the previous screenshot, where we start in the bottom-right corner. Here's how we created `THREE.Shape`:

```
function drawShape() {
  // create a basic shape
  var shape = new THREE.Shape();

  // startpoint
  shape.moveTo(10, 10);

  // straight line upwards
  shape.lineTo(10, 40);

  // the top of the figure, curve to the right
  shape.bezierCurveTo(15, 25, 25, 25, 30, 40);

  // spline back down
  shape.splineThru(
    [new THREE.Vector2(32, 30),
      new THREE.Vector2(28, 20),
      new THREE.Vector2(30, 10),
    ])
```

```
        // curve at the bottom
        shape.quadraticCurveTo(20, 15, 10, 10);

        // add 'eye' hole one
        var hole1 = new THREE.Path();
        hole1.absellipse(16, 24, 2, 3, 0, Math.PI * 2, true);
        shape.holes.push(hole1);

        // add 'eye hole 2'
        var hole2 = new THREE.Path();
        hole2.absellipse(23, 24, 2, 3, 0, Math.PI * 2, true);
        shape.holes.push(hole2);

        // add 'mouth'
        var hole3 = new THREE.Path();
        hole3.absarc(20, 16, 2, 0, Math.PI, true);
        shape.holes.push(hole3);

        // return the shape
        return shape;
    }
```

In this piece of code, you can see that we created the outline of this shape using lines, curves, and splines. After that, we punched a number of holes in this shape using the holes property of THREE.Shape. In this section, though, we're talking about THREE.ShapeGeometry and not THREE.Shape. To create a geometry from THREE.Shape, we need to pass in THREE.Shape (returned in our case from the drawShape() function) as the argument to THREE.ShapeGeometry, as follows:

```
new THREE.ShapeGeometry(drawShape());
```

The result from this function is a geometry that can be used to create a mesh. There is also an alternative way of creating THREE.ShapeGeometry when you already have a shape. You can call shape.makeGeometry(options), which will return an instance of THREE.ShapeGeometry (for an explanation of the options, see the next table).

Let's first look at the parameters you can pass in to THREE.ShapeGeometry:

Property	Mandatory	Description
shapes	Yes	These are one or more THREE.Shape objects that are used to create THREE.Geometry. You can either pass in a single THREE.Shape object or an array of THREE.Shape objects.

Property	Mandatory	Description
options	No	You can also pass in some `options` that are applied to all the shapes passed in with the `shapes` argument. An explanation of these options is given here: • `curveSegments`: This property determines how smooth the curves created from the shape are. The default value is 12. • `material`: This is the `materialIndex` property used for the faces created for the specified shapes. When you use `THREE.MeshFaceMaterial` together with this geometry, the `materialIndex` property determines which of the materials passed in is used for the faces of the shapes passed in. • `UVGenerator`: When you use a texture with your material, the UV mapping determines what part of a texture is used for a specific face. With the `UVGenerator` property, you can pass in your own object that will create the UV settings for the faces that are created for the shapes passed in. More information on UV settings can be found in *Chapter 10, Loading and Working with Textures*. If none are specified, `THREE.ExtrudeGeometry.WorldUVGenerator` is used.

The most important part of `THREE.ShapeGeometry` is `THREE.Shape`, which you use to create the shape, so let's look at the list of drawing functions you can use to create `THREE.Shape` (note that these are actually functions of the `THREE.Path` object, from which `THREE.Shape` extends):

Name	Description
moveTo(x,y)	Move the drawing position to the *x* and *y* coordinates specified.
lineTo(x,y)	Draw a line from the current position (for example, set by the moveTo function) to the *x* and *y* coordinates provided.

Name	Description
quadraticCurveTo(aCPx, aCPy, x, y)	You can use two different ways of specifying curves. You can use this quadraticCurveTo function, or you can use the bezierCurveTo function (see the next table row). The difference between these two functions is how you specify the curvature of the curve. The following figure explains the differences between these two options: 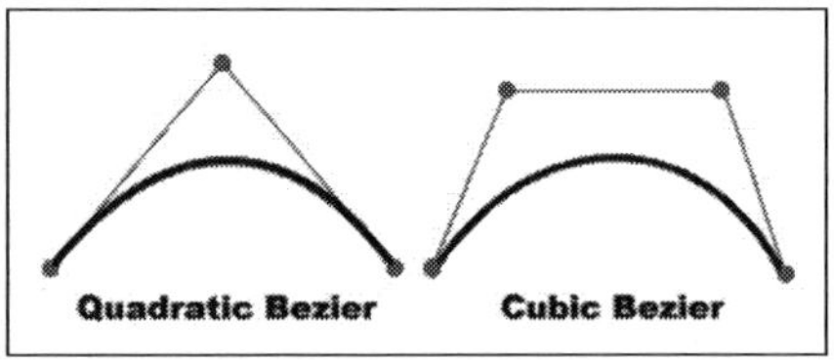 For a quadratic curve, we need to specify one additional point (using the aCPx and aCPy arguments), and the curve is based solely on that point and, of course, the specified end point (from the x and y arguments). For a cubic curve (used by the bezierCurveTo function), you specify two additional points to define the curve. The start point is the current position of the path.
bezierCurveTo(aCPx1, aCPy1, aCPx2, aCPy2, x, y)	This draws a curve based on the arguments supplied. For an explanation, see the previous table entry. The curve is drawn based on the two coordinates that define the curve (aCPx1, aCPy1, aCPx2, and aCPy2) and the end coordinate (x and y). The start point is the current position of the path.
splineThru(pts)	This function draws a fluid line through the set of coordinates provided (pts). This argument should be an array of THREE.Vector2 objects. The start point is the current position of the path.
arc(aX, aY, aRadius, aStartAngle, aEndAngle, aClockwise)	This draws a circle (or part of a circle). The circle starts from the current position of the path. Here, aX and aY are used as offsets from the current position. Note that aRadius sets the size of the circle and aStartAngle and aEndAngle define how large a part of the circle is drawn. The Boolean property aClockwise determines whether the circle is drawn clockwise or counterclockwise.
absArc(aX, aY, aRadius, aStartAngle, aEndAngle, AClockwise)	See the description of arc. The position is absolute instead of relative to the current position.

Name	Description
ellipse(aX, aY, xRadius, yRadius, aStartAngle, aEndAngle, aClockwise)	See the description of arc. As an addition, with the ellipse function, we can separately set the *x* radius and the *y* radius.
absEllipse(aX, aY, xRadius, yRadius, aStartAngle, aEndAngle, aClockwise)	See the description of ellipse. The position is absolute instead of relative to the current position.
fromPoints(vectors)	If you pass in an array of THREE.Vector2 (or THREE.Vector3) objects into this function, Three.js will create a path using straight lines from the supplied vectors.
holes	The holes property contains an array of THREE.Shape objects. Each of the objects in this array is rendered as a hole. A good example of this is the example we saw at the beginning of this section. In that code fragment, we added three THREE.Shape objects to this array. One for the left eye, one for the right eye, and one for the mouth of our main THREE.Shape object.

In this example, we created THREE.ShapeGeometry from a THREE.Shape object using the new THREE.ShapeGeometry(drawShape())) constructor. The THREE.Shape object itself also has a few helper functions you can use to create geometries. They are as follows:

Name	Description
makeGeometry(options)	This returns THREE.ShapeGeometry from THREE.Shape. For more information on the available options, look at the properties of THREE.ShapeGeometry, which we discussed earlier.
createPointsGeometry(divisions)	This converts the shape to a set of points. The divisions property defines how many points are returned. If this value is higher, more points are returned and the resulting line is smoother. The divisions apply to each part of the path separately.
createSpacedPointsGeometry(divisions)	Even this converts the shape into a set of points, but this time, apply the division to the complete path at once.

When you create a set of points, use `createPointsGeometry` or `createSpacedPointsGeometry`; you can use the created points to draw a line, as follows:

```
new THREE.Line( shape.createPointsGeometry(10), new
    THREE.LineBasicMaterial( { color: 0xff3333, linewidth: 2 } ) );
```

When you click on the **asPoints** or **asSpacedPoints** buttons in the example, you'll see something like this:

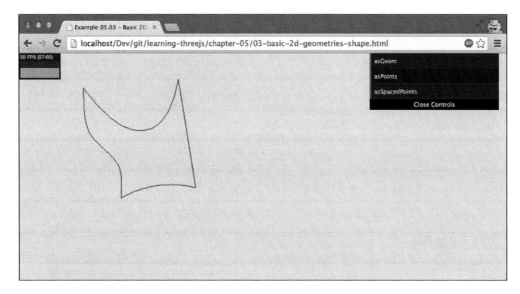

That's it for the two-dimensional shapes. The next part will show and explain the basic three-dimensional shapes.

Three-dimensional geometries

In this section on the basic three-dimensional geometries, we'll start with the geometry we've already seen a couple of times: `THREE.BoxGeometry`.

THREE.BoxGeometry

`THREE.BoxGeometry` is a very simple 3D geometry that allows you to create a box by specifying its width, height, and depth. We've added an example, `05-basic-3d-geometries-cube.html`, where you can play around with these properties. The following screenshot shows this geometry:

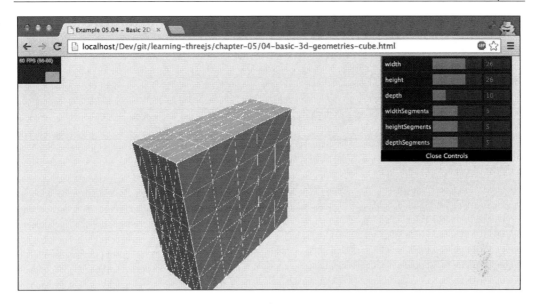

As you can see in this example, by changing the `width`, `height`, and `depth` properties of `THREE.BoxGeometry`, you can control the size of the resulting mesh. These three properties are also mandatory when you create a new cube, as follows:

```
new THREE.BoxGeometry(10,10,10);
```

In the example, you can also see a couple of other properties that you can define on the cube. The following table explains all the properties:

Property	Mandatory	Description
Width	Yes	This is the width of the cube. This is the length of the vertices of the cube along the x axis.
height	Yes	This is the height of the cube. This is the length of the vertices of the cube along the y axis.
depth	Yes	This is the depth of the cube. This is the length of the vertices of the cube along the z axis.
widthSegments	No	This is the number of segments into which we divide a face along the cube's x axis. The default value is 1.
heightSegments	No	This is the number of segments into which we divide a face along the cube's y axis. The default value is 1.
depthSegments	No	This is the number of segments into which we divide a face along the cube's z axis. The default value is 1.

By increasing the various segment properties, you divide the six main faces of the cube into smaller faces. This is useful if you want to set specific material properties on parts of the cube using THREE.MeshFaceMaterial. THREE.BoxGeometry is a very simple geometry. Another simple one is THREE.SphereGeometry.

THREE.SphereGeometry

With SphereGeometry, you can create a three-dimensional sphere. Let's dive straight into the example, 06-basic-3d-geometries-sphere.html:

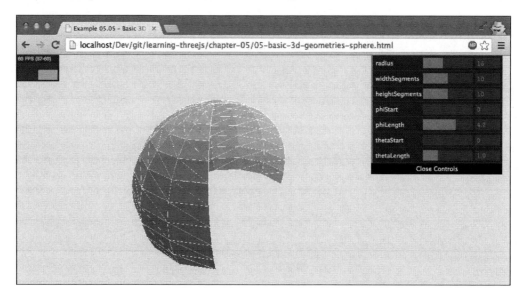

In the previous screenshot, we show you a half-open sphere that was created based on THREE.SphereGeometry. This geometry is a very flexible one and can be used to create all kinds of sphere-related geometries. A basic THREE.SphereGeometry, though, can be created as easily as this: new THREE.SphereGeometry(). The following properties can be used to tune what the resulting mesh looks like:

Property	Mandatory	Description
radius	No	This is used to set the radius for the sphere. This defines how large the resulting mesh will be. The default value is 50.
widthSegments	No	This is the number of segments to be used vertically. More segments means a smoother surface. The default value is 8 and the minimum value is 3.

Property	Mandatory	Description
heightSegments	No	This is the number of segments to be used horizontally. The more the segments, the smoother the surface of the sphere. The default value is 6 and the minimum value is 2.
phiStart	No	This determines where to start drawing the sphere along its *x* axis. This can range from 0 to 2 * PI. The default value is 0.
phiLength	No	This determines how far from phiStart the sphere is be drawn. 2 * PI will draw a full sphere and 0.5 * PI will draw an open quarter sphere. The default value is 2 * PI.
thetaStart	No	This determines where to start drawing the sphere along its *x*-axis. This can range from 0 to PI, and the default value is 0.
thetaLength	No	This determines how far from phiStart the sphere is drawn. The PI value is a full sphere, whereas 0.5 * PI will draw only the top half of the sphere. The default value is PI.

The radius, widthSegments, and heightSegments properties should be clear. We've already seen these kinds of properties in other examples. The phiStart, phiLength, thetaStart, and thetaLength properties are a bit harder to understand without looking at an example. Luckily though, you can experiment with these properties from the menu in the 06-basic-3d-geometries-sphere.html example and create interesting geometries such as these:

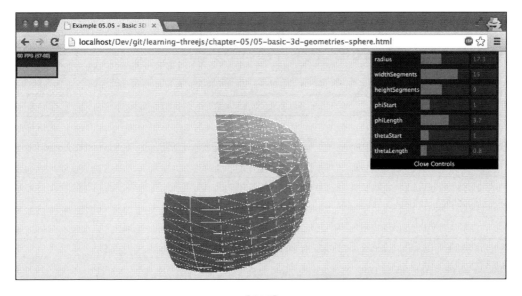

The next one on the list is THREE.CylinderGeometry.

THREE.CylinderGeometry

With this geometry, we can create cylinders and cylinder-like objects. As for all the other geometries, we also have an example (07-basic-3d-geometries-cylinder.html) that lets you experiment with the properties of this geometry, the screenshot for which is as follows:

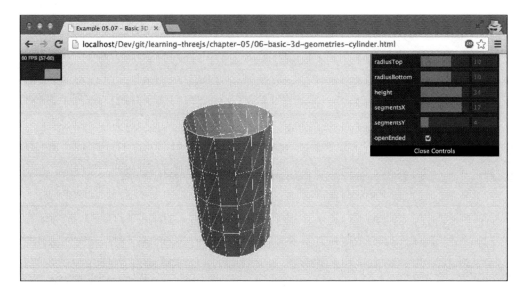

When you create THREE.CylinderGeometry, there aren't any mandatory arguments. So you can create a cylinder by just calling new THREE.CylinderGeometry().
You can pass in a number of properties, as you can see in the example, to alter the appearance of this cylinder. The properties are explained in this table:

Property	Mandatory	Description
radiusTop	No	This sets the size this cylinder will have at the top. The default value is 20.
radiusBottom	No	This sets the size this cylinder will have at the bottom. The default value is 20.
height	No	This property sets the height of the cylinder. The default height is 100.
radialSegments	No	This determines the number of segments along the radius of the cylinder. This defaults to 8. More segments means a smoother cylinder.

Property	Mandatory	Description
heightSegments	No	This determines the number of segments along the height of the cylinder. The default value is 1. More segments means more faces.
openEnded	No	This determines whether or not the mesh is closed at the top and the bottom. The default value is false.

These are all very basic properties you can use to configure the cylinder. One interesting aspect, though, is when you use a negative radius for the top (or for the bottom). If you do this, you can use this geometry to create an hourglass-like shape, as shown in the following screenshot. One thing to note here, as you can see from the colors, is that the top half in this case is turned inside out. If you use a material that isn't configured with THREE.DoubleSide, you won't see the top half.

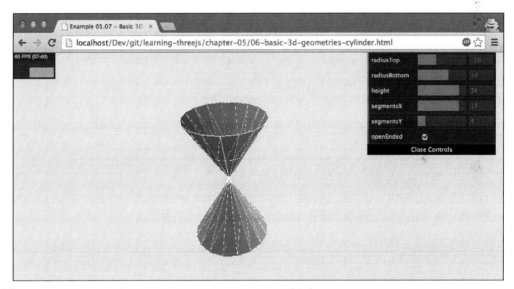

The next geometry is THREE.TorusGeometry, which you can use to create donut-like shapes.

THREE.TorusGeometry

A torus is a simple shape that looks like a donut. The following screenshot, which you can get yourself by opening the `08-basic-3d-geometries-torus.html` example, shows `THREE.TorusGeometry` in action:

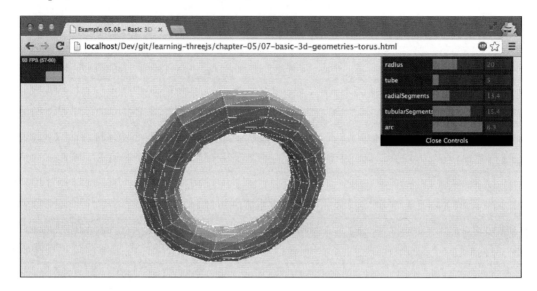

Just like most of the simple geometries, there aren't any mandatory arguments when creating `THREE.TorusGeometry`. The following table lists the arguments you can specify when you create this geometry:

Property	Mandatory	Description
`radius`	No	This sets the size of the complete torus. The default value is `100`.
`tube`	No	This sets the radius of the tube (the actual donut). The default value for this attribute is `40`.
`radialSegments`	No	This determines the number of segments to be used along the length of the torus. The default value is `8`. See the effect of changing this value in the demo.
`tubularSegments`	No	This determines the number of segments to be used along the width of the torus. The default value is `6`. See the effect of changing this value in the demo.
`arc`	No	With this property, you can control whether the torus is drawn full circle. The default of this value is `2 * PI` (a full circle).

Most of these are very basic properties that you've already seen. The `arc` property, however, is a very interesting one. With this property, you define whether the donut makes a full circle or only a partial one. By experimenting with this property, you can create very interesting meshes, such as the following one with an arc set to `0.5 * PI`:

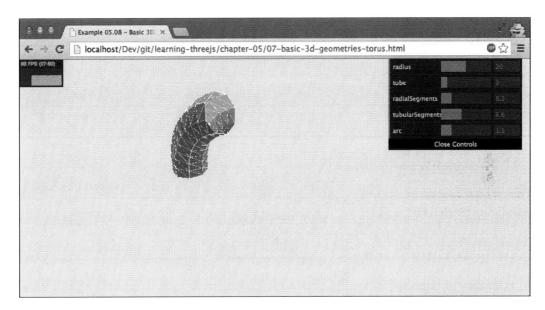

`THREE.TorusGeometry` is a very straightforward geometry. In the next section, we'll look at a geometry that almost shares its name but is much less straightforward: `THREE.TorusKnotGeometry`.

THREE.TorusKnotGeometry

With THREE.TorusKnotGeometry, you can create a torus knot. A torus knot is a special kind of knot that looks like a tube that winds around itself a couple of times. The best way to explain this is by looking at the 09-basic-3d-geometries-torus-knot.html example. The following screenshot shows this geometry:

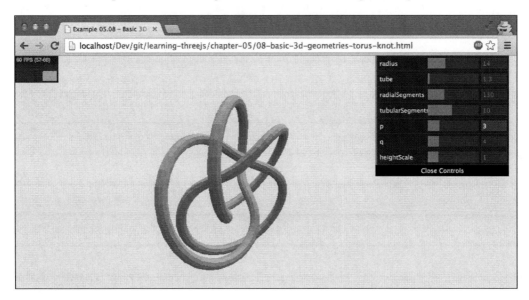

If you open this example and play around with the p and q properties, you can create all kinds of beautiful geometries. The p property defines how often the knot winds around its axis, and q defines how much the knot winds around its interior. If this sounds a bit vague, don't worry. You don't need to understand these properties to create beautiful knots, such as the one shown in the following screenshot (for those interested in the details, Wikipedia has a good article on this subject at http://en.wikipedia.org/wiki/Torus_knot):

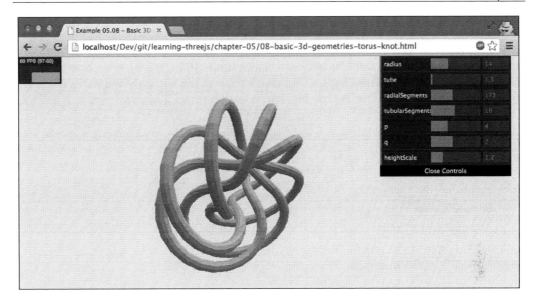

With the example for this geometry, you can play around with the following properties and see the effect various combinations of p and q have on this geometry:

Property	Mandatory	Description
radius	No	This sets the size of the complete torus. The default value is 100.
tube	No	This sets the radius of the tube (the actual donut). The default value for this attribute is 40.
radialSegments	No	This determines the number of segments to be used along the length of the torus knot. The default value is 64. See the effect of changing this value in the demo.
tubularSegments	No	This determines the number of segments to be used along the width of the torus knot. The default value is 8. See the effect of changing this value in the demo.
p	No	This defines the shape of the knot, and the default value is 2.
q	No	This defines the shape of the knot, and the default value is 3.
heightScale	No	With this property, you can stretch out the torus knot. The default value is 1.

The next geometry on the list is the last one of the basic geometries:
`THREE.PolyhedronGeometry`.

THREE.PolyhedronGeometry

With this geometry, you can easily create polyhedrons. A polyhedron is a geometry that has only flat faces and straight edges. Most often, though, you won't use this geometry directly. Three.js provides a number of specific polyhedrons you can use directly without having to specify the vertices and the faces of THREE. PolyhedronGeometry. We'll discuss these polyhedrons later on in this section. If you do want to use THREE. PolyhedronGeometry directly, you have to specify the vertices and the faces (just as we did for the cube in *Chapter 3, Working with the Different Light Sources Available in Three.js*). For instance, we can create a simple tetrahedron (also see THREE. TetrahedronGeometry in this chapter) like this:

```
var vertices = [
   1,  1,  1,
  -1, -1,  1,
  -1,  1, -1,
   1, -1, -1
];

var indices = [
  2, 1, 0,
  0, 3, 2,
  1, 3, 0,
  2, 3, 1
];

polyhedron = createMesh(new THREE.PolyhedronGeometry(vertices,
    indices, controls.radius, controls.detail));
```

To construct THREE.PolyhedronGeometry, we pass in the vertices, indices, radius, and detail properties. The resulting THREE.PolyhedronGeometry object is shown in the 10-basic-3d-geometries-polyhedron.html example (select type as: **Custom** in the menu in the top-right corner):

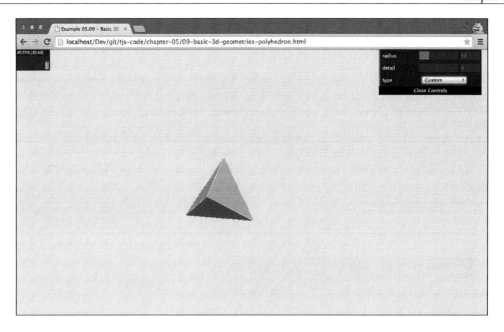

When you create a polyhedron, you can pass in the following four properties:

Property	Mandatory	Description
vertices	Yes	These are the points that make up the polyhedron.
indices	Yes	These are the faces that need to be created from the vertices.
radius	No	This is the size of the polyhedron. This defaults to 1.
detail	No	With this property, you can add additional detail to the polyhedron. If you set this to 1, each triangle in the polyhedron will be split into four smaller triangles. If you set this to 2, those four smaller triangles will each be again split into four smaller triangles, and so on.

At the beginning of this section, we mentioned that Three.js comes with a couple of polyhedrons out of the box. In the following subsections, we'll quickly show you these.

All these polyhedron types can be viewed by looking at the 09-basic-3d-geometries-polyhedron.html example.

THREE.IcosahedronGeometry

THREE.IcosahedronGeometry creates a polyhedron that has 20 identical triangular faces created from 12 vertices. When creating this polyhedron, all you need to specify are the radius and detail levels. This screenshot shows a polyhedron created using THREE.IcosahedronGeometry:

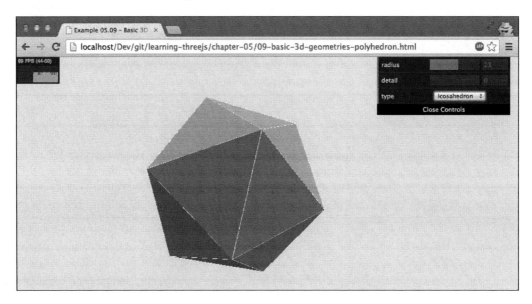

THREE.TetrahedronGeometry

The tetrahedron is one of the simplest polyhedrons. This polyhedron only contains four triangular faces created from four vertices. You create THREE. TetrahedronGeometry just like the other polyhedrons provided by Three.js, by specifying the radius and detail levels. Here's a screenshot that shows a tetrahedron created using THREE.TetrahedronGeometry:

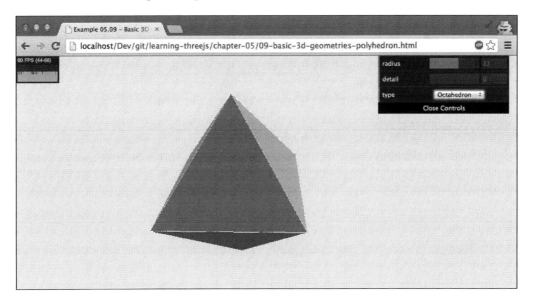

THREE.Octahedron Geometry

Three.js also provides an implementation of an octahedron. As the name implies, this polyhedron has 8 faces. These faces are created from 6 vertices. The following screenshot shows this geometry:

THREE.DodecahedronGeometry

The final polyhedron geometry provided by Three.js is `THREE.DodecahedronGeometry`. This polyhedron has 12 faces. The following screenshot shows this geometry:

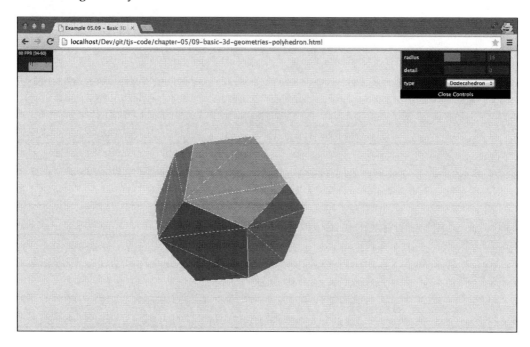

That's the end of this chapter on the basic two-dimensional and three-dimensional geometries provided by Three.js.

Summary

In this chapter, we discussed all of the standard geometries Three.js has to offer. As you saw, there are a whole lot of geometries you can use right out of the box. To best learn how to use the geometries, experiment with the geometries. Use the examples in this chapter to get to know the properties you can use to customize the standard set of geometries available from Three.js. It is also a good thing that when you start with geometries, you choose a basic material; don't go directly for the complex materials, but start simple with THREE.MeshBasicMaterial with the wireframe set to true, or THREE.MeshNormalMaterial. That way, you'll get a much better picture of the true shape of a geometry. For two-dimensional shapes, it's important to remember that they are placed on the x-y plane. If you want to have a two-dimensional shape horizontally, you'll have to rotate the mesh around the x axis for -0.5 * PI. And finally, take care that if you're rotating a two-dimensional shape, or a three-dimensional shape that is *open* (for example, a cylinder or a tube), remember to set the material to THREE.DoubleSide. If you don't do this, the inside or the back of your geometry won't be shown.

In this chapter, we focused on simple, straightforward meshes. Three.js also provides ways to create complex geometries. In the following chapter, you'll learn how to create these.

6

Advanced Geometries and Binary Operations

In the previous chapter, we showed you all the basic geometries provided by Three.js. Besides these basic geometries, Three.js also offers a set of more advanced and specialized objects. In this chapter, we'll show you these advanced geometries and cover the following subjects:

- How to use advanced geometries such as `THREE.ConvexGeometry`, `THREE.LatheGeometry`, and `THREE.TubeGeometry`.

- How to create 3D shapes from 2D shapes using `THREE.ExtrudeGeometry`. We'll do this based on a 2D shape drawn using functionality provided by Three.js, and we'll show an example where we create a 3D shape based on an externally loaded SVG image.

- If you want to create custom shapes yourself, you can easily amend the ones we've discussed in the previous chapters. Three.js, however, also offers a `THREE.ParamtericGeometry` object. With this object, you can create a geometry based on a set of equations.

- Finally, we'll look at how you can create 3D text effects using `THREE.TextGeometry`.

- Additionally, we'll also show you how you can create new geometries from existing ones using binary operations provided by the Three.js extension, ThreeBSP.

We'll start with the first one from this list, `THREE.ConvexGeometry`.

THREE.ConvexGeometry

With `THREE.ConvexGeometry`, we can create a convex hull around a set of points. A convex hull is the minimal shape that encompasses all these points. The easiest way to understand this is by looking at an example. If you open up the `01-advanced-3d-geometries-convex.html` example, you'll see the convex hull for a random set of points. The following screenshot shows this geometry:

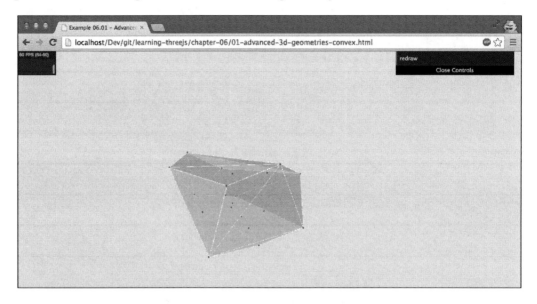

In this example, we generate a random set of points and based on these points we create `THREE.ConvexGeometry`. In the example, you can click on **redraw**, which will generate 20 new points and draw the convex hull. We also add each of these points as a small `THREE.SphereGeometry` object to clearly show how a convex hull works. `THREE.ConvexGeometry` isn't included in the standard Three.js distribution, so you have to include an additional JavaScript file to use this geometry. At the top of your HTML page, add the following:

```
<script src="../libs/ConvexGeometry.js"></script>
```

The following piece of code shows how these points were created and added to the scene:

```
function generatePoints() {
  // add 10 random spheres
  var points = [];
  for (var i = 0; i < 20; i++) {
```

```
    var randomX = -15 + Math.round(Math.random() * 30);
    var randomY = -15 + Math.round(Math.random() * 30);
    var randomZ = -15 + Math.round(Math.random() * 30);
    points.push(new THREE.Vector3(randomX, randomY, randomZ));
  }

  var group = new THREE.Object3D();
  var material = new THREE.MeshBasicMaterial({color: 0xff0000,
    transparent: false});
  points.forEach(function (point) {
    var geom = new THREE.SphereGeometry(0.2);
    var mesh = new THREE.Mesh(geom, material);
    mesh.position.clone(point);
    group.add(mesh);
  });

  // add the points as a group to the scene
  scene.add(group);
}
```

As you can see in this snippet of code, we create 20 random points (`THREE.Vector3`), which we push into an array. Next, we iterate this array and create `THREE.SphereGeometry`, whose position we set to one of these points (`position.clone(point)`). All the points are added to a group (more on this in *Chapter 7, Particles, Sprites, and the Point Cloud*), so we can rotate them easily by just rotating the group.

Once you have this set of points, creating `THREE.ConvexGeometry` is very easy, as shown in the following code snippet:

```
// use the same points to create a convexgeometry
var convexGeometry = new THREE.ConvexGeometry(points);
convexMesh = createMesh(convexGeometry);
scene.add(convexMesh);
```

An array containing vertices (of the `THREE.Vector3` type) is the only argument `THREE.ConvexGeometry` takes. Here's one final note on the `createMesh()` function (which is a function we created ourselves in *Chapter 5, Learning to Work with Geometries*) we call here. In the previous chapter, we used this method to create a mesh using `THREE.MeshNormalMaterial`. For this example, we changed this to a translucent green `THREE.MeshBasicMaterial` to better show the convex hull we created and the individual points that make up this geometry.

The next complex geometry is `THREE.LatheGeometry`, which can be used to create vase-like shapes.

THREE.LatheGeometry

THREE.LatheGeometry allows you to create shapes from a smooth curve. This curve is defined by a number of points (also called knots) and is most often called a spline. This spline is rotated around the central *z* axis of the object and results in vase-like and bell-like shapes. Once again, the easiest way to understand what THREE.LatheGeometry looks like is by looking at an example. This geometry is shown in 02-advanced-3d-geometries-lathe.html. The following screenshot taken from the example shows this geometry:

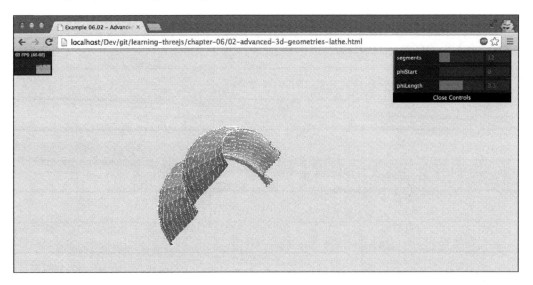

In the preceding screenshot, you can see the spline as the set of small red spheres. The positions of these spheres are passed in to THREE.LatheGeometry, together with a couple of other arguments. In this example, we rotate this spline for half a circle, and based on this spline, we extract the shape you can see. Before we look at all the arguments, let's look at the code used to create the spline and how THREE.LatheGeometry uses this spline:

```
function generatePoints(segments, phiStart, phiLength) {
  // add 10 random spheres
  var points = [];
  var height = 5;
  var count = 30;
  for (var i = 0; i < count; i++) {
    points.push(new THREE.Vector3((Math.sin(i * 0.2) + Math.cos(i
      * 0.3)) * height + 12, 0, ( i - count ) + count / 2));
  }
```

```
        . . .

        // use the same points to create a LatheGeometry
        var latheGeometry = new THREE.LatheGeometry (points, segments,
          phiStart, phiLength);
        latheMesh = createMesh(latheGeometry);
        scene.add(latheMesh);
      }
```

In this piece of JavaScript, you can see that we generate 30 points whose *x* coordinate is based on a combination of sine and cosine functions while the *z* coordinate is based on the `i` and `count` variables. This creates the spline visualized by the red dots in the preceding screenshot.

Based on these points, we can create `THREE.LatheGeometry`. Besides the array of vertices, `THREE.LatheGeometry` takes a couple of other arguments. The following table lists all the arguments:

Property	Mandatory	Description
points	Yes	These are the points that make up the spline used to generate the bell/vase shape.
segments	No	These are the number of segments used when creating the shape. The higher this number, the more *round* the resulting shape will be. The default value for this is 12.
phiStart	No	This determines where to start on a circle when generating the shape. This can range from 0 to 2*PI. The default value is 0.
phiLength	No	This defines how fully generated the shape is. For instance, a quarter shape will be 0.5*PI. The default value is the full 360 degrees or 2*PI.

In the next section, we'll look at an alternative way of creating geometries by extracting a 3D geometry from a 2D shape.

Creating a geometry by extruding

Three.js provides a couple of ways in which we can extrude a 2D shape to a 3D shape. By extruding, we mean stretching out a 2D shape along its *z* axis to convert it to 3D. For instance, if we extrude `THREE.CircleGeometry`, we get a shape that looks like a cylinder, and if we extrude `THREE.PlaneGeometry`, we get a cube-like shape.

The most versatile way of extruding a shape is using the `THREE.ExtrudeGeometry` object.

THREE.ExtrudeGeometry

With THREE.ExtrudeGeometry, you can create a 3D object from a 2D shape. Before we dive into the details of this geometry, let's first look at an example: 03-extrude-geometry.html. The following screenshot taken from the example shows this geometry:

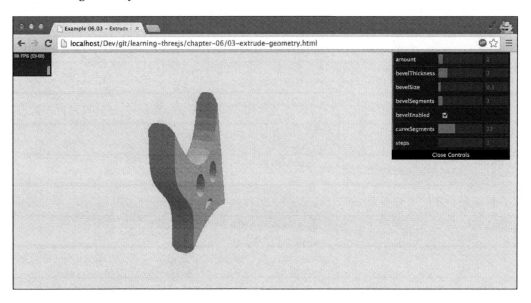

In this example, we took the 2D shape we created in the previous chapter and used THREE.ExtrudeGeometry to convert it to 3D. As you can see in this screenshot, the shape is extruded along the *z* axis, which results in a 3D shape. The code to create THREE.ExtrudeGeometry is very easy:

```
var options = {
  amount: 10,
  bevelThickness: 2,
  bevelSize: 1,
  bevelSegments: 3,
  bevelEnabled: true,
  curveSegments: 12,
  steps: 1
};

shape = createMesh(new THREE.ExtrudeGeometry(drawShape(),
  options));
```

In this code, we created the shape with the `drawShape()` function just as we did in the previous chapter. This shape is passed on to the `THREE.ExtrudeGeometry` constructor together with an `options` object. With the `options` object, you can define exactly how the shape should be extruded. The following table explains the options you can pass in to `THREE.ExtrudeGeometry`.

Property	Mandatory	Description
shapes	Yes	One or more shapes (`THREE.Shape` objects) are required to extrude the geometry from. See the preceding chapter on how to create such a shape.
amount	No	This determines how far (the depth) the shape should be extruded. The default value is `100`.
bevelThickness	No	This determines the depth of the bevel. The bevel is the rounded corner between the front and back faces and the extrusion. This value defines how deep into the shape the bevel goes. The default value is `6`.
bevelSize	No	This determines the height of the bevel. This is added to the normal height of the shape. The default value is `bevelThickness - 2`.
bevelSegments	No	This defines the number of segments that will be used by the bevel. The more the number of segments used, the smoother the bevel will look. The default value is `3`.
bevelEnabled	No	If this is set to `true`, a bevel is added. The default value is `true`.
curveSegments	No	This determines how many segments will be used when extruding the curves of shapes. The more the number of segments used, the smoother the curves will look. The default value is `12`.
steps	No	This defines the number of segments into the extrusion will be divided along its depth. The default value is `1`. A higher value will result in more individual faces.
extrudePath	No	This is the path (`THREE.CurvePath`) along which the shape should be extruded. If this isn't specified, the shape is extruded along the z axis.
material	No	This is the index of the material to use for the front and the back faces. Use the `THREE.SceneUtils.createMultiMaterialObject` function to create the mesh if you want separate materials for the front and back faces.

Property	Mandatory	Description
extrudeMaterial	No	This is the index of the materials to use for the bevel and the extrusion. Use the THREE.SceneUtils.createMultiMaterialObject function to create the mesh if you want separate materials for the front and back faces.
uvGenerator	No	When you use a texture with your material, the UV mapping determines what part of a texture is used for a specific face. With the uvGenerator property, you can pass in your own object that will create the UV settings for the faces that are created for the shapes that are passed in. More information on UV settings can be found in *Chapter 10, Loading and Working with Textures*. If none are specified, THREE.ExtrudeGeometry.WorldUVGenerator is used.
frames	No	A frenet frame is used to calculate the tangents, normal, and binormals of a spline. This is used when extruding along extrudePath. You don't need to specify this since Three.js provides its own implementation, THREE.TubeGeometry.FrenetFrames, which is also used as default. More information on frenet frames can be found at http://en.wikipedia.org/wiki/Differential_geometry_of_curves#Frenet_frame.

You can experiment with these options using the menu from the 03-extrude-geometry.html example.

In this example, we extruded the shape along its *z* axis. As you would have seen in the options, you can also extrude a shape along a path with the extrudePath option. In the following geometry, THREE.TubeGeometry, we'll do just that.

THREE.TubeGeometry

THREE.TubeGeometry creates a tube that extrudes along a 3D spline. You specify the path using a number of vertices, and THREE.TubeGeometry will create the tube. An example which you can experiment with can be found in the sources for this chapter (04-extrude-tube.html). The following screenshot shows this example:

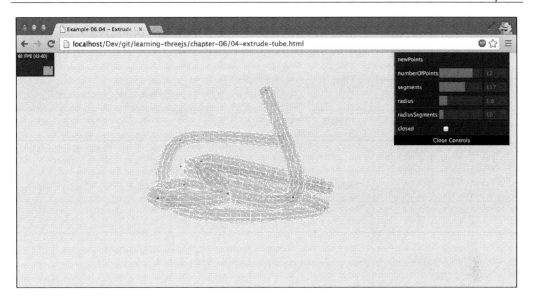

As you can see in this example, we generate a number of random points and use those points to draw the tube. With the controls in the upper-right corner, we can define how the tube looks or generate a new tube by clicking on the **newPoints** button. The code needed to create a tube is very simple, as follows:

```
var points = [];
for (var i = 0 ; i < controls.numberOfPoints ; i++) {
  var randomX = -20 + Math.round(Math.random() * 50);
  var randomY = -15 + Math.round(Math.random() * 40);
  var randomZ = -20 + Math.round(Math.random() * 40);

  points.push(new THREE.Vector3(randomX, randomY, randomZ));
}

var tubeGeometry = new THREE.TubeGeometry(new THREE.SplineCurve3
  (points), segments, radius, radiusSegments, closed);

var tubeMesh = createMesh(tubeGeometry);
scene.add(tubeMesh);
```

What we need to do first is get a set of vertices of the THREE.Vector3 type just like we did for THREE.ConvexGeometry and THREE.LatheGeometry. Before we can use these points, however, to create the tube, we first need to convert these points to THREE.SplineCurve3. In other words, we need to define a smooth curve through the points we defined. We can do this simply by passing in the array of vertices to the constructor of THREE.SplineCurve3. With this spline and the other arguments (which we'll explain in a bit), we can create the tube and add it to the scene.

THREE.TubeGeometry takes some other arguments besides THREE.SplineCurve3. The following table lists all the arguments for THREE.TubeGeometry:

Property	Mandatory	Description
path	Yes	This is THREE.SplineCurve3 that describes the path this tube should follow.
segments	No	These are the segments used to build up the tube. The default value is 64. The longer the path, the more segments you should specify.
radius	No	This is the radius of the tube. The default value is 1.
radiusSegments	No	This is the number of segments to be used along the length of the tube. The default value is 8. The more you use, the more *round* the tube will look.
closed	No	If this is set to true, the start of the tube and the end will be connected together. The default value is false.

The last extrude example we'll show in this chapter isn't really a different geometry. In the next section, we'll show you how you can use THREE.ExtrudeGeometry to create extrusions from existing SVG paths.

Extrude from SVG

When we discussed THREE.ShapeGeometry, we mentioned that SVG follows pretty much the same approach of drawing shapes. SVG has a very close match with how Three.js handles shapes. In this section, we'll look at how you can use a small library from https://github.com/asutherland/d3-threeD to convert SVG paths to a Three.js shape.

For the `05-extrude-svg.html` example, I've taken an SVG drawing of the Batman logo and used `ExtrudeGeometry` to convert it to 3D, as shown in the following screenshot:

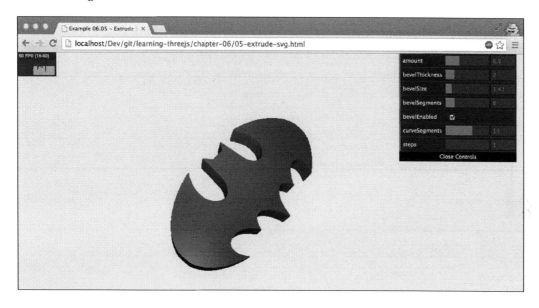

First, let's look at what the original SVG code looks like (you can also see this for yourself when looking at the source code for this example):

```
<svg version="1.0" xmlns="http://www.w3.org/2000/svg"
  xmlns:xlink="http://www.w3.org/1999/xlink" x="0px" y="0px"
  width="1152px" height="1152px" xml:space="preserve">
<g>
<path  id="batman-path" style="fill:rgb(0,0,0);" d="M 261.135
  114.535 C 254.906 116.662 247.491 118.825 244.659 119.344 C
  229.433 122.131 177.907 142.565 151.973 156.101 C 111.417
  177.269 78.9808 203.399 49.2992 238.815 C 41.0479 248.66
  26.5057 277.248 21.0148 294.418 C 14.873 313.624 15.3588
  357.341 21.9304 376.806 C 29.244 398.469 39.6107 416.935
  52.0865 430.524 C 58.2431 437.23 63.3085 443.321 63.3431
  444.06 ... 261.135 114.535 "/>
</g>
</svg>
```

Unless you're an SVG guru, this will probably mean nothing to you. Basically though, what you see here are a set of drawing instructions. For instance, C 277.987 119.348 279.673 116.786 279.673 115.867 tells the browser to draw a cubic Bezier curve, and L 489.242 111.787 tells us that we should draw a line to that specific position. Luckily though, we won't have to write the code to interpret this ourselves. With the d3-threeD library, we can convert this automatically. This library was originally created to be used together with the excellent **D3.js** library, but with some small adaptions, we can also use this specific functionality standalone.

> **SVG** stands for **Scalable Vector Graphics**. This is an XML-based standard that can be used to create vector-based 2D images for the Web. This is an open standard that is supported by all of the modern browsers. Directly working with SVG and manipulating it from JavaScript, however, isn't very straightforward. Luckily, there are a couple of open source JavaScript libraries that make working with SVG a lot easier. **Paper.js**, **Snap.js**, **D3.js**, and **Raphael.js** are some of the best.

The following code fragment shows how we can load in the SVG you saw earlier, convert it to THREE.ExtrudeGeometry, and show it on screen:

```
function drawShape() {
  var svgString = document.querySelector("#batman-
    path").getAttribute("d");
  var shape = transformSVGPathExposed(svgString);
  return shape;
}

var options = {
  amount: 10,
  bevelThickness: 2,
  bevelSize: 1,
  bevelSegments: 3,
  bevelEnabled: true,
  curveSegments: 12,
  steps: 1
};

shape = createMesh(new THREE.ExtrudeGeometry(drawShape(),
  options));
```

In this code fragment, you'll see a call to the `transformSVGPathExposed` function. This function is provided by the d3-threeD library and takes an SVG string as an argument. We get this SVG string directly from the SVG element with the following expression: `document.querySelector("#batman-path").getAttribute("d")`. In SVG, the `d` attribute contains the path statements used to draw a shape. Add a nice-looking shiny material and a spotlight and you've recreated this example.

The last geometry we'll discuss in this section is `THREE.ParametricGeometry`. With this geometry, you can specify a couple of functions that are used to programmatically create geometries.

THREE.ParametricGeometry

With `THREE.ParametricGeometry`, you can create a geometry based on an equation. Before we dive into our own example, a good thing to start with is to look at the examples already provided by Three.js. When you download the Three.js distribution, you get the `examples/js/ParametricGeometries.js` file. In this file, you can find a couple of examples of equations you can use together with `THREE.ParametricGeometry`. The most basic example is the function to create a plane:

```
function plane(u, v) {
  var x = u * width;
  var y = 0;
  var z = v * depth;
  return new THREE.Vector3(x, y, z);
}
```

This function is called by `THREE.ParametricGeometry`. The u and v values will range from `0` to `1` and will be called a large number of times for all the values from `0` to `1`. In this example, the u value is used to determine the *x* coordinate of the vector and the v value is used to determine the *z* coordinate. When this is run, you'll have a basic plane with a width of `width` and a depth of `depth`.

In our example, we do something similar. However, instead of creating a flat plane, we create a wave-like pattern, as you can see in the 06-parametric-geometries.html example. The following screenshot shows this example:

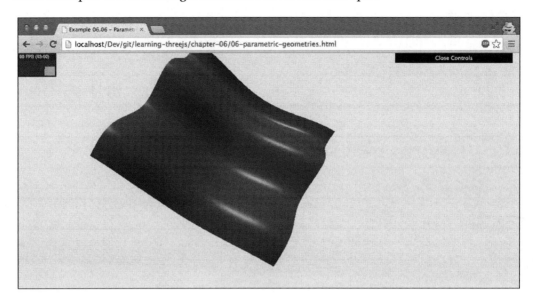

To create this shape, we passed in the following function to THREE.ParametricGeometry:

```
radialWave = function (u, v) {
  var r = 50;

  var x = Math.sin(u) * r;
  var z = Math.sin(v / 2) * 2 * r;
  var y = (Math.sin(u * 4 * Math.PI) + Math.cos(v * 2 * Math.PI))
    * 2.8;

  return new THREE.Vector3(x, y, z);
}

var mesh = createMesh(new THREE.ParametricGeometry(radialWave,
  120, 120, false));
```

As you can see in this example, with a few lines of code, we can create really interesting geometries. In this example, you can also see the arguments we can pass in to THREE.ParametricGeometry. These are explained in the following table:

Property	Mandatory	Description
`function`	Yes	This is the function that defines the position of each vertex based on the u and v values provided
`slices`	Yes	This defines the number of parts the u value should be divided into
`stacks`	Yes	This defines the number of parts the v value should be divided into

I'd like to make a final note on how to use the `slices` and `stacks` properties before moving on to the final part of this chapter. We mentioned that the u and v properties are passed in to the `function` argument provided, and that the values of these two properties range from 0 to 1. With the `slices` and `stacks` properties, we can define how often the passed-in function is called. If, for instance, we set `slices` to 5 and `stacks` to 4, the function will be called with the following values:

```
u:0/5, v:0/4
u:1/5, v:0/4
u:2/5, v:0/4
u:3/5, v:0/4
u:4/5, v:0/4
u:5/5, v:0/4
u:0/5, v:1/4
u:1/5, v:1/4
...
u:5/5, v:3/4
u:5/5, v:4/4
```

So, the higher this value, the more vertices you get to specify and the smoother your created geometry will be. You can use the menu in the top-right corner of the `06-parametric-geometries.html` example to see this effect.

For more examples, you can look at the `examples/js/ParametricGeometries.js` file in the Three.js distribution. This file contains functions to create the following geometries:

- Klein bottle
- Plane
- Flat mobius strip
- 3d mobius strip
- Tube
- Torus knot
- Sphere

The last part of this chapter deals with creating 3D text objects.

Creating 3D text

In the last part of this chapter, we'll have a quick look at how you can create 3D text effects. First, we'll look at how to render text using the fonts provided by Three.js, and after that, we'll have a quick look at how you can use your own fonts for this.

Rendering text

Rendering text in Three.js is very easy. All you have to do is define the font you want to use and the basic extrude properties we saw when we discussed THREE. ExtrudeGeometry. The following screenshot shows the `07-text-geometry.html` example on how to render text in Three.js:

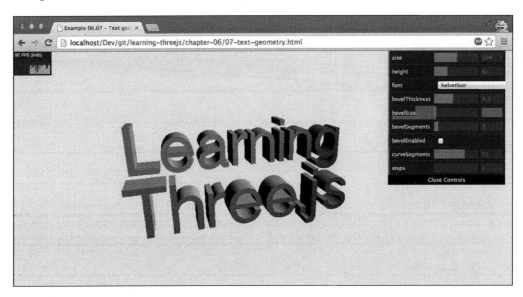

The code required to create this 3D text is as follows:

```
var options = {
  size: 90,
  height: 90,
  weight: 'normal',
  font: 'helvetiker',
  style: 'normal',
  bevelThickness: 2,
  bevelSize: 4,
```

```
    bevelSegments: 3,
    bevelEnabled: true,
    curveSegments: 12,
    steps: 1
};

// the createMesh is the same function we saw earlier
text1 = createMesh(new THREE.TextGeometry("Learning", options));
text1.position.z = -100;
text1.position.y = 100;
scene.add(text1);

text2 = createMesh(new THREE.TextGeometry("Three.js", options));
scene.add(text2);
};
```

Let's look at all the options we can specify for THREE.TextGeometry:

Property	Mandatory	Description
size	No	This is the size of the text. The default value is 100.
height	No	This is the length (depth) of the extrusion. The default value is 50.
weight	No	This is the weight of the font. The possible values are normal and bold. The default value is normal.
font	No	This is the name of the font to be used. The default value is helvetiker.
style	No	This is the weight of the font. The possible values are normal and italic. The default value is normal.
bevelThickness	No	This is the depth of the bevel. The bevel is the rounded corner between the front and back faces and the extrusion. The default value is 10.
bevelSize	No	This is the height of the bevel. The default value is 8.
bevelSegments	No	This defines the number of segments that will be used by the bevel. The more segments there are, the smoother the bevel will look. The default value is 3.
bevelEnabled	No	If this is set to true, a bevel is added. The default value is false.

Property	Mandatory	Description
curveSegments	No	This defines the number segments used when extruding the curves of shapes. The more segments there are, the smoother the curves will look. The default value is 4.
steps	No	This defines the number of segments the extrusion will be divided into. The default value is 1.
extrudePath	No	This is the path along which the shape should be extruded. If this isn't specified, the shape is extruded along the z axis.
material	No	This is the index of the material to be used for the front and back faces. Use the THREE.SceneUtils.createMultiMaterialObject function to create the mesh.
extrudeMaterial	No	This is the index of the material to be used for the bevel and the extrusion. Use the THREE.SceneUtils.createMultiMaterialObject function to create the mesh.
uvGenerator	No	When you use a texture with your material, the UV mapping determines what part of a texture is used for a specific face. With the UVGenerator property, you can pass in your own object that will create the UV settings for the faces that are created for the passed-in shapes. More information on UV settings can be found in *Chapter 10, Loading and Working with Textures*. If none are specified, THREE.ExtrudeGeometry.WorldUVGenerator is used.
frames	No	A frenet frame is used to calculate the tangents, normal, and binormals of a spline. This is used when extruding along extrudePath. You don't need to specify this because Three.js provides its own implementation, THREE.TubeGeometry.FrenetFrames, which is also used as default. More information on frenet frames can be found at http://en.wikipedia.org/wiki/Differential_geometry_of_curves#Frenet_frame.

The fonts that are included in Three.js are also added to the sources for this book. You can find them in the assets/fonts folder.

If you want to render fonts in 2D, for instance, to use them as a texture for a material, you shouldn't use THREE.TextGeometry. THREE.TextGeometry, which internally uses THREE.ExtrudeGeometry to build the 3D text, and the JavaScript fonts introduce a lot of overhead. Rendering a simple 2D font is better than just using the HTML5 canvas. With context.font, you can set the font to be used, and with context.fillText, you can output text to the canvas. You can then use this canvas as input for your texture. We will show you how to do this in *Chapter 10, Loading and Working with Textures*.

It's also possible to use other fonts with this geometry, but you first need to convert them to JavaScript. How to do this is shown in the next section.

Adding custom fonts

There are a couple of fonts provided by Three.js that you can use in your scenes. These fonts are based on the fonts provided by **typeface.js** (http://typeface. neocracy.org:81/). Typeface.js is a library that can convert TrueType and OpenType fonts to JavaScript. The resulting JavaScript file can be included in your page, and the font can then be used in Three.js.

To convert an existing OpenType or TrueType font, you can use the web page at http://typeface.neocracy.org:81/fonts.html. On this page, you can upload a font, and it will be converted to JavaScript for you. Note that this doesn't work for all types of fonts. The simpler the font (more straight lines), the better the chance is that it will be rendered correctly when used in Three.js.

To include that font, just add the following line at the top of your HTML page:

```
<script type="text/javascript" src="../assets/fonts/bitstream
  _vera_sans_mono_roman.typeface.js">
</script>
```

This will load the font and make it available to Three.js. If you want to know the name of the font (to use with the font property), you can print out the font cache to the console using the following line of JavaScript:

```
console.log(THREE.FontUtils.faces);
```

This will print out something like the following:

```
▼ Object
  ▼ bitstream vera sans mono: Object
    ▶ normal: Object
    ▶ __proto__: Object
  ▼ helvetiker: Object
    ▶ bold: Object
    ▶ normal: Object
    ▶ __proto__: Object
  ▶ __proto__: Object
```

Here, you can see that we can use the `helvetiker` font with `weight` as `either bold` or `normal`, and the `bitstream vera sans mono` font with `weight` as `normal`. Note that each font weight comes in its separate JavaScript file and needs to be loaded separately. An alternative way of determining the font name is by looking at the JavaScript source file for the font. At the end of the file, you'll find a property with the name `familyName` as shown in the following code. This property also contains the name of the font:

```
"familyName":"Bitstream Vera Sans Mono"
```

In the next part of this chapter, we'll introduce the ThreeBSP library to create very interesting-looking geometries using the binary operations: `intersect`, `subtract`, and `union`.

Using binary operations to combine meshes

In this section, we'll look at a different way of creating geometries. In this chapter, so far, and in the previous chapter, we used the default geometries provided by Three.js to create interesting-looking geometries. With the default set of properties, you can create beautiful models, but you are limited to what Three.js provides. In this section, we'll show you how you can combine these standard geometries to create new ones—a technique known as **Constructive Solid Geometry** (**CSG**) To do this, we use the Three.js extension ThreeBSP, which you can find online at `https://github.com/skalnik/ThreeBSP`. This additional library provides the following three functions:

Name	Description
`intersect`	This function allows you to create a new geometry based on the intersection of two existing geometries. The area where both geometries overlap will define the shape of this new geometry.
`union`	The union function can be used to combine two geometries and create a new one. You can compare this with the `mergeGeometry` functionality we'll look at in *Chapter 8, Creating and Loading Advanced Meshes and Geometries*.
`subtract`	The subtract function is the opposite of the union function. You can create a new geometry by removing the overlapping area from the first geometry.

In the following sections, we'll look at each of these functions in more detail. The following screenshot shows an example of what you can create by just using the union and subtract functionalities one after the other.

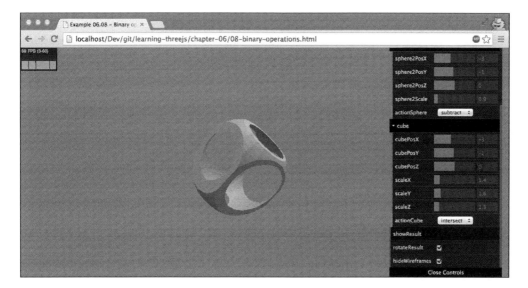

To use this library, we need to include it in our page. This library is written in CoffeeScript, a more user-friendly variant of JavaScript. To get this working, we have two options. We can add the CoffeeScript file and compile it on the fly, or we can precompile it to JavaScript and include it directly. For the first approach, we need to do the following:

```html
<script type="text/javascript" src="../libs/coffee-script.js">
  </script>
<script type="text/coffeescript" src="../libs/ThreeBSP.coffee">
  </script>
```

The `ThreeBSP.coffee` file contains the functionality we need for this example, and `coffee-script.js` can interpret the Coffee language used for ThreeBSP. A final step we need to take is make sure the `ThreeBSP.coffee` file has been parsed completely before we start using the ThreeBSP functionality. For this, we add the following to the bottom of the file:

```
<script type="text/coffeescript">
  onReady();
</script>
```

We rename our initial `onload` function to `onReady` like this:

```
function onReady() {
  // Three.js code
}
```

If we precompile CoffeeScript to JavaScript using the CoffeeScript command-line tool, we can include the resulting JavaScript file directly. Before we can do this, though, we need to install CoffeeScript. You can follow the installation instructions on the CoffeeScript website at `http://coffeescript.org/`. Once you've installed CoffeeScript, you can use the following command line to convert the CoffeeScript ThreeBSP file to JavaScript:

```
coffee --compile ThreeBSP.coffee
```

This command creates a `ThreeBSP.js` file that we can include in our example just as we do with the other JavaScript file. In our examples, we use this second approach because it'll load quicker than compiling the CoffeeScript each time we load the page. For this, all we need to do is add the following to the top of our HTML page:

```
<script type="text/javascript" src="../libs/ThreeBSP.js"></script>
```

Now that the ThreeBSP library is loaded, we can use the functions it provides.

The subtract function

Before we start with the `subtract` function, there is one important step you need to keep in mind. These three functions use the absolute position of the mesh for calculations. So, if you group meshes together or use multiple materials before applying these functions, you'll probably get strange results. For the best and most predictable result, make sure you're working with ungrouped meshes.

Let's start by demonstrating the `subtract` functionality. For this, we've provided an example, `08-binary-operations.html`. With this example, you can experiment with the three operations. When you first open the example on binary operations, you'll see something like the following start screen:

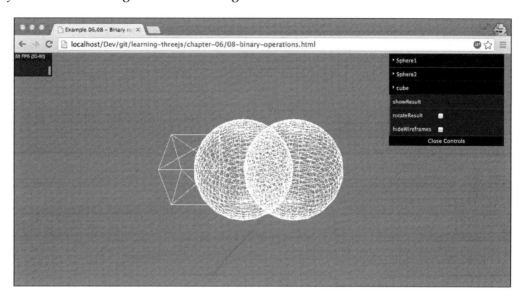

There are three wireframes: a cube and two spheres. **Sphere1**, the center sphere, is the object on which all operations are executed, **Sphere2** is on the right-hand side, and **Cube** is on the left-hand side. On **Sphere2** and **Cube**, you can define one of four actions: **subtract**, **union**, **intersect**, and **none**. These actions are applied from the point of view of **Sphere1**. When we set **Sphere2** to subtract and select **showResult** (and hide the wireframes), the result will show **Sphere1** minus the area where **Sphere1** and **Sphere2** overlap. Note that a few of these operations might take a couple of seconds to complete after you've pushed the **showResult** button, so be patient while the *busy* indicator is visible.

The following screenshot shows the result action of a sphere after subtracting another sphere:

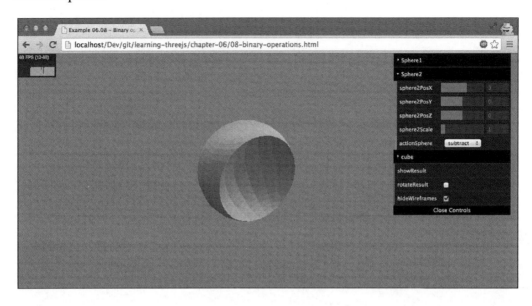

In this example, first the action defined for **Sphere2** is executed, and next, the action for **Cube** is executed. So, if we subtract both **Sphere2** and **Cube** (which we scale a bit along the *x* axis), we get the following result:

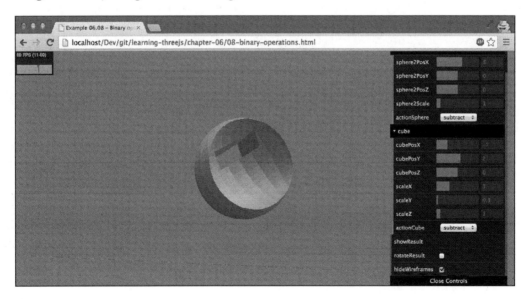

The best way to understand the `subtract` functionality is to just play around with the example. The ThreeBSP code to accomplish this is very simple and, in this example, is implemented in the `redrawResult` function, which we call whenever the **showResult** button from the example is clicked on:

```
function redrawResult() {
  scene.remove(result);
  var sphere1BSP = new ThreeBSP(sphere1);
  var sphere2BSP = new ThreeBSP(sphere2);
  var cube2BSP = new ThreeBSP(cube);

  var resultBSP;

  // first do the sphere
  switch (controls.actionSphere) {
    case "subtract":
      resultBSP = sphere1BSP.subtract(sphere2BSP);
    break;
    case "intersect":
      resultBSP = sphere1BSP.intersect(sphere2BSP);
    break;
    case "union":
      resultBSP = sphere1BSP.union(sphere2BSP);
    break;
    case "none": // noop;
  }

  // next do the cube
  if (!resultBSP) resultBSP = sphere1BSP;
  switch (controls.actionCube) {
    case "subtract":
      resultBSP = resultBSP.subtract(cube2BSP);
    break;
    case "intersect":
      resultBSP = resultBSP.intersect(cube2BSP);
    break;
    case "union":
      resultBSP = resultBSP.union(cube2BSP);
    break;
    case "none": // noop;
  }

  if (controls.actionCube === "none" && controls.actionSphere ===
    "none") {
```

```
    // do nothing
  } else {
    result = resultBSP.toMesh();
    result.geometry.computeFaceNormals();
    result.geometry.computeVertexNormals();
    scene.add(result);
  }
}
```

The first thing we do in this code is wrap our meshes (the wireframes you can see) in a `ThreeBSP` object. This allows us to apply the `subtract`, `intersect`, and `union` functions on these objects. Now, we can just call the specific function we want on the `ThreeBSP` object wrapped around the center sphere (`sphere1BSP`), and the result from this function will contain all the information we need to create a new mesh. To create this mesh, we just call the `toMesh()` function on the `sphere1BSP` object. On the resulting object, we have to make sure that all the normals are computed correctly by first calling `computeFaceNormals` and then calling `computeVertexNormals()`. These compute functions need to be called since by running one of the binary operations, the vertices and faces of the geometry are changed and this affects the normals of the faces. Explicitly recalculating them will make sure your new object is shaded smoothly (when shading on the material has been set to `THREE.SmoothShading`) and rendered correctly. Finally, we add the result to the scene.

For `intersect` and `union`, we use exactly the same approach.

The intersect function

With everything we explained in the previous section, there isn't much left to explain for the `intersect` function. With this function, only the part of the meshes that overlap is left. The following screenshot is an example where both the sphere and the cube are set to intersect:

If you look at the example and play around with the settings, you'll see that it's very easy to create these kinds of objects. And remember, this can be applied to every mesh you can create, even the complex ones we saw in this chapter, such as THREE. ParametricGeometry and THREE.TextGeometry.

The subtract and intersect functions work great together. The example we showed at the beginning of this section was created by first subtracting a smaller sphere to create a hollow sphere. After that, we used the cube to intersect with this hollow sphere to get the following result (a hollow cube with rounded corners):

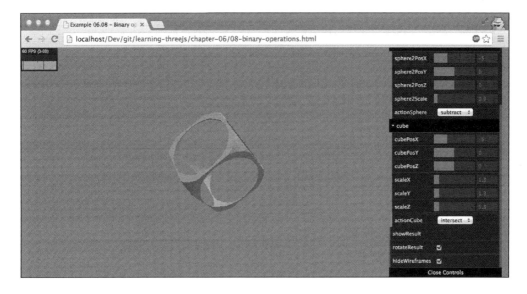

The last function provided by ThreeBSP is the `union` function.

The union function

The final function is the least interesting one of those offered by ThreeBSP. With this function, we can combine two meshes together to create a new one. So, when we apply this to the two spheres and the cube, we'll get a single object—a result of the union function:

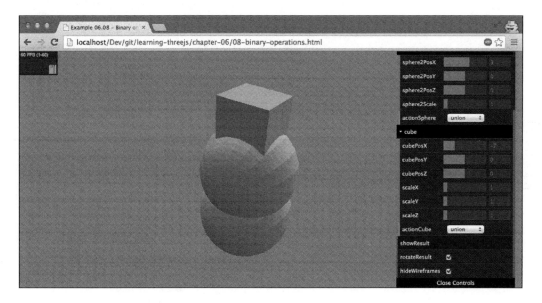

This is not really that useful because this functionality is also provided by Three.js (see *Chapter 8, Creating and Loading Advanced Meshes and Geometries*, where we explain how to use `THREE.Geometry.merge`), which also offers slightly better performance. If you enable rotation, you can see that this union is applied from the perspective of the center sphere since it is rotating around the center of that sphere. The same applies to the other two operations.

Summary

We saw a lot in this chapter. We introduced a couple of advanced geometries and even showed you how you can create interesting-looking geometries using a couple of simple binary operations. We showed you how you can create really beautiful shapes using advanced geometries such as THREE.ConvexGeometry, THREE.TubeGeometry, and THREE.LatheGeometry and experiment with these geometries to get the results you're looking for. A very nice feature is that we can also convert existing SVG paths to Three.js. Remember, though, that you still might need to fine-tune the paths using tools such as GIMP, Adobe Illustrator, or Inkscape.

If you want to create 3D text, you need to specify the font to use. Three.js comes with a couple of fonts you can use, but you can also create your own fonts. However, remember that complex fonts often won't convert correctly. And finally, with ThreeBSP, you have access to three binary operations you can apply to your mesh: union, subtract, and intersect. With union, you combine two meshes together; with subtract, you remove the overlapping part of the meshes from the source mesh; and with intersect, only the overlapping part is kept.

Until now, we looked at solid (or wireframe) geometries, where vertices are connected to each other to form faces. In the following chapter, we'll look at an alternative way of visualizing geometries using something called particles. With particles, we don't render complete geometries—we just render the vertices as points in space. This allows you to create great-looking 3D effects that perform well.

7

Particles, Sprites, and the Point Cloud

In the previous chapters, we discussed the most important concepts, objects, and APIs that Three.js has to offer. In this chapter, we'll look into the only concept we've skipped until now: particles. With particles (sometimes also called sprites), it is very easy to create many small objects that you can use to simulate rain, snow, smoke, and other interesting effects. For instance, you can render individual geometries as a set of particles and control these particles separately. In this chapter, we'll explore the various particle features provided by Three.js. To be more specific, we'll look at the following subjects in this chapter:

- Creating and styling particles using `THREE.SpriteMaterial`
- Using a point cloud to create a grouped set of particles
- Creating a point cloud from existing geometries
- Animating particles and the particle system
- Using a texture to style the particles
- Using the canvas to style a particle with `THREE.SpriteCanvasMaterial`

Let's start by exploring what a particle is and how you can create one. Before we get started, though, a quick note on some of the names used in this chapter. In recent versions of Three.js, the names of the objects related to particles have changed. `THREE.PointCloud`, which we use in this chapter, used to be called `THREE.ParticleSystem`, `THREE.Sprite` used to be called `THREE.Particle`, and also the materials have undergone some name changes. So, if you see online examples using these old names, remember that they are talking about the same concepts. In this chapter, we use the new naming convention introduced in the latest versions of Three.js.

Understanding particles

Like we do with most new concepts, we'll start with an example. In the sources for this chapter, you'll find an example with the name `01-particles.html`. Open this example and you'll see a grid of very uninteresting-looking white cubes, as shown in the following screenshot:

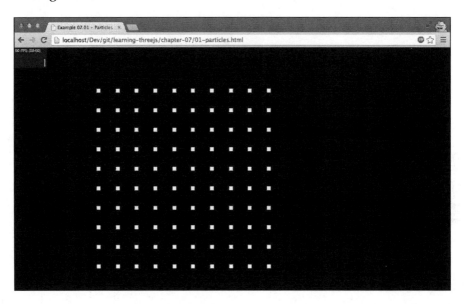

What you see in this screenshot are 100 sprites. A sprite is a 2D plane that always faces the camera. If you create a sprite without any properties, they are rendered as small, white, two-dimensional squares. These sprites were created with the following lines of code:

```
function createSprites() {
  var material = new THREE.SpriteMaterial();
  for (var x = -5; x < 5; x++) {
    for (var y = -5; y < 5; y++) {
      var sprite = new THREE.Sprite(material);
      sprite.position.set(x * 10, y * 10, 0);
      scene.add(sprite);
    }
  }
}
```

In this example, we create the sprites manually using the THREE.Sprite(material) constructor. The only item we pass in is a material. This has to be either THREE. SpriteMaterial or THREE.SpriteCanvasMaterial. We'll look at both of these materials in more depth in the rest of this chapter.

Before we move on to more interesting particles, let's look a bit closer at the THREE. Sprite object. A THREE.Sprite object extends from the THREE.Object3D object just as THREE.Mesh does. This means that most of the properties and functions you know from THREE.Mesh can be used on THREE.Sprite. You can set its position using the position attribute, scale it using the scale property, and move it relatively using the translate properties.

Note that in older versions of Three.js, you were unable to use THREE. Sprite objects with THREE.WebGLRenderer and could use it only with THREE.CanvasRenderer. In the current version, THREE. Sprite objects can be used with both renderers.

With THREE.Sprite, you can very easily create a set of objects and move them around the scene. This works great when you're working with a small number of objects, but you'll quickly run into performance issues when you want to work with a high number of THREE.Sprite objects because each of the objects needs to be managed separately by Three.js. Three.js provides an alternative way of handling a large number of sprites (or particles) using THREE.PointCloud. With THREE. PointCloud, Three.js doesn't have to manage many individual THREE.Sprite objects, but only the THREE.PointCloud instance.

To get the same result as the screenshot we saw earlier, but this time using THREE. PointCloud, we do the following:

```
function createParticles() {

  var geom = new THREE.Geometry();
  var material = new THREE.PointCloudMaterial({size: 4,
    vertexColors: true, color: 0xffffff});

  for (var x = -5; x < 5; x++) {
    for (var y = -5; y < 5; y++) {
      var particle = new THREE.Vector3(x * 10, y * 10, 0);
      geom.vertices.push(particle);
      geom.colors.push(new THREE.Color(Math.random() * 0x00ffff));
    }
  }

  var cloud = new THREE.PointCloud(geom, material);
  scene.add(cloud);
}
```

As you can see, for each particle (each point in the cloud), we need to create a vertex (represented by THREE.Vector3), add it to THREE.Geometry, use THREE.Geometry together with THREE.PointCloudMaterial to create THREE.PointCloud, and add cloud to the scene. An example of THREE.PointCloud in action (with colored squares) can be found in the 02-particles-webgl.html example. The following screenshot shows this example:

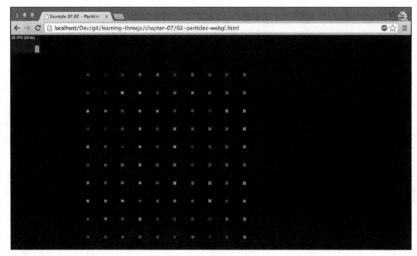

In the following sections, we'll explore THREE.PointCloud further.

Particles, THREE.PointCloud, and THREE.PointCloudMaterial

At the end of the previous section, we quickly introduced THREE.PointCloud. The constructor of THREE.PointCloud takes two properties: a geometry and a material. The material is used to color and texture the particles (as we'll see later on), and the geometry defines where the individual particles are positioned. Each vertex and each point used to define the geometry is shown as a particle. When we create THREE.PointCloud based on THREE.BoxGeometry, we get 8 particles, one for each corner of the cube. Normally, though, you won't create THREE.PointCloud from one of the standard Three.js geometries, but add the vertices manually to a geometry created from scratch (or use an externally loaded model) just like we did at the end of the previous section. In this section, we'll dive a bit deeper into this approach and look at how you can use THREE.PointCloudMaterial to style the particles. We'll explore this using the 03-basic-point-cloud.html example. The following screenshot shows this example:

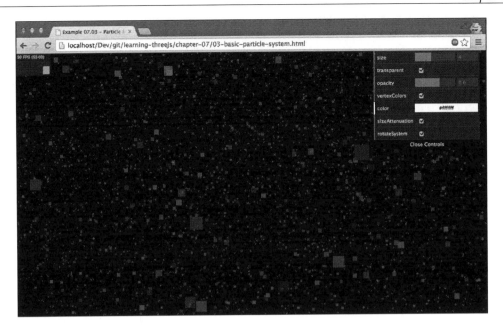

In this example, we create THREE.PointCloud, which we fill with 15,000 particles. All the particles are styled with THREE.PointCloudMaterial. To create THREE. PointCloud, we used the following code:

```
function createParticles(size, transparent, opacity, vertexColors,
  sizeAttenuation, color) {



  var geom = new THREE.Geometry();
  var material = new THREE.PointCloudMaterial({size: size,
    transparent: transparent, opacity: opacity, vertexColors:
    vertexColors, sizeAttenuation: sizeAttenuation, color:
    color});

  var range = 500;
  for (var i = 0; i < 15000; i++) {
    var particle = new THREE.Vector3(Math.random() * range - range
      / 2, Math.random() * range - range / 2, Math.random() *
      range - range / 2);
    geom.vertices.push(particle);
    var color = new THREE.Color(0x00ff00);
    color.setHSL(color.getHSL().h, color.getHSL().s, Math.random()
      * color.getHSL().l);
    geom.colors.push(color);
  }
```

```
    cloud = new THREE.PointCloud(geom, material);
    scene.add(cloud);
}
```

In this listing, we first create `THREE.Geometry`. We'll add the particles, represented as `THREE.Vector3`, to this geometry. For this, we've created a simple loop that creates `THREE.Vector3` at a random position and adds it. In this same loop, we also specify the array of colors, `geom.colors`, that are used when we set the `vertexColors` property of `THREE.PointCloudMaterial` to `true`. The last thing to do is create `THREE.PointCloudMaterial` and add it to the scene.

The following table explains all the properties you can set on `THREE.PointCloudMaterial`:

Name	Description
color	This is the color of all the particles in `ParticleSystem`. Setting the `vertexColors` property to true and specifying the colors using the colors property of the geometry overrides this property (to be more precise, the color of a vertex will be multiplied with this value to determine the final color). The default value is `0xFFFFFF`.
map	With this property, you can apply a texture to the particles. You can, for instance, make them look like snowflakes. This property isn't shown in this example but is explained later on in this chapter.
size	This is the size of the particle. The default value is `1`.
sizeAnnutation	If this is set to false, all the particles will have the same size regardless of how far from the camera they are positioned. If this is set to true, the size is based on the distance from the camera. The default value is `true`.
vertexColors	Normally, all the particles in `THREE.PointCloud` have the same color. If this property is set to `THREE.VertexColors` and the colors array in the geometry has been filled, the colors from that array will be used instead (also see the color entry in this table). The default value is `THREE.NoColors`.
opacity	This, together with the transparent property, sets the opacity of the particle. The default value is `1` (no opacity).
transparent	If this is set to true, the particle will be rendered with the opacity set by the opacity property. The default value is `false`.
blending	This is the blend mode to use when rendering the particle. See *Chapter 9, Animations and Moving the Camera,* for more information on blend modes.
fog	This determines whether the particles are affected by fog added to the scene. This defaults to `true`.

The previous example provides a simple control menu that you can use to experiment with the properties specific to THREE.ParticleCloudMaterial.

So far, we've only rendered the particles as small cubes, which is the default behavior. There are, however, a few additional ways you can use to style the particles:

- We can apply THREE.SpriteCanvasMaterial (which only works for THREE.CanvasRenderer) to use the results from an HTML canvas element as a texture
- Use THREE.SpriteMaterial and a HTML5-based texture to use the output of an HTML canvas when working with THREE.WebGLRenderer
- Load an external image file (or use the HTML5 canvas) with the map property of THREE.PointCloudMaterial to style all particles of THREE.ParticleCloud

In the next section, we look into how you can do this.

Styling particles with the HTML5 canvas

Three.js offers three different ways you can use an HTML5 canvas to style your particles. If you use THREE.CanvasRenderer, you can directly reference an HTML5 canvas from THREE.SpriteCanvasMaterial. When you use THREE.WebGLRenderer, you need to take a couple of extra steps to use an HTML5 canvas to style your particles. In the following two sections, we'll show you the different approaches.

Using HTML5 canvas with THREE. CanvasRenderer

With THREE.SpriteCanvasMaterial, you can use the output from an HTML5 canvas as a texture for your particles. This material is specifically created for THREE.CanvasRenderer and only works when you use this specific renderer. Before we look at how to use this material, let's first look at the attributes you can set on this material:

Name	Description
color	This is the color of the particle. Depending on the specified blending mode, this affects the color of the canvas image.
program	This is a function that takes a canvas context as a parameter. This function is called when the particle is rendered. The output from the calls to this 2D drawing context is shown as the particle.

Name	Description
opacity	This determines the opacity of the particle. The default value is 1, and there is no opacity.
transparent	This determines whether the particle is transparent or not. This works together with the opacity property.
blending	This is the blend mode to be used. See *Chapter 9, Animations and Moving the Camera* for more details.
rotation	This property allows you to rotate the contents of the canvas. You'll usually need to set this to PI to correctly align the contents of the canvas. Note that this property can't be passed in to the constructor of the material, but needs to be set explicitly.

To see THREE.SpriteCanvasMaterial in action, you can open the 04-program-based-sprites.html example. The following screenshot shows this example:

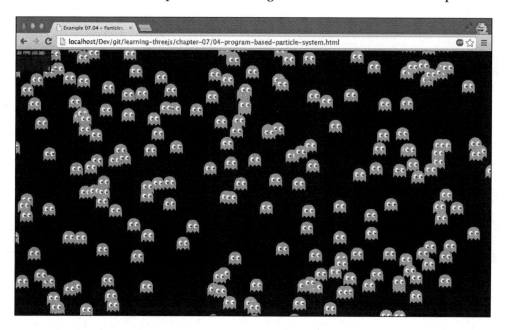

In this example, the particles are created in the createSprites function:

```
function createSprites() {

  var material = new THREE.SpriteCanvasMaterial({
    program: draw,
    color: 0xffffff});
  material.rotation = Math.PI;
```

```
  var range = 500;
  for (var i = 0; i < 1000; i++) {
    var sprite = new THREE.Sprite(material);
    sprite.position = new THREE.Vector3(Math.random() * range -
      range / 2, Math.random() * range - range / 2, Math.random()
      * range - range / 2);
    sprite.scale.set(0.1, 0.1, 0.1);
    scene.add(sprite);
  }
}
```

This code looks a lot like the code we saw in the previous section. The main change is that because we're working with THREE.CanvasRenderer, we create THREE.Sprite objects directly, instead of using THREE.PointCloud. In this code, we also define THREE.SpriteCanvasMaterial with a program attribute that points to the draw function. This draw function defines what a particle will look like (in our case, a ghost from *Pac-Man*):

```
var draw = function(ctx) {
  ctx.fillStyle = "orange";
  ...
  // lots of other ctx drawing calls
  ...
  ctx.beginPath();
  ctx.fill();
}
```

We won't dive into the actual canvas code required to draw our shape. What's important here is that we define a function that accepts a 2D canvas context (ctx) as its parameter. Everything that is drawn onto that context is used as the shape for THREE.Sprite.

Using HTML5 canvas with WebGLRenderer

If we want to use an HTML5 canvas with THREE.WebGLRenderer, we can take two different approaches. We can use THREE.PointCloudMaterial and create THREE.PointCloud, or we can use THREE.Sprite and the map property of THREE.SpriteMaterial.

Let's start with the first approach and create THREE.PointCloud. In the attributes for THREE.PointCloudMaterial, we mentioned the map property. With the map property, we can load a texture for the particle. With Three.js, this texture can also be the output from an HTML5 canvas. An example showing this concept is 05a-program-based-point-cloud-webgl.html. The following screenshot shows this example:

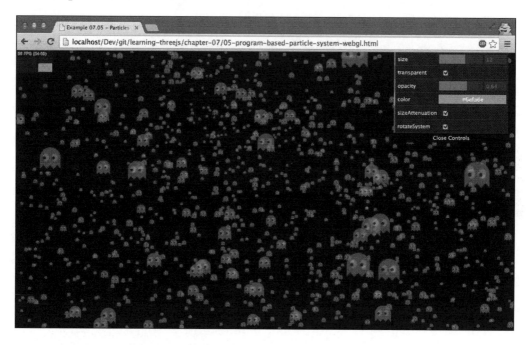

Let's look at the code we wrote to get this effect. Most of the code is the same as our previous WebGL example, so we won't go into too much detail. The important code changes that were made to get this example are shown here:

```
var getTexture = function() {
  var canvas = document.createElement('canvas');
  canvas.width = 32;
  canvas.height = 32;

  var ctx = canvas.getContext('2d');
  ...
  // draw the ghost
  ...
  ctx.fill();
  var texture = new THREE.Texture(canvas);
  texture.needsUpdate = true;
```

```
      return texture;
  }

  function createPointCloud(size, transparent, opacity,
    sizeAttenuation, color) {

    var geom = new THREE.Geometry();


    var material = new THREE.PointCloudMaterial ({size: size,
      transparent: transparent, opacity: opacity, map: getTexture(),
      sizeAttenuation: sizeAttenuation, color: color});


    var range = 500;
    for (var i = 0; i < 5000; i++) {
      var particle = new THREE.Vector3(Math.random() * range -
        range / 2, Math.random() * range - range / 2,
        Math.random() * range - range / 2);
      geom.vertices.push(particle);
    }

    cloud = new THREE.PointCloud(geom, material);
    cloud.sortParticles = true;
    scene.add(cloud);
  }
```

In `getTexture`, the first of these two JavaScript functions, we create `THREE.Texture` based on an HTML5 canvas element. In the second function, `createPointCloud`, we assign this texture to the `map` property of `THREE.PointCloudMaterial`. In this function, you can also see that we set the `sortParticles` property of `THREE. PointCloud` to `true`. This property makes sure that before the particles are rendered, they are sorted according to their z position on screen. If you see partly overlapping particles or incorrect transparency, setting this property to `true` will (in most cases) fix that. You should note, though, that setting this property to `true` will affect the performance of your scene. When this is set to true, Three.js will have to determine the distance to the camera for each individual particle. For a `THREE.PointCloud` object that is very large, this can have a big impact on performance.

While we're talking about the properties of `THREE.PointCloud`, there is one additional property you can set on `THREE.PointCloud`: `FrustumCulled`. If this property is set to true, it means that if particles fall outside the visible camera range, they aren't rendered. This can be used to improve performance and frame rate if needed.

The result of this is that everything we draw to the canvas in the getTexture() method is used for the particles in THREE.PointCloud. In the following section, we'll look a bit deeper into how this works with textures we load from external files. Note that in this example, we only see a very small part of what is possible with textures. In *Chapter 10, Loading and Working with Textures*, we'll dive into the details of what can be done with textures.

At the beginning of this section, we mentioned that we could also use THREE.Sprite together with the map property to create a canvas-based particle. For this, we use the same approach to create THREE.Texture as we saw in the previous example. This time, however, we assign it to THREE.Sprite like this:

```
function createSprites() {
  var material = new THREE.SpriteMaterial({
    map: getTexture(),
    color: 0xffffff
  });

  var range = 500;
  for (var i = 0; i < 1500; i++) {
    var sprite = new THREE.Sprite(material);
    sprite.position.set(Math.random() * range - range / 2,
      Math.random() * range - range / 2, Math.random() * range -
      range / 2);
    sprite.scale.set(4,4,4);
    scene.add(sprite);
  }
}
```

Here, you can see that we use a standard THREE.SpriteMaterial object and assign the output of the canvas as THREE.Texture to the map property of the material. You can view an example of this by opening 05b-program-based-sprites-webgl.html in your browser. Both of these approaches have their own advantages and disadvantages. With THREE.Sprite, you have more control over the individual particle, but it becomes less performant and more complex when you're working with a large number of particles. With THREE.PointCloud, you can easily manage a large number of particles, but have less control over each individual particle.

Using textures to style particles

In the previous example, we saw how you could style `THREE.PointCloud` and individual `THREE.Sprite` objects using an HTML5 canvas. Since you can draw anything you want and even load external images, you can use this approach to add all kinds of styles to the particle system. There is, however, a more direct way to use an image to style your particles. You can use the `THREE.ImageUtils. loadTexture()` function to load an image as `THREE.Texture`. `THREE.Texture` can then be assigned to the `map` property of a material.

In this section, we'll show you two examples and explain how to create them. Both these examples use an image as a texture for your particles. In the first example, we create a simulation of rain, `06-rainy-scene.html`. The following screenshot shows this example:

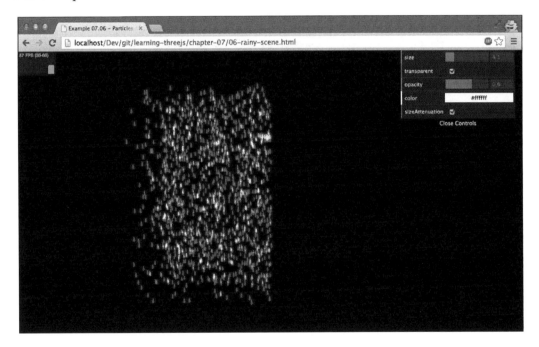

The first thing we need to do is get a texture that will represent our raindrop. You can find a couple of examples in the assets/textures/particles folder. In *Chapter 9, Animations and Moving the Camera*, we will explain all the details and requirements for textures. For now, all you need to know is that the texture should be square and preferably a power of 2 (for example, 64 x 64, 128 x 128, 256 x 256). For this example, we'll use this texture:

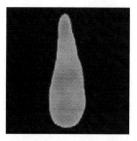

This image uses a black background (needed for correct blending) and shows the shape and color of a raindrop. Before we can use this texture in THREE. PointCloudMaterial, we first need to load it. This can be done with the following line of code:

```
var texture = THREE.ImageUtils.loadTexture("../assets/textures/
    particles/raindrop-2.png");
```

With this line of code, Three.js will load the texture, and we can use it in our material. For this example, we defined the material like this:

```
var material = new THREE.PointCloudMaterial({size: 3, transparent:
    true, opacity: true, map: texture, blending:
    THREE.AdditiveBlending, sizeAttenuation: true, color:
    0xffffff});
```

In this chapter, we've discussed all of these properties. The main thing to understand here is that the map property points to the texture we loaded with the THREE.ImageUtils.loadTexture() function, and we specify THREE. AdditiveBlending as the blending mode. This blending mode means that when a new pixel is drawn, the color of the background pixel is added to the color of this new pixel. For our raindrop texture, this means that the black background won't be shown. A logical alternative would be to replace the black from our texture with a transparent background, but that doesn't work with particles and WebGL unfortunately.

That takes care of styling THREE.PointCloud. What you'll also see when you open up this example is that the particles themselves are moving. In the previous examples, we moved the entire particle system; this time, we position the individual particles within THREE.PointCloud. Doing this is actually very simple. Each particle is represented as a vertex that makes up the geometry that was used to create THREE.PointCloud. Let's look at how we add the particles for THREE.PointCloud:

```
var range = 40;
for (var i = 0; i < 1500; i++) {
  var particle = new THREE.Vector3(Math.random() * range - range /
    2, Math.random() * range * 1.5, Math.random() * range - range
    / 2);

  particle.velocityX = (Math.random() - 0.5) / 3;
  particle.velocityY = 0.1 + (Math.random() / 5);
  geom.vertices.push(particle);
}
```

This isn't that different from the previous examples we saw. Here, we added two additional properties to each particle (THREE.Vector3): velocityX and velocityY. The first one defines how a particle (a raindrop) moves horizontally, and the second one defines how fast the raindrop falls down. The horizontal velocity ranges from -0.16 to +0.16, and the vertical speed ranges from 0.1 to 0.3. Now that each raindrop has its own speed, we can move the individual particles inside the render loop:

```
var vertices = system2.geometry.vertices;
vertices.forEach(function (v) {
  v.x = v.x - (v.velocityX);
  v.y = v.y - (v.velocityY);

  if (v.x <= -20 || v.x >= 20) v.velocityX = v.velocityX * -1;
  if (v.y <= 0) v.y = 60;
});
```

In this piece of code, we get all vertices (particles) from the geometry that was used to create THREE.PointCloud. For each of the particles, we take velocityX and velocityY and use them to change the current position of the particle. The last two lines make sure the particles stay within the range we've defined. If the v.y position drops below zero, we add the raindrop back to the top, and if the v.x position reaches any of the edges, we make it bounce back by inverting the horizontal velocity.

Let's look at another example. This time, we won't make rain, but we'll make snow. Additionally, we won't be using just a single texture, but we'll use five separate images (taken from the Three.js examples). Let's start by looking at the result again (see `07-snowy-scene.html`):

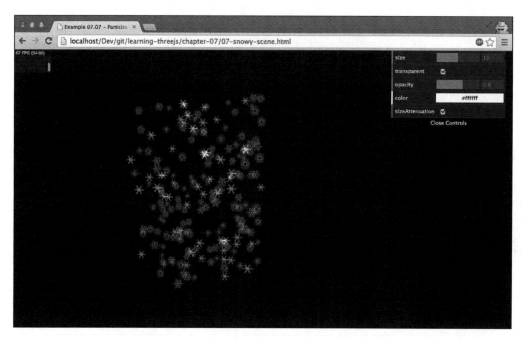

In the preceding screenshot, you can see that instead of using just a single image as texture, we've used multiple images. You might wonder how we did this. As you probably remember, we can only have a single material for `THREE.PointCloud`. If we want to have multiple materials, we just have to make multiple particle systems, as follows:

```
function createPointClouds(size, transparent, opacity,
  sizeAttenuation, color) {

  var texture1 = THREE.ImageUtils.loadTexture
    ("../assets/textures/particles/snowflake1.png");
  var texture2 = THREE.ImageUtils.loadTexture
    ("../assets/textures/particles/snowflake2.png");
  var texture3 = THREE.ImageUtils.loadTexture
    ("../assets/textures/particles/snowflake3.png");
  var texture4 = THREE.ImageUtils.loadTexture
    ("../assets/textures/particles/snowflake5.png");

  scene.add(createPointCloud("system1", texture1, size,
    transparent, opacity, sizeAttenuation, color));
```

```
    scene.add(createPointCloud ("system2", texture2, size,
        transparent, opacity, sizeAttenuation, color));
    scene.add(createPointCloud ("system3", texture3, size,
        transparent, opacity, sizeAttenuation, color));
    scene.add(createPointCloud ("system4", texture4, size,
        transparent, opacity, sizeAttenuation, color));
}
```

Here, you can see that we load the textures separately and pass all the information on how to create THREE.PointCloud to the createPointCloud function. This function looks like this:

```
function createPointCloud(name, texture, size, transparent,
    opacity, sizeAttenuation, color) {
    var geom = new THREE.Geometry();

    var color = new THREE.Color(color);
    color.setHSL(color.getHSL().h, color.getHSL().s, (Math.random())
        * color.getHSL().l);

    var material = new THREE.PointCloudMaterial({size: size,
        transparent: transparent, opacity: opacity, map: texture,
        blending: THREE.AdditiveBlending, depthWrite: false,
        sizeAttenuation: sizeAttenuation, color: color});

    var range = 40;
    for (var i = 0; i < 50; i++) {
        var particle = new THREE.Vector3(Math.random() * range - range
            / 2, Math.random() * range * 1.5, Math.random() * range -
            range / 2);
        particle.velocityY = 0.1 + Math.random() / 5;
        particle.velocityX = (Math.random() - 0.5) / 3;
        particle.velocityZ = (Math.random() - 0.5) / 3;
        geom.vertices.push(particle);
    }

    var cloud = new THREE.ParticleCloud(geom, material);
    cloud.name = name;
    cloud.sortParticles = true;
    return cloud;
}
```

The first thing we do in this function is define the color in which the particles for this specific texture should be rendered. This is done by randomly changing the *lightness* of the passed-in color. Next, the material is created in the same manner we did before. The only change here is that the depthWrite property is set to false. This property defines whether this object affects the WebGL depth buffer. By setting this to false, we make sure that the various point clouds don't interfere with each other. If this property isn't set to false, you'll see that the black background from the texture is sometimes shown when a particle is in front of a particle from another THREE.PointCloud object. The last step taken in this piece of code is randomly placing the particles and adding a random speed to each particle. In the render loop, we can now update the position of all the particles from each THREE.PointCloud object like this:

```
scene.children.forEach(function (child) {
  if (child instanceof THREE.ParticleSystem) {
    var vertices = child.geometry.vertices;
    vertices.forEach(function (v) {
      v.y = v.y - (v.velocityY);
      v.x = v.x - (v.velocityX);
      v.z = v.z - (v.velocityZ);

      if (v.y <= 0) v.y = 60;
      if (v.x <= -20 || v.x >= 20) v.velocityX = v.velocityX * -1;
      if (v.z <= -20 || v.z >= 20) v.velocityZ = v.velocityZ * -1;
    });
  }
});
```

With this approach, we can have particles that have different textures. This approach, however, is a bit limited. The more different textures we want, the more point clouds we'll have to create and manage. If you have a limited set of particles with different styles, you'd better use the THREE.Sprite object we showed at the beginning of this chapter.

Working with sprite maps

At the beginning of this chapter, we used a THREE.Sprite object to render single particles with THREE.CanvasRenderer and THREE.WebGLRenderer. These sprites were positioned somewhere in the 3D world, and their size was based on the distance from the camera (this is also sometimes called **billboarding**). In this section, we'll show an alternative use of the THREE.Sprite object. We'll show you how you can use THREE.Sprite to create a layer similar to **head-up display (HUD)** for your 3D content using an extra THREE.OrthographicCamera instance. We will also show you how to select the image for a THREE.Sprite object using a sprite map.

As an example, we're going to create a simple THREE.Sprite object that moves from left to right over the screen. In the background, we'll render a 3D scene with a moving camera to illustrate that THREE.Sprite moves independently of the camera. The following screenshot shows what we'll be creating for the first example (08-sprites.html):

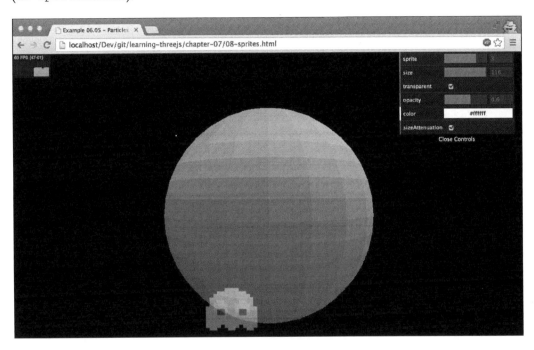

If you open this example in your browser, you'll see a Pac-Man ghost-like sprite moving across the screen and changing color and form whenever it hits the right edge. The first thing we'll do is look at how we create THREE.OrthographicCamera and a separate scene to render THREE.Sprite in:

```
var sceneOrtho = new THREE.Scene();
var cameraOrtho = new THREE.OrthographicCamera( 0,
  window.innerWidth, window.innerHeight, 0, -10, 10 );
```

Next, let's look at the construction of THREE.Sprite and how the various shapes the sprite can take are loaded:

```
function getTexture() {
  var texture = new THREE.ImageUtils.loadTexture("../assets/
    textures/particles/sprite-sheet.png");
  return texture;
}
```

```
function createSprite(size, transparent, opacity, color,
   spriteNumber) {
  var spriteMaterial = new THREE.SpriteMaterial({
    opacity: opacity,
    color: color,
    transparent: transparent,
    map: getTexture()});


  // we have 1 row, with five sprites
  spriteMaterial.map.offset = new THREE.Vector2(1/5 *
    spriteNumber, 0);
  spriteMaterial.map.repeat = new THREE.Vector2(1/5, 1);
  spriteMaterial.blending = THREE.AdditiveBlending;

  // makes sure the object is always rendered at the front
  spriteMaterial.depthTest = false;
  var sprite = new THREE.Sprite(spriteMaterial);
  sprite.scale.set(size, size, size);
  sprite.position.set(100, 50, 0);
  sprite.velocityX = 5;

  sceneOrtho.add(sprite);
}
```

In the `getTexture()` function, we load a texture. However, instead of loading five different images for each *ghost*, we load a single texture that contains all the sprites. The texture looks like this:

With the `map.offset` and the `map.repeat` properties, we select the correct sprite to show on screen. With the `map.offset` property, we determine the offset for the x axis (u) and the y axis (v) for the texture we loaded. The scale for these properties runs from 0 to 1. In our example, if we want to select the third ghost, we set the u-offset (x axis) to 0.4, and, because we've only got one row, we don't need to change the v-offset (y axis). If we only set this property, the texture shows the third, fourth, and fifth ghosts compressed together on screen. To only show one ghost, we need to zoom in. We do this by setting the `map.repeat` property for the u-value to 1/5. This means that we zoom in (only for the x axis) to only show 20 percent of the texture, which is exactly one ghost.

The final step we need to take is update the `render` function:

```
webGLRenderer.render(scene, camera);
webGLRenderer.autoClear = false;
webGLRenderer.render(sceneOrtho, cameraOrtho);
```

We first render the scene with the normal camera and the moving sphere, and after that, we render the scene containing our sprite. Note that we need to set the `autoClear` property of the WebGLRenderer to `false`. If we don't do this, Three.js will clear the scene before it renders the sprite, and the sphere wouldn't show up.

The following table shows an overview of all the properties of THREE. `SpriteMaterial` we used in the previous examples:

Name	Description
color	This is the color of the sprite.
map	This is the texture to be used for this sprite. This can be a sprite sheet, as shown in the example in this section.
sizeAnnutation	If this is set to `false`, the size of the sprite won't be affected by the distance it's removed from the camera. The default value is `true`.
opacity	This sets the transparency of the sprite. The default value is 1 (no opacity).
blending	This defines the blend mode to be used when rendering the sprite. See *Chapter 9, Animations and Moving the Camera,* for more information on blend modes.
fog	This determines whether the sprite is affected by fog added to the scene. This defaults to `true`.

You can also set the `depthTest` and `depthWrite` properties on this material. For more information on these properties, see *Chapter 4, Working with Three.js Materials.*

We can, of course, also use a sprite map when positioning THREE.Sprites in 3D (as we did at the beginning of this chapter). An example (09-sprites-3D.html) of this is shown in the following screenshot:

With the properties we saw in the previous table, we can very easily create the effect we see in the preceding screenshot:

```
function createSprites() {

  group = new THREE.Object3D();
  var range = 200;
  for (var i = 0; i < 400; i++) {
    group.add(createSprite(10, false, 0.6, 0xffffff, i % 5,
      range));
  }
  scene.add(group);
}

function createSprite(size, transparent, opacity, color,
  spriteNumber, range) {


  var spriteMaterial = new THREE.SpriteMaterial({
    opacity: opacity,
```

```
        color: color,
        transparent: transparent,
        map: getTexture()}
    );

    // we have 1 row, with five sprites
    spriteMaterial.map.offset = new THREE.Vector2(0.2*spriteNumber,
        0);
    spriteMaterial.map.repeat = new THREE.Vector2(1/5, 1);
    spriteMaterial.depthTest = false;

    spriteMaterial.blending = THREE.AdditiveBlending;

    var sprite = new THREE.Sprite(spriteMaterial);
    sprite.scale.set(size, size, size);
    sprite.position.set(Math.random() * range - range / 2,
        Math.random() * range - range / 2, Math.random() * range -
        range / 2);
    sprite.velocityX = 5;

    return sprite;
}
```

In this example, we create 400 sprites based on the sprite sheet we showed earlier. You'll probably know and understand most of the properties and concepts shown here. As we've added the separate sprites to a group, rotating them is very easy and can be done like this:

```
group.rotation.x+=0.1;
```

In this chapter, so far we've mainly looked at creating sprites and point clouds from scratch. An interesting option, though, is to create THREE.PointCloud from an existing geometry.

Creating THREE.PointCloud from an advanced geometry

As you remember, THREE.PointCloud renders each particle based on the vertices from the supplied geometry. This means that if we provide a complex geometry (for example, a torus knot or a tube), we can create THREE.PointCloud based on the vertices from that specific geometry. For this last section of this chapter, we'll create a torus knot, like the one we saw in the previous chapter, and render it as THREE.PointCloud.

We've already explained the torus knot in the previous chapter, so we won't go into much detail here. We're using the exact code from the previous chapter, and we've added a single menu option that you can use to transform the rendered mesh into THREE.PointCloud. You can find the example (10-create-particle-system-from-model.html) in the sources for this chapter. The following screenshot shows the example:

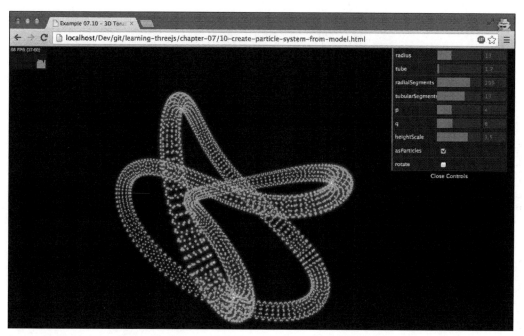

As you can see in the preceding screenshot, every vertex used to generate the torus knot is used as a particle. In this example, we've added a nice-looking material, based on a HTML canvas, to create this glowing effect. We'll only look at the code to the create the material and the particle system as we've already discussed the other properties in this chapter:

```
function generateSprite() {

  var canvas = document.createElement('canvas');
  canvas.width = 16;
  canvas.height = 16;

  var context = canvas.getContext('2d');
```

```
  var gradient = context.createRadialGradient(canvas.width / 2,
    canvas.height / 2, 0, canvas.width / 2, canvas.height / 2,
    canvas.width / 2);

  gradient.addColorStop(0, 'rgba(255,255,255,1)');
  gradient.addColorStop(0.2, 'rgba(0,255,255,1)');
  gradient.addColorStop(0.4, 'rgba(0,0,64,1)');
  gradient.addColorStop(1, 'rgba(0,0,0,1)');

  context.fillStyle = gradient;
  context.fillRect(0, 0, canvas.width, canvas.height);

  var texture = new THREE.Texture(canvas);
  texture.needsUpdate = true;
  return texture;
}

function createPointCloud(geom) {
  var material = new THREE.PointCloudMaterial({
    color: 0xffffff,
    size: 3,
    transparent: true,
    blending: THREE.AdditiveBlending,
    map: generateSprite()
  });

  var cloud = new THREE.PointCloud(geom, material);
  cloud.sortParticles = true;
  return cloud;
}

// use it like this
var geom = new THREE.TorusKnotGeometry(...);
var knot = createPointCloud(geom);
```

In this code fragment, you can see two functions: `createPointCloud()` and `generateSprite()`. In the first function, we create a simple `THREE.PointCloud` object directly from the geometry provided (in this example, a torus knot) and set the texture (the `map` property) to a glowing dot (generated on an HTML5 canvas element) with the `generateSprite()` function, which looks like this:

Summary

That's a wrap for this chapter. We've explained what particles, sprites, and particle systems are and how you can style these objects with the available materials. In this chapter, you saw how you can use `THREE.Sprite` directly with `THREE.CanvasRenderer` and `THREE.WebGLRenderer`. If you want to create a large number of particles, however, you should use `THREE.PointCloud`. With `THREE.PointCloud`, all the particles share the same material, and the only property you can change for an individual particle is their color by setting the `vertexColors` property of the material to `THREE.VertexColors` and providing a color value in the `colors` array of `THREE.Geometry` used to create `THREE.PointCloud`. We also showed how you can easily animate particles by changing their position. This works the same for an individual `THREE.Sprite` instance and the vertices from the geometry used to create `THREE.PointCloud`.

So far, we have created meshes based on geometries provided by Three.js. This works great for simple models such as spheres and cubes but isn't the best approach when you want to create complex 3D models. For those models, you'd usually use a 3D modeling application such as Blender or 3D Studio Max. In the next chapter, you'll learn how you can load and display models created by such 3D modeling applications.

8
Creating and Loading Advanced Meshes and Geometries

In this chapter, we'll look at a couple of different ways that you can create advanced and complex geometries and meshes. In *Chapter 5*, *Learning to Work with Geometries*, and *Chapter 6*, *Advanced Geometries and Binary Operations* ,we showed you how to create a few advanced geometries using the built-in objects from Three.js. In this chapter, we'll use the following two approaches to create advanced geometries and meshes:

- **Grouping and merging**: The first approach we explain uses built-in functionality from Three.js to group and merge existing geometries. This creates new meshes and geometries from existing objects.

- **Loading from external**: In this section, we'll explain how you can load meshes and geometries from external sources. For instance, we'll show you how you can use Blender to export meshes in a format Three.js supports.

We start with the *group and merge* approach. With this approach, we use the standard Three.js grouping and the `THREE.Geometry.merge()` function to create new objects.

Geometry grouping and merging

In this section, we'll look at two basic features of Three.js: grouping objects together and merging multiple meshes into a single mesh. We'll start with grouping objects.

Grouping objects together

In some of the previous chapters, you already saw this when working with multiple materials. When you create a mesh from a geometry using multiple materials, Three. js creates a group. Multiple copies of your geometry are added to this group, each with their own specific material. This group is returned, so it looks like a mesh that uses multiple materials. In truth, however, it is a group that contains a number of meshes.

Creating groups is very easy. Every mesh you create can contain child elements, which can be added using the add function. The effect of adding a child object to a group is that you can move, scale, rotate, and translate the parent object, and all the child objects will also be affected. Let's look at an example (`01-grouping.html`). The following screenshot shows this example:

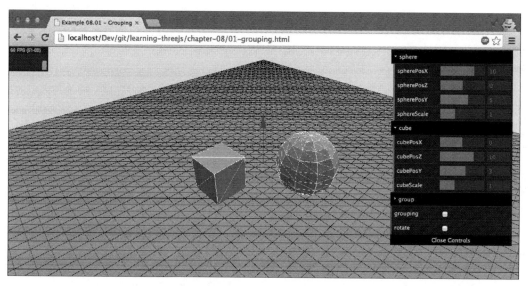

In this example, you can use the menu to move the sphere and the cube around. If you check the **rotate** option, you'll see these two meshes rotating around their center. This isn't anything new and is not very exciting. However, these two objects haven't been added to the scene directly, but have been added as a group. The following code encapsulates this discussion:

```
sphere = createMesh(new THREE.SphereGeometry(5, 10, 10));
cube = createMesh(new THREE.BoxGeometry(6, 6, 6));

group = new THREE.Object3D();
group.add(sphere);
```

```
group.add(cube);

scene.add(group);
```

In this code snippet, you can see that we create THREE.Object3D. This is the base class of THREE.Mesh and THREE.Scene, but by itself, it doesn't contain anything or cause anything to be rendered. Note that in the latest version of Three.js, a new object called THREE.Group was introduced to support grouping. This object is exactly the same as a THREE.Object3D object, and you can replace new THREE.Object3D() in the previous code with new THREE.Group() for the same effect. In this example, we use the add function to add the sphere and cube to this object, and then we add it to the scene. If you look at the example, you can still move the cube and sphere around and scale and rotate these two objects. You can also do these things on the group they are in. If you look at the group menu, you'll see position and scale options. You can use these to scale and move the entire group around. The scale and position of the objects inside this group are relative to the scale and position of the group itself.

Scale and position are very straightforward. One thing to keep in mind, though, is that when you rotate a group, it doesn't rotate the objects inside it separately; it rotates the entire group around its own center (in our example, you rotate the entire group around the center of the group object). In this example, we placed an arrow using the THREE.ArrowHelper object at the center of the group to indicate the rotation point:

```
var arrow = new THREE.ArrowHelper(new THREE.Vector3(0, 1, 0),
    group.position, 10, 0x0000ff);
scene.add(arrow);
```

If you check both the **grouping** and **rotate** checkboxes, the group will rotate. You'll see the sphere and cube rotating around the center of the group (indicated by the arrow), as follows:

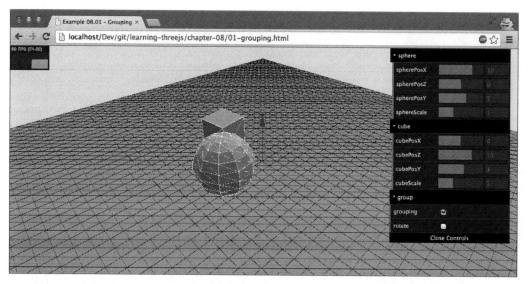

When using a group, you can still refer to, modify, and position the individual geometries. The only thing you need to remember is that all positions, rotations, and translations are done relative to the parent object. In the next section, we'll look at merging, where you'll combine multiple separate geometries and end up with a single THREE.Geometry object.

Merging multiple meshes into a single mesh

In most cases, using groups allows you to easily manipulate and manage a large number of meshes. When you're dealing with a very large number of objects, however, performance will become an issue. With groups, you're still working with individual objects that each need to be handled and rendered separately. With THREE.Geometry.merge(), you can merge geometries together and create a combined one. In the following example, you can see how this works and the effect it has on performance. If you open the 02-merging.html example, you see a scene with a set of randomly distributed semitransparent cubes. With the slider in the menu, you can set the number of cubes you want in the scene and redraw the scene by clicking on the **redraw** button. Depending on the hardware you're running on, you'll see a performance degradation as the number of cubes increases. In our case, as you can see in the following screenshot, this happens at around 4,000 objects, where the refresh rate drops to around 40 fps instead of the normal 60 fps:

As you can see, there is a certain limit to the number of meshes you can add to the scene. Normally, though, you probably wouldn't need that many meshes, but when creating specific games (for example, something like *Minecraft*) or advanced visualizations, you might need to manage a large number of individual meshes. With THREE.Geometry.merge(), you can solve this problem. Before we look at the code, let's run this same example, but this time, with the **combine** box checked. With this option flagged, we merge all the cubes into a single THREE.Geometry and add that one instead, as shown in the following screenshot:

As you can see, we can easily render 20,000 cubes without any drop in performance. To do this, we use the following couple of lines of code:

```
var geometry = new THREE.Geometry();
for (var i = 0; i < controls.numberOfObjects; i++) {
  var cubeMesh = addcube();
  cubeMesh.updateMatrix();
  geometry.merge(cubeMesh.geometry,cubeMesh.matrix);
}
scene.add(new THREE.Mesh(geometry, cubeMaterial));
```

In this code snippet, the addCube() function returns THREE.Mesh. In older versions of Three.js, we could use the THREE.GeometryUtils.merge function to also merge THREE.Mesh objects into THREE.Geometry objects. With the latest version, this functionality has been deprecated in favor of the THREE.Geometry.merge function. To make sure the merged-in THREE.Geometry object is positioned and rotated correctly, we not only provide THREE.Geometry to the merge function, but also its transformation matrix. When we add this matrix to the merge function, the cube we merge in will be positioned correctly.

We do this 20,000 times and are left with a single geometry that we add to the scene. If you look at the code, you can probably see a couple of drawbacks of this approach. Since you're left with a single geometry, you can't apply a material to each individual cube. This, however, can be somewhat solved using THREE.MeshFaceMaterial. The biggest drawback, however, is that you lose control over the individual cubes. If you want to move, rotate, or scale a single cube, you can't (unless you search for the correct faces and vertices and position them individually).

With the grouping and merging approach, you can create large and complex geometries using the basic geometries provided by Three.js. If you want to create more advanced geometries, then using the programmatic approach provided by Three.js isn't always the best and easiest option. Three.js, luckily, offers a couple of other options to create geometries. In the next section, we'll look at how you can load geometries and meshes from external resources.

Loading geometries from external resources

Three.js can read a number of 3D file formats and import geometries and meshes defined in those files. The following table shows the file formats that are supported by Three.js:

Format	Description
JSON	Three.js has its own JSON format you can use to declaratively define a geometry or a scene. Even though this isn't an official format, it's very easy to use and comes in very handy when you want to reuse complex geometries or scenes.
OBJ or MTL	OBJ is a simple 3D format first developed by **Wavefront Technologies**. It's one of the most widely adopted 3D file formats and is used to define the geometry of an object. MTL is a companion format to OBJ. In an MTL file, the material of the objects in an OBJ file is specified. Three.js also has a custom OBJ exporter, called OBJExporter.js, should you want to export your models to OBJ from Three.js.
Collada	Collada is a format for defining *digital assets* in an XML-based format. This is also a widely used format that is supported by pretty much all 3D applications and rendering engines.
STL	**STL** stands for **STereoLithography** and is widely used for rapid prototyping. For instance, models for 3D printers are often defined as STL files. Three.js also has a custom STL exporter, called STLExporter.js, should you want to export your models to STL from Three.js.
CTM	CTM is a file format created by **openCTM**. It's used as a format for storing 3D triangle-based meshes in a compact format.
VTK	VTK is the file format defined by **Visualization Toolkit** and is used to specify vertices and faces. There are two formats available: a binary one and a text-based ASCII one. Three.js only supports the ASCII-based format.
AWD	AWD is a binary format for 3D scenes and is most often used with the `http://away3d.com/` engine. Note that this loader doesn't support compressed AWD files.
Assimp	Open asset import library (also called **Assimp**) is a standard way to import various 3D model formats. With this loader, you can import models from a large range of 3D formats that have been converted using **assimp2json**, details of which are available at `https://github.com/acgessler/assimp2json`.
VRML	**VRML** stands for **Virtual Reality Modeling Language**. This is a text-based format that allows you to specify 3D objects and worlds. It has been superseded by the X3D file format. Three.js doesn't support loading X3D models, but these models can be easily converted to other formats. More information can be found at `http://www.x3dom.org/?page_id=532#`.

Format	Description
Babylon	Babylon is a 3D JavaScript game library. It stores models in its own internal format. More information about this can be found at `http://www.babylonjs.com/`.
PDB	This is a very specialized format, created by **Protein Data Bank**, that is used to specify what proteins look like. Three.js can load and visualize proteins specified in this format.
PLY	This format is called the **Polygon** file format. This is most often used to store information from 3D scanners.

In the next chapter, we'll revisit some of these formats (and look at two additional ones, MD2 and glTF) when we look at animations. For now, we start with the first one on the list, the internal format of Three.js.

Saving and loading in Three.js JSON format

You can use Three.js' JSON format for two different scenarios in Three.js. You can use it to save and load a single THREE.Mesh, or you can use it to save and load a complete scene.

Saving and loading THREE.Mesh

To demonstrate saving and loading, we created a simple example based on THREE.TorusKnotGeometry. With this example, you can create a torus knot, just like we did in *Chapter 5, Learning to Work with Geometries,* and using the **save** button from the **Save & Load** menu, you can save the current geometry. For this example, we save using the HTML5 local storage API. This API allows us to easily store persistent information in the client's browser and retrieve it at a later time (even after the browser has been shut down and restarted).

We will look at the 03-load-save-json-object.html example. The following screenshot shows this example:

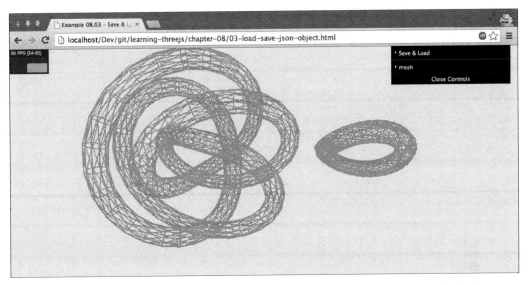

Exporting in JSON from Three.js is very easy and doesn't require you to include any additional libraries. The only thing you need to do to export THREE.Mesh as JSON is the following:

```
var result = knot.toJSON();
localStorage.setItem("json", JSON.stringify(result));
```

Before saving it, we first convert the result from the toJSON function, a JavaScript object, to a string using the JSON.stringify function. This results in a JSON string that looks like this (most of the vertices and faces are left out):

```
{
  "metadata": {
    "version": 4.3,
    "type": "Object",
    "generator": "ObjectExporter"
  },
  "geometries": [{
    "uuid": "53E1B290-3EF3-4574-BD68-E65DFC618BA7",
    "type": "TorusKnotGeometry",
    "radius": 10,
    "tube": 1,
    "radialSegments": 64,
    "tubularSegments": 8,
    "p": 2,
```

```
    "q": 3,
    "heightScale": 1
  }],
  ...
}
```

As you can see, Three.js saves all the information about `THREE.Mesh`. To save this information using the HTML5 local storage API, all we have to do is call the `localStorage.setItem` function. The first argument is the key value (`json`) that we can later use to retrieve the information we passed in as the second argument.

Loading `THREE.Mesh` back into Three.js also requires just a couple of lines of code, as follows:

```
var json = localStorage.getItem("json");

if (json) {
  var loadedGeometry = JSON.parse(json);
  var loader = new THREE.ObjectLoader();

  loadedMesh = loader.parse(loadedGeometry);
  loadedMesh.position.x -= 50;
  scene.add(loadedMesh);
}
```

Here, we first get the JSON from local storage using the name we saved it with (`json` in this case). For this, we use the `localStorage.getItem` function provided by the HTML5 local storage API. Next, we need to convert the string back to a JavaScript object (`JSON.parse`) and convert the JSON object back to `THREE.Mesh`. Three.js provides a helper object called `THREE.ObjectLoader`, which you can use to convert JSON to `THREE.Mesh`. In this example, we used the `parse` method on the loader to directly parse a JSON string. The loader also provides a `load` function, where you can pass in the URL to a file containing the JSON definition.

As you can see here, we only saved `THREE.Mesh`. We lose everything else. If you want to save the complete scene, including the lights and the cameras, you can use `THREE.SceneExporter`.

Saving and loading a scene

If you want to save a complete scene, you use the same approach as we saw in the previous section for the geometry. `04-load-save-json-scene.html` is a working example showing this. The following screenshot shows this example:

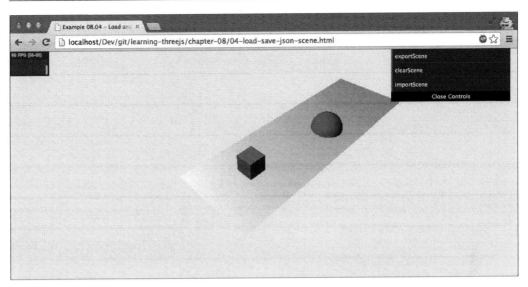

In this example, you've got three options: **exportScene**, **clearScene**, and **importScene**. With **exportScene**, the current state of the scene will be saved in the browser's local storage. To test the import functionality, you can remove the scene by clicking on the **clearScene** button and load it from local storage with the **importScene** button. The code to do all this is very simple, but before you can use it, you have to import the required exporter and loader from the Three.js distribution (look at the examples/js/exporters and examples/js/loaders directories):

```
<script type="text/javascript" src="../libs/SceneLoader.js">
  </script>
<script type="text/javascript" src="../libs/SceneExporter.js">
  </script>
```

With these JavaScript imports included in the page, you can export a scene with the following code:

```
var exporter = new THREE.SceneExporter();
var sceneJson = JSON.stringify(exporter.parse(scene));
localStorage.setItem('scene', sceneJson);
```

This approach is exactly the same as we used in the previous section—only this time, we use THREE.SceneExporter() to export a complete scene. The resulting JSON looks like this:

```
{
  "metadata": {
    "formatVersion": 3.2,
```

```
    "type": "scene",
    "generatedBy": "SceneExporter",
    "objects": 5,
    "geometries": 3,
    "materials": 3,
    "textures": 0
},
"urlBaseType": "relativeToScene", "objects": {
    "Object_78B22F27-C5D8-46BF-A539-A42207DDDCA8": {
        "geometry": "Geometry_5",
        "material": "Material_1",
        "position": [15, 0, 0],
        "rotation": [-1.5707963267948966, 0, 0],
        "scale": [1, 1, 1],
        "visible": true
    }
    ... // removed all the other objects for legibility
},
"geometries": {
    "Geometry_8235FC68-64F0-45E9-917F-5981B082D5BC": {
        "type": "cube",
        "width": 4,
        "height": 4,
        "depth": 4,
        "widthSegments": 1,
        "heightSegments": 1,
        "depthSegments": 1
    }
    ... // removed all the other objects for legibility
}
... other scene information like textures
```

When you load this JSON again, Three.js just recreates the objects exactly as they were exported. Loading a scene is done like this:

```
var json = (localStorage.getItem('scene'));
var sceneLoader = new THREE.SceneLoader();
sceneLoader.parse(JSON.parse(json), function(e) {
  scene = e.scene;
}, '.');
```

The last argument passed into the loader ('.') defines the relative URL. For instance, if you've got materials that use textures (for example, external images), those will be retrieved using this relative URL. In this example, where we don't use textures, we just pass in the current directory. Just as with THREE.ObjectLoader, you can also load a JSON file from a URL using the load function.

There are many different 3D programs you can use to create complex meshes. A popular open source one is Blender (www.blender.org). Three.js has an exporter for Blender (and for Maya and 3D Studio Max) that directly exports to the JSON format of Three.js. In the next section, we'll walk you through getting Blender configured to use this exporter and show you how you can export a complex model in Blender and show it in Three.js.

Working with Blender

Before we get started with the configuration, we'll show the result that we'll be aiming for. In the following screenshot, you can see a simple Blender model that we exported with the Three.js plugin and imported in Three.js with THREE.JSONLoader:

Installing the Three.js exporter in Blender

To get Blender to export Three.js models, we first need to add the Three.js exporter to Blender. The following steps are for Mac OS X but are pretty much the same on Windows and Linux. You can download Blender from `www.blender.org` and follow the platform-specific installation instructions. After installation, you can add the Three.js plugin. First, locate the `addons` directory from your Blender installation using a terminal window:

```
jos@Joss-MacBook-Pro.local:~/Downloads/Blender/blender.app/Contents/MacOS/2.68/scripts/addons$ ls -l | head
total 3104
drwxr-xr-x@  6 jos  staff     204 Jul 24 16:13 add_curve_extra_objects
-rw-r--r--@  1 jos  staff   26032 Jul 24 16:13 add_curve_ivygen.py
drwxr-xr-x@  5 jos  staff     170 Jul 24 16:13 add_curve_sapling
drwxr-xr-x@  7 jos  staff     238 Jul 24 16:13 add_mesh_BoltFactory
-rw-r--r--@  1 jos  staff   27994 Jul 24 16:13 add_mesh_ant_landscape.py
drwxr-xr-x@ 14 jos  staff     476 Jul 24 16:13 add_mesh_extra_objects
-rw-r--r--@  1 jos  staff   35389 Jul 24 16:13 add_mesh_pipe_joint.py
-rw-r--r--@  1 jos  staff   27191 Jul 24 16:13 add_mesh_solid.py
-rw-r--r--@  1 jos  staff   13200 Jul 24 16:13 animation_add_corrective_shape_key.py
jos@Joss-MacBook-Pro.local:~/Downloads/Blender/blender.app/Contents/MacOS/2.68/scripts/addons$ ▮
```

On my Mac, it's located here: `./blender.app/Contents/MacOS/2.70/scripts/addons`. For Windows, this directory can be found at the following location: `C:\Users\USERNAME\AppData\Roaming\Blender Foundation\Blender\2.7X\scripts\addons`. And for Linux, you can find this directory here: `/home/USERNAME/.config/blender/2.7X/scripts/addons`.

Next, you need to get the Three.js distribution and unpack it locally. In this distribution, you can find the following folder: `utils/exporters/blender/2.65/scripts/addons/`. In this directory, there is a single subdirectory with the name `io_mesh_threejs`. Copy this directory to the `addons` folder of your Blender installation.

Now, all we need to do is start Blender and enable the exporter. In Blender, open **Blender User Preferences (File | User Preferences)**. In the window that opens, select the **Addons** tab, and in the search box, type `three`. This will show the following screen:

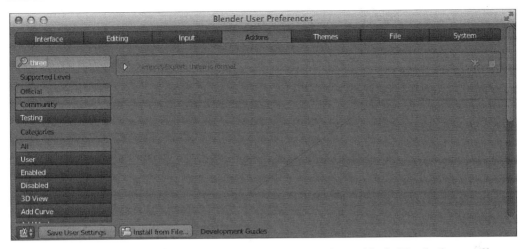

At this point, the Three.js plugin is found, but it is still disabled. Check the small checkbox to the right, and the Three.js exporter will be enabled. As a final check to see whether everything is working correctly, open the **File** | **Export** menu option, and you'll see Three.js listed as an export option. This is shown in the following screenshot:

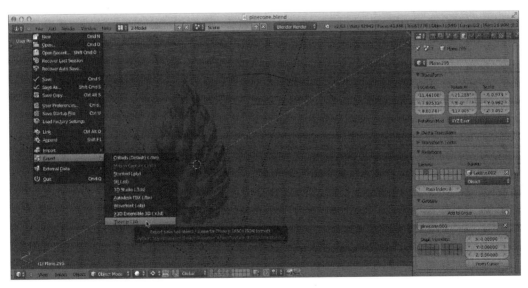

With the plugin installed, we can load our first model.

Loading and exporting a model from Blender

As an example, we've added a simple Blender model named `misc_chair01.blend` in the `assets/models` folder, which you can find in the sources for this book. In this section, we'll load this model and show the minimal steps it takes to export this model to Three.js.

First, we need to load this model in Blender. Use **File | Open** and navigate to the folder containing the `misc_chair01.blend` file. Select this file and click on **Open**. This will show you a screen that looks somewhat like this:

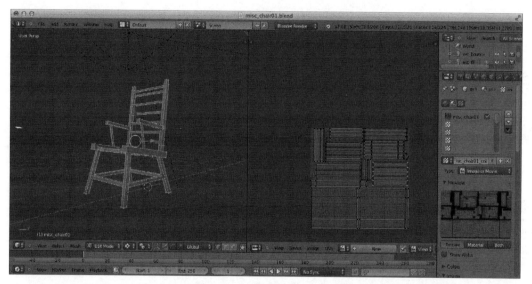

Exporting this model to the Three.js JSON format is pretty straightforward. From the **File** menu, open **Export | Three.js**, type in the name of the export file, and select **Export Three.js**. This will create a JSON file in a format Three.js understands. A part of the contents of this file is shown next:

```
{

    "metadata" :
    {
        "formatVersion" : 3.1,
        "generatedBy"   : "Blender 2.7 Exporter",
        "vertices"      : 208,
        "faces"         : 124,
        "normals"       : 115,
        "colors"        : 0,
```

```
        "uvs"            : [270,151],
        "materials"      : 1,
        "morphTargets"   : 0,
        "bones"          : 0
    },
    ...
```

However, we aren't completely done. In the previous screenshot, you can see that the chair contains a wooden texture. If you look through the JSON export, you can see that the export for the chair also specifies a material, as follows:

```
"materials": [{
  "DbgColor": 15658734,
  "DbgIndex": 0,
  "DbgName": "misc_chair01",
  "blending": "NormalBlending",
  "colorAmbient": [0.53132, 0.25074, 0.147919],
  "colorDiffuse": [0.53132, 0.25074, 0.147919],
  "colorSpecular": [0.0, 0.0, 0.0],
  "depthTest": true,
  "depthWrite": true,
  "mapDiffuse": "misc_chair01_col.jpg",
  "mapDiffuseWrap": ["repeat", "repeat"],
  "shading": "Lambert",
  "specularCoef": 50,
  "transparency": 1.0,
  "transparent": false,
  "vertexColors": false
}],
```

This material specifies a texture, `misc_chair01_col.jpg`, for the `mapDiffuse` property. So, besides exporting the model, we also need to make sure the texture file is also available to Three.js. Luckily, we can save this texture directly from Blender.

In Blender, open the **UV/Image Editor** view. You can select this view from the drop-down menu on the left-hand side of the **File** menu option. This will replace the top menu with the following:

Make sure the texture you want to export is selected, `misc_chair_01_col.jpg` in our case (you can select a different one using the small image icon). Next, click on the **Image** menu and use the **Save as Image** menu option to save the image. Save it in the same folder where you saved the model using the name specified in the JSON export file. At this point, we're ready to load the model into Three.js.

The code to load this into Three.js at this point looks like this:

```
var loader = new THREE.JSONLoader();
loader.load('../assets/models/misc_chair01.js', function (geometry,
mat) {
  mesh = new THREE.Mesh(geometry, mat[0]);

  mesh.scale.x = 15;
  mesh.scale.y = 15;
  mesh.scale.z = 15;

  scene.add(mesh);

}, '../assets/models/');
```

We've already seen `JSONLoader` before, but this time, we use the `load` function instead of the `parse` function. In this function, we specify the URL we want to load (points to the exported JSON file), a callback that is called when the object is loaded, and the location, `../assets/models/`, where the texture can be found (relative to the page). This callback takes two parameters: `geometry` and `mat`. The `geometry` parameter contains the model, and the `mat` parameter contains an array of material objects. We know that there is only one material, so when we create `THREE.Mesh`, we directly reference that material. If you open the `05-blender-from-json.html` example, you can see the chair we just exported from Blender.

Using the Three.js exporter isn't the only way of loading models from Blender into Three.js. Three.js understands a number of 3D file formats, and Blender can export in a couple of those formats. Using the Three.js format, however, is very easy, and if things go wrong, they are often quickly found.

In the following section, we'll look at a couple of the formats Three.js supports and also show a Blender-based example for the OBJ and MTL file formats.

Importing from 3D file formats

At the beginning of this chapter, we listed a number of formats that are supported by Three.js. In this section, we'll quickly walk through a couple of examples for those formats. Note that for all these formats, an additional JavaScript file needs to be included. You can find all these files in the Three.js distribution in the `examples/js/loaders` directory.

The OBJ and MTL formats

OBJ and MTL are companion formats and often used together. The OBJ file defines the geometry, and the MTL file defines the materials that are used. Both OBJ and MTL are text-based formats. A part of an OBJ file looks like this:

```
v -0.032442 0.010796 0.025935
v -0.028519 0.013697 0.026201
v -0.029086 0.014533 0.021409
usemtl Material
s 1
f 2731 2735 2736 2732
f 2732 2736 3043 3044
```

The MTL file defines materials like this:

```
newmtl Material
Ns 56.862745
Ka 0.000000 0.000000 0.000000
Kd 0.360725 0.227524 0.127497
Ks 0.010000 0.010000 0.010000
Ni 1.000000
d 1.000000
illum 2
```

The OBJ and MTL formats by Three.js are understood well and are also supported by Blender. So, as an alternative, you could choose to export models from Blender in the OBJ/MTL format instead of the Three.js JSON format. Three.js has two different loaders you can use. If you only want to load the geometry, you can use OBJLoader. We used this loader for our example (06-load-obj.html). The following screenshot shows this example:

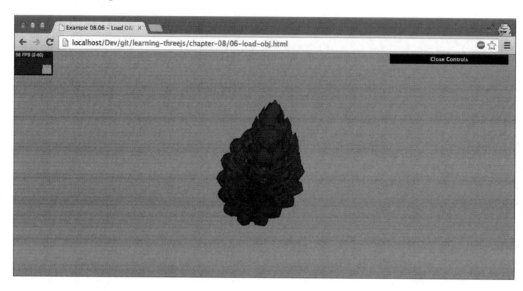

To import this in Three.js, you have to add the OBJLoader JavaScript file:

```
<script type="text/javascript" src="../libs/OBJLoader.js">
  </script>
```

Import the model like this:

```
var loader = new THREE.OBJLoader();
loader.load('../assets/models/pinecone.obj', function (loadedMesh) {
  var material = new THREE.MeshLambertMaterial({color: 0x5C3A21});

  // loadedMesh is a group of meshes. For
  // each mesh set the material, and compute the information
  // three.js needs for rendering.
  loadedMesh.children.forEach(function (child) {
    child.material = material;
    child.geometry.computeFaceNormals();
    child.geometry.computeVertexNormals();
  });
```

```
mesh = loadedMesh;
loadedMesh.scale.set(100, 100, 100);
loadedMesh.rotation.x = -0.3;
scene.add(loadedMesh);
});
```

In this code, we use `OBJLoader` to load the model from a URL. Once the model is loaded, the callback we provide is called, and we add the model to the scene.

 Usually, a good first step is to print out the response from the callback to the console to understand how the loaded object is built up. Often with these loaders, the geometry or mesh is returned as a hierarchy of groups. Understanding this makes it much easier to place and apply the correct material and take any other additional steps. Also, look at the position of a couple of vertices to determine whether you need to scale the model up or down and where to position the camera. In this example, we've also made the calls to `computeFaceNormals` and `computeVertexNormals`. This is required to ensure that the material used (`THREE.MeshLambertMaterial`) is rendered correctly.

The next example (`07-load-obj-mtl.html`) uses `OBJMTLLoader` to load a model and directly assign a material. The following screenshot shows this example:

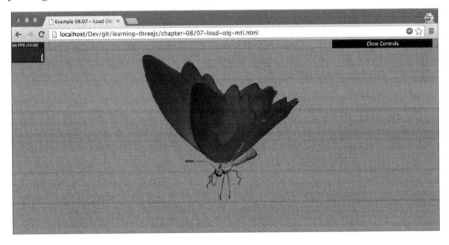

First, we need to add the correct loaders to the page:

```html
<script type="text/javascript" src="../libs/OBJLoader.js">
  </script>
<script type="text/javascript" src="../libs/MTLLoader.js">
  </script>
<script type="text/javascript" src="../libs/OBJMTLLoader.js">
  </script>
```

We can load the model from the OBJ and MTL files like this:

```
var loader = new THREE.OBJMTLLoader();
loader.load('../assets/models/butterfly.obj', '../assets/
  models/butterfly.mtl', function(object) {
  // configure the wings
  var wing2 = object.children[5].children[0];
  var wing1 = object.children[4].children[0];

  wing1.material.opacity = 0.6;
  wing1.material.transparent = true;
  wing1.material.depthTest = false;
  wing1.material.side = THREE.DoubleSide;

  wing2.material.opacity = 0.6;
  wing2.material.depthTest = false;
  wing2.material.transparent = true;
  wing2.material.side = THREE.DoubleSide;

  object.scale.set(140, 140, 140);
  mesh = object;
  scene.add(mesh);

  mesh.rotation.x = 0.2;
  mesh.rotation.y = -1.3;
});
```

The first thing to mention before we look at the code is that if you receive an OBJ file, an MTL file, and the required texture files, you'll have to check how the MTL file references the textures. These should be referenced relative to the MTL file and not as an absolute path. The code itself isn't that different from the one we saw for THREE. ObjLoader. We specify the location of the OBJ file, the location of the MTL file, and the function to call when the model is loaded. The model we've used as an example in this case is a complex model. So, we set some specific properties in the callback to fix some rendering issues, as follows:

- The opacity in the source files was set incorrectly, which caused the wings to be invisible. So, to fix that, we set the opacity and transparent properties ourselves.

- By default, Three.js only renders one side of an object. Since we look at the wings from two sides, we need to set the side property to the THREE. DoubleSide value.

- The wings caused some unwanted artifacts when they needed to be rendered on top of each other. We've fixed that by setting the `depthTest` property to `false`. This has a slight impact on performance but can often solve some strange rendering artifacts.

But, as you can see, you can easily load complex models directly into Three.js and render them in real time in your browser. You might need to fine-tune some material properties though.

Loading a Collada model

Collada models (extension is `.dae`) are another very common format for defining scenes and models (and animations, as we'll see in the following chapter). In a Collada model, it is not just the geometry that is defined, but also the materials. It's even possible to define light sources.

To load Collada models, you have to take pretty much the same steps as for the OBJ and MTL models. You start by including the correct loader:

```
<script type="text/javascript" src="../libs/ColladaLoader.js">
  </script>
```

For this example, we'll load the following model:

Loading a truck model is once again pretty simple:

```
var mesh;
loader.load("../assets/models/dae/Truck_dae.dae", function
  (result) {
  mesh = result.scene.children[0].children[0].clone();
  mesh.scale.set(4, 4, 4);
  scene.add(mesh);
});
```

The main difference here is the result of the object that is returned to the callback. The `result` object has the following structure:

```
var result = {

  scene: scene,
  morphs: morphs,
  skins: skins,
  animations: animData,
  dae: {
    ...
  }
};
```

In this chapter, we're interested in the objects that are in the `scene` parameter. I first printed out the scene to the console to look where the mesh was that I was interested in, which was `result.scene.children[0].children[0]`. All that was left to do was scale it to a reasonable size and add it to the scene. A final note on this specific example—when I loaded this model for the first time, the materials didn't render correctly. The reason was that the textures used the `.tga` format, which isn't supported in WebGL. To fix this, I had to convert the `.tga` files to `.png` and edit the XML of the `.dae` model to point to these `.png` files.

As you can see, for most complex models, including materials, you often have to take some additional steps to get the desired results. By looking closely at how the materials are configured (using `console.log()`) or replacing them with test materials, problems are often easy to spot.

Loading the STL, CTM, VTK, AWD, Assimp, VRML, and Babylon models

We're going to quickly skim over these file formats as they all follow the same principles:

1. Include `[NameOfFormat]Loader.js` in your web page.
2. Use `[NameOfFormat]Loader.load()` to load a URL.
3. Check what the response format for the callback looks like and render the result.

We have included an example for all these formats:

Name	Example	Screenshot
STL	08-load-STL.html	
CTM	09-load-CTM.html	
VTK	10-load-vtk.html	

Name	Example	Screenshot
AWD	`11-load-awd.html`	
Assimp	`12-load-assimp.html`	
VRML	`13-load-vrml.html`	

Name	Example	Screenshot
Babylon	The Babylon loader is slightly different from the other loaders in this table. With this loader, you don't load a single THREE. Mesh or THREE. Geometry instance, but with this loader, you load a complete scene, including lights. 14-load-babylon.html	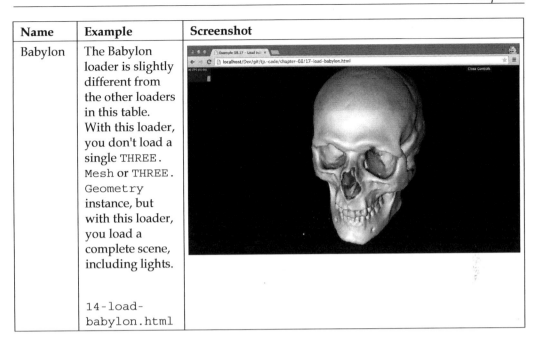

If you look at the source code for these examples, you might see that for some of them, we need to change some material properties or do some scaling before the model is rendered correctly. The reason we need to do this is because of the way the model is created in its external application, giving it different dimensions and grouping than we normally use in Three.js.

We've almost shown all the supported file formats. In the next two sections, we'll take a different approach. First, we'll look at how to render proteins from Protein Data Bank (PDB format), and finally we'll use a model defined in the PLY format to create a particle system.

Show proteins from Protein Data Bank

Protein Data Bank (www.rcsb.org) contains detailed information about many different molecules and proteins. Besides the explanation of these proteins, they also provide a way to download the structure of these molecules in the PDB format. Three.js provides a loader for files specified in the PDB format. In this section, we'll give an example of how you can parse PDB files and visualize them with Three.js.

The first thing we always need to do to load in a new file format is include the correct loader in Three.js, as follows:

```
<script type="text/javascript" src="../libs/PDBLoader.js">
  </script>
```

With this loader included, we're going to create the following 3D model of the molecule description provided (see the `15-load-ptb.html` example):

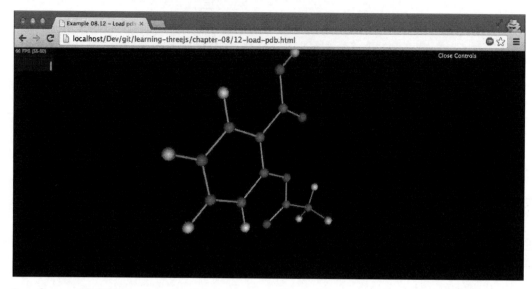

Loading a PDB file is done in the same manner as the previous formats, as follows:

```
var loader = new THREE.PDBLoader();
var group = new THREE.Object3D();
loader.load("../assets/models/diamond.pdb", function (geometry,
  geometryBonds) {
  var i = 0;

  geometry.vertices.forEach(function (position) {
    var sphere = new THREE.SphereGeometry(0.2);
    var material = new THREE.MeshPhongMaterial({color:
      geometry.colors[i++]});
    var mesh = new THREE.Mesh(sphere, material);
    mesh.position.copy(position);
    group.add(mesh);
  });

  for (var j = 0; j < geometryBonds.vertices.length; j += 2) {
    var path = new THREE.SplineCurve3([geometryBonds.vertices[j],
      geometryBonds.vertices[j + 1]]);
    var tube = new THREE.TubeGeometry(path, 1, 0.04)
```

```
        var material = new THREE.MeshPhongMaterial({color: 0xcccccc});
        var mesh = new THREE.Mesh(tube, material);
        group.add(mesh);
    }
    console.log(geometry);
    console.log(geometryBonds);

    scene.add(group);
});
```

As you can see from this example, we instantiate THREE.PDBLoader, pass in the model file we want to load, and provide a callback that is called when the model is loaded. For this specific loader, the callback function is called with two arguments: geometry and geometryBonds. The vertices from the geometry argument supplied contain the positions of the individual atoms, and geometryBounds is used for the connections between the atoms.

For each vertex, we create a sphere with the color that is also supplied by the model:

```
var sphere = new THREE.SphereGeometry(0.2);
var material = new THREE.MeshPhongMaterial({color:
    geometry.colors[i++] });
var mesh = new THREE.Mesh(sphere, material);
mesh.position.copy(position);
group.add(mesh)
```

Each connection is defined like this:

```
var path = new THREE.SplineCurve3([geometryBonds.vertices[j],
    geometryBonds.vertices[j + 1]]);
var tube = new THREE.TubeGeometry(path, 1, 0.04)
var material = new THREE.MeshPhongMaterial({color: 0xcccccc});
var mesh = new THREE.Mesh(tube, material);
group.add(mesh);
```

For the connection, we first create a 3D path using the THREE.SplineCurve3 object. This path is used as input for THREE.Tube and used to create the connection between the atoms. All the connections and atoms are added to a group, and this group is added to the scene. There are many models you can download from Protein Data Bank.

The following image shows the structure of a diamond:

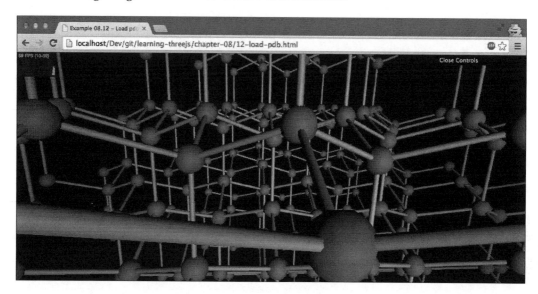

Creating a particle system from a PLY model

Working with the PLY format isn't that much different from the other formats. You include the loader, provide a callback, and visualize the model. For this last example, however, we're going to do something different. Instead of rendering the model as a mesh, we'll use the information from this model to create a particle system (see the 15-load-ply.html example). The following screenshot shows this example:

The JavaScript code to render the preceding screenshot is actually very simple, as follows:

```
var loader = new THREE.PLYLoader();
var group = new THREE.Object3D();
loader.load("../assets/models/test.ply", function (geometry) {
  var material = new THREE.PointCloudMaterial({
    color: 0xffffff,
    size: 0.4,
    opacity: 0.6,
    transparent: true,
    blending: THREE.AdditiveBlending,
    map: generateSprite()
  });

  group = new THREE.PointCloud(geometry, material);
  group.sortParticles = true;

  scene.add(group);
});
```

As you can see, we use `THREE.PLYLoader` to load the model. The callback returns `geometry`, and we use this geometry as input for `THREE.PointCloud`. The material we use is the same as the one we used for the last example in the previous chapter. As you can see, with Three.js, it is very easy to combine models from various sources and render them in different ways, all with a few lines of code.

Summary

Using models from external sources isn't that hard to do in Three.js. Especially for simple models, you only have to take a few simple steps. When working with external models, or creating them using grouping and merging, it is good to keep a couple of things in mind. The first thing you need to remember is that when you group objects, they still remain available as individual objects. Transformations applied to the parent also affect the children, but you can still transform the children individually. Besides grouping, you can also merge geometries together. With this approach, you lose the individual geometries and get a single new geometry. This is especially useful when you're dealing with thousands of geometries you need to render and you're running into performance issues.

Three.js supports a large number of external formats. When using these format loaders, it's a good idea to look through the source code and log out the information received in the callback. This will help you to understand the steps you need to take to get the correct mesh and set it to the correct position and scale. Often, when the model doesn't show correctly, this is caused by its material settings. It could be that incompatible texture formats are used, opacity is incorrectly defined, or the format contains incorrect links to the texture images. It is usually a good idea to use a test material to determine whether the model itself is loaded correctly and log the loaded material to the JavaScript console to check for unexpected values. It is also possible to export meshes and scenes, but remember that `GeometryExporter, SceneExporter,` and `SceneLoader` of Three.js are still work in progress.

The models you worked with in this chapter, and in the previous chapters, are mostly static models. They aren't animated, don't move around, and don't change shape. In the next chapter, you'll learn how you can animate your models to make them come to life. Besides animations, the following chapter will also explain the various camera controls provided by Three.js. With a camera control, you can move, pan, and rotate the camera around your scene.

9
Animations and Moving the Camera

In the previous chapters, we have seen some simple animations, but nothing too complex. In *Chapter 1, Creating Your First 3D Scene with Three.js*, we introduced the basic rendering loop, and in the chapter following that, we used that to rotate some simple objects and show a couple of other basic animation concepts. In this chapter, we're going to look in more detail at how animation is supported by Three.js. We will look in detail at the following four subjects:

- Basic animation
- Moving the camera
- Morphing and skinning
- Loading external animations

We start with the basic concepts behind animations.

Basic animations

Before we look at the examples, let's do a quick recap of what was shown in *Chapter 1, Creating Your First 3D Scene with Three.js*, on the render loop. To support animations, we need to tell Three.js to render the scene every so often. For this, we use the standard HTML5 `requestAnimationFrame` functionality, as follows:

```
render();

function render() {
```

```
    // render the scene
    renderer.render(scene, camera);
    // schedule the next rendering using requestAnimationFrame
    requestAnimationFrame(render);
}
```

With this code, we only need to call the `render()` function once when were done initializing the scene. In the `render()` function itself, we use `requestAnimationFrame` to schedule the next rendering. This way, the browser will make sure the `render()` function is called at the correct interval (usually around 60 times a second). Before `requestAnimationFrame` was added to browsers, `setInterval(function, interval)` or `setTimeout(function, interval)` were used. These would call the specified function once every set interval. The problem with this approach is that it doesn't take into account what else is going on. Even if your animation isn't shown or is in a hidden tab, it is still called and is still using resources. Another issue is that these functions update the screen whenever they are called, not when it is the best time for the browser, which means higher CPU usage. With `requestAnimationFrame`, we don't tell the browser when it needs to update the screen; we ask the browser to run the supplied function when it's most opportune. Usually, this results in a frame rate of about 60 fps. With `requestAnimationFrame`, your animations will run more smoothly and will be more CPU- and GPU-friendly, and you don't have to worry about timing issues yourself.

Simple animations

With this approach, we can very easily animate objects by changing their rotation, scale, position, material, vertices, faces, and anything else you can imagine. In the next render loop, Three.js will render the changed properties. A very simple example, based on the one we already saw in *Chapter 1, Creating Your First 3D Scene with Three.js*, is available in `01-basic-animation.html`. The following screenshot shows this example:

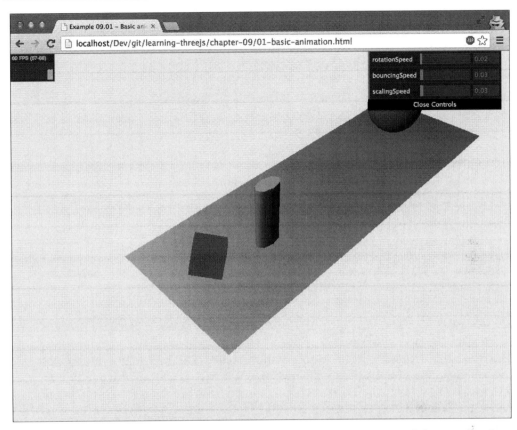

The render loop for this is very simple. Just change the properties of the involved meshes, and Three.js handles the rest. Here's how we do this:

```
function render() {
  cube.rotation.x += controls.rotationSpeed;
  cube.rotation.y += controls.rotationSpeed;
  cube.rotation.z += controls.rotationSpeed;

  step += controls.bouncingSpeed;
```

```
sphere.position.x = 20 + ( 10 * (Math.cos(step)));
sphere.position.y = 2 + ( 10 * Math.abs(Math.sin(step)));

scalingStep += controls.scalingSpeed;
var scaleX = Math.abs(Math.sin(scalingStep / 4));
var scaleY = Math.abs(Math.cos(scalingStep / 5));
var scaleZ = Math.abs(Math.sin(scalingStep / 7));
cylinder.scale.set(scaleX, scaleY, scaleZ);

renderer.render(scene, camera);
requestAnimationFrame(render);
}
```

Nothing spectacular here, but it nicely shows the concept behind the basic animations we discuss in this book. In the next section, we'll take a quick sidestep. Besides animations, an important aspect, which you'll quickly run into when working with Three.js in more complex scenes, is the ability to select objects on screen using the mouse.

Selecting objects

Even though not directly related to animations, since we'll be looking into cameras and animations in this chapter, it is a nice addition to the subjects explained in this chapter. What we'll show here is how you can select an object from the scene using the mouse. We'll first look at the code required for this before we look at the example:

```
var projector = new THREE.Projector();

function onDocumentMouseDown(event) {
  var vector = new THREE.Vector3(event.clientX / window.innerWidth
    ) * 2 - 1, -( event.clientY / window.innerHeight ) * 2 + 1,
    0.5);
  vector = vector.unproject(camera);

  var raycaster = new THREE.Raycaster(camera.position,
    vector.sub(camera.position).normalize());

  var intersects = raycaster.intersectObjects([sphere, cylinder,
    cube]);
```

```
    if (intersects.length > 0) {
      intersects[ 0 ].object.material.transparent = true;
      intersects[ 0 ].object.material.opacity = 0.1;
    }
}
```

In this code, we use `THREE.Projector` together with `THREE.Raycaster` to determine whether we've clicked on a specific object. What happens when we click on the screen is the following:

1. First, `THREE.Vector3` is created based on the position where we've clicked on the screen.

2. Next, with the `vector.unproject` function, we convert the clicked position on screen to coordinates in our Three.js scene. In other words, we unproject from screen coordinates to world coordinates.

3. Next, we create `THREE.Raycaster`. With `THREE.Raycaster`, we can cast rays into our scene. In this case, we emit a ray from the position of the camera (`camera.position`) to the position we clicked on in the scene.

4. Finally, we use the `raycaster.intersectObjects` function to determine whether any of the supplied objects are hit by this ray.

The result from this final step contains information on any object that is hit by this ray. The following information is provided:

```
distance: 49.9047088522448
face: THREE.Face3
faceIndex: 4
object: THREE.Mesh
point: THREE.Vector3
```

The mesh that was clicked on is the object, and `face` and `faceIndex` point to the face of the mesh that was selected. The `distance` value is measured from the camera to the clicked object, and `point` is the exact position on the mesh where it was clicked. You can test this out in the `02-selecting-objects.html` example. Any object you click on will become transparent and the details of the selection will be printed to the console.

If you want to see the path of the ray that is cast, you can enable the showRay property from the menu. The following screenshot shows the ray that was used to select the blue sphere:

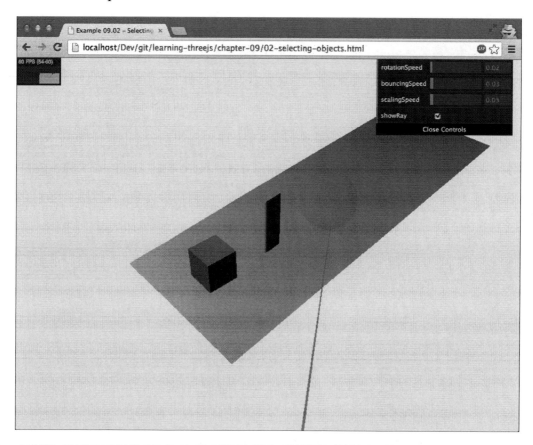

Now that we've finished this small intermission, let's get back to our animations. Until now, we've changed the properties in our render loop to animate an object. In the next section, we'll look at a small library that makes defining animations a lot easier.

Animating with Tween.js

Tween.js is a small JavaScript library that you can download from https://github.com/sole/tween.js/ and that you can use to easily define the transition of a property between two values. All the intermediate points between the start and end values are calculated for you. This process is called **tweening**.

For instance, you can use this library to change the *x* position of a mesh from 10 to 3 in 10 seconds, as follows:

```
var tween = new TWEEN.Tween({x: 10}).to({x: 3},
  10000).easing(TWEEN.Easing.Elastic.InOut).onUpdate( function ()
  {
  // update the mesh
})
```

In this example, we've created `TWEEN.Tween`. This tween will make sure that the *x* property is changed from 10 to 3 over a period of 10,000 milliseconds. Tween.js also allows you to define how this property is changed over time. This can be done using linear, quadratic, or any of the other possibilities (see `http://sole.github.io/tween.js/examples/03_graphs.html` for a complete overview). The way the value is changed over time is called **easing**. With Tween.js, you configure this using the `easing()` function.

Using this library from Three.js is very simple. If you open up the `03-animation-tween.html` example, you can see the Tween.js library in action. The following screenshot shows a still image of the example:

In this example, we've taken a particle cloud from *Chapter 7, Particles, Sprites, and the Point Cloud*, and animated all the particles down to the ground. The position of these particles is based on a tween created with the Tween.js library, as follows:

```
// first create the tweens
var posSrc = {pos: 1}
var tween = new TWEEN.Tween(posSrc).to({pos: 0}, 5000);
tween.easing(TWEEN.Easing.Sinusoidal.InOut);

var tweenBack = new TWEEN.Tween(posSrc).to({pos: 1}, 5000);
tweenBack.easing(TWEEN.Easing.Sinusoidal.InOut);

tween.chain(tweenBack);
tweenBack.chain(tween);


var onUpdate = function () {
  var count = 0;
  var pos = this.pos;

  loadedGeometry.vertices.forEach(function (e) {
    var newY = ((e.y + 3.22544) * pos) - 3.22544;
    particleCloud.geometry.vertices[count++].set(e.x, newY, e.z);
  });

  particleCloud.sortParticles = true;
};

tween.onUpdate(onUpdate);
tweenBack.onUpdate(onUpdate);
```

With this piece of code, we create two tweens: `tween` and `tweenBack`. The first one defines how the position property transitions from 1 to 0, and the second one does the opposite. With the `chain()` function, we chain these two tweens to each other, so these tweens will start looping when started. The final thing we define here is the `onUpdate` method. In this method, we walk through all the vertices of the particle system and change their position according to the position provided by the tween (`this.pos`).

We start the tween when the model is loaded, so at the end of the following function, we call the `tween.start()` function:

```
var loader = new THREE.PLYLoader();
loader.load( "../assets/models/test.ply", function (geometry) {
  ...
  tween.start()
  ...
});
```

When the tween is started, we need to tell the Tween.js library when we want it to update all the tweens it knows about. We do this by calling the `TWEEN.update()` function:

```
function render() {
  TWEEN.update();
  webGLRenderer.render(scene, camera);
  requestAnimationFrame(render);
}
```

With these steps in place, the tween library will take care of positioning the various points of the point cloud. As you can see, using this library is much easier than having to manage the transitions yourself.

Besides animating and changing objects, we can also animate a scene by moving the camera around. In the previous chapters, we already did this a couple of times by manually updating the position of the camera. Three.js also provides a number of additional ways of updating the camera.

Working with the camera

Three.js has a number of camera controls you can use to control the camera throughout a scene. These controls are located in the Three.js distribution and can be found in the `examples/js/controls` directory. In this section, we'll look in more detail at the following controls:

Name	Description
FirstPersonControls	These are controls that behave like those in first-person shooters. Move around with the keyboard and look around with the mouse.
FlyControls	These are flight simulator-like controls. Move and steer with the keyboard and the mouse.

Name	Description
RollControls	This is a simpler version of FlyControls. Allows you to move around and roll around the z axis.
TrackBallControls	These are the most used controls, allowing you to use the mouse (or the trackball) to easily move, pan, and zoom around the scene.
OrbitControls	This simulates a satellite in orbit around a specific scene. This allows you to move around with the mouse and keyboard.

These controls are the most useful controls available. Besides these, Three.js also provides a number of additional controls you can use (but which aren't explained in this book). Using these controls, however, is done in the same manner as the ones explained in the previous table:

Name	Description
DeviceOrientationControls	This controls the movement of the camera based on the orientation of the device. It internally uses the HTML device orientation API (http://www.w3.org/TR/orientation-event/).
EditorControls	These are controls that are specifically created for online 3D editors. This is used by the Three.js online editor, which you can find at http://threejs.org/editor/.
OculusControls	These are controls that allow you to use an Oculus Rift device to look around in your scene.
OrthographicTrackballControls	This is the same control as TrackBallControls but specifically created to be used with THREE.OrthographicCamera.
PointerLockControls	This is a simple control that locks the mouse using the DOM element on which the scene is rendered. This provides basic functionality for a simple 3D game.
TransformControls	This is an internal control used by the Three.js editor.

Name	Description
VRControls	This is a control that uses the `PositionSensorVRDevice` API to control the scene. More information on this standard can be found at `https://developer.mozilla.org/en-US/docs/Web/API/Navigator.getVRDevices`.

Besides using these camera controls, you can of course also move the camera yourself by setting `position` and change where it is pointed to using the `lookAt()` function.

> If you've worked with an older version of Three.js, you might be missing a specific camera control named `THREE.PathControls`. With this control, it was possible to define a path (for example using `THREE.Spline`) and move the camera along that path. In the last version of Three.js, this control was removed because of code complexity. The people behind Three.js are currently working on a replacement, but one isn't available yet.

The first of the controls we'll look at is `TrackballControls`.

TrackballControls

Before you can use `TrackballControls`, you first need to include the correct JavaScript file into your page:

```
<script type="text/javascript" src="../libs/TrackballControls.js">
  </script>
```

With this included, we can create the controls and attach them to the camera, as follows:

```
var trackballControls = new THREE.TrackballControls(camera);
trackballControls.rotateSpeed = 1.0;
trackballControls.zoomSpeed = 1.0;
trackballControls.panSpeed = 1.0;
```

Updating the position of the camera is something we do in the render loop, as follows:

```
var clock = new THREE.Clock();
function render() {
  var delta = clock.getDelta();
  trackballControls.update(delta);
  requestAnimationFrame(render);
  webGLRenderer.render(scene, camera);
}
```

In the preceding code snippet, we see a new Three.js object, THREE.Clock. The THREE.Clock object can be used to exactly calculate the elapsed time that a specific invocation or rendering loop takes to complete. You can do this by calling the clock.getDelta() function. This function will return the elapsed time between this call and the previous call to getDelta(). To update the position of the camera, we call the trackballControls.update() function. In this function, we need to provide the time that has passed since the last time this update function was called. For this, we use the getDelta() function from the THREE.Clock object. You might wonder why we don't just pass in the frame rate (1/60 seconds) to the update function. The reason is that with requestAnimationFrame, we can expect 60 fps, but this isn't guaranteed. Depending on all kinds of external factors, the frame rate might change. To make sure the camera turns and rotates smoothly, we need to pass in the exact elapsed time.

A working example for this can be found in 04-trackball-controls-camera.html. The following screenshot shows a still image of this example:

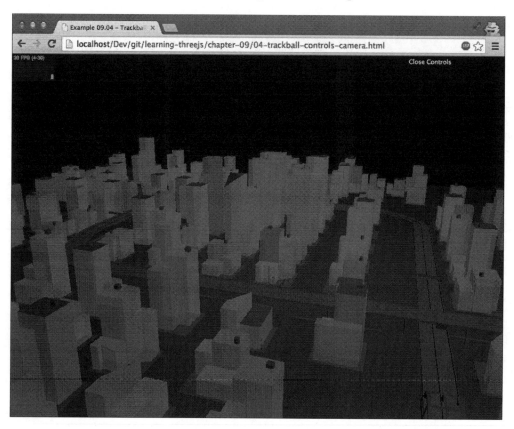

You can control the camera in the following manner:

Control	Action
Left mouse button and move	Rotate and roll the camera around the scene
Scroll wheel	Zoom in and zoom out
Middle mouse button and move	Zoom in and zoom out
Right mouse button and move	Pan around the scene

There are a couple of properties that you can use to fine-tune how the camera acts. For instance, you can set how fast the camera rotates with the rotateSpeed property and disable zooming by setting the noZoom property to true. In this chapter, we won't go into detail on what each property does as they are pretty much self-explanatory. For a complete overview of what is possible, look at the source of the TrackballControls.js file where these properties are listed.

FlyControls

The next control we'll look at is FlyControls. With FlyControls, you can fly around a scene using controls also found in flight simulators. An example can be found in 05-fly-controls-camera.html. The following screenshot shows a still image of this example:

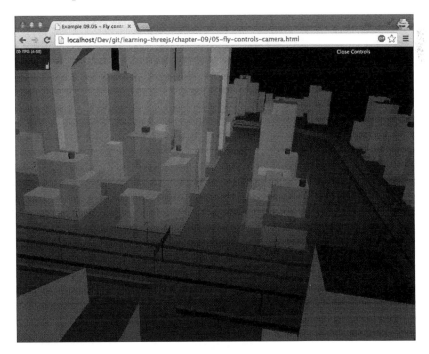

Enabling `FlyControls` works in the same manner as `TrackballControls`. First, load the correct JavaScript file:

```
<script type="text/javascript" src="../libs/FlyControls.js">
  </script>
```

Next, we configure the controls and attach it to the camera, as follows:

```
var flyControls = new THREE.FlyControls(camera);
flyControls.movementSpeed = 25;
flyControls.domElement = document.querySelector('#WebGL-output');
flyControls.rollSpeed = Math.PI / 24;
flyControls.autoForward = true;
flyControls.dragToLook = false;
```

Once again, we won't look into all the specific properties. Look at the source of the `FlyControls.js` file for that. Let's just pick out the properties you need to configure to get this control working. The property that needs to be set correctly is the `domElement` property. This property should point to the element in which we render the scene. For the examples in this book, we use the following element for our output:

```
<div id="WebGL-output"></div>
```

We set the property like this:

```
flyControls.domElement = document.querySelector('#WebGL-output');
```

If we don't set this property correctly, moving the mouse around will result in strange behavior.

You can control the camera with `THREE.FlyControls` in the following manner:

Control	Action
Left and middle mouse button	Start moving forward
Right mouse button	Move backwards
Mouse movement	Look around
W	Start moving forward
S	Move backwards
A	Move left
D	Move right
R	Move up
F	Move down

Control	Action
Left, right, up, and down arrows	Look left, right, up, and down
G	Roll left
E	Roll right

The next control we'll look at is THREE.RollControls.

RollControls

RollControls behaves much the same as FlyControls, so we won't go into detail here. RollControls can be created like this:

```
var rollControls = new THREE.RollControls(camera);
rollControls.movementSpeed = 25;
rollControls.lookSpeed = 3;
```

If you want to play around with this control, look at the 06-roll-controls-camera.html example. Note that if you only see a black screen, move the mouse to the bottom of your browser, and the cityscape will pan into view. This camera can be moved around with the following controls:

Control	Action
Left mouse button	Move forward
Right mouse button	Move backwards
Left, right, up, and down arrows	Move left, right, forward, and backwards
W	Move forward
A	Move left
S	Move backwards
D	Move right
Q	Roll left
E	Roll right
R	Move up
F	Move down

The last of the basic controls we'll look at is FirstPersonControls.

FirstPersonControls

As the name implies, FirstPersonControls allows you to control the camera just like in a first-person shooter. The mouse is used to look around and the keyboard is used to walk around. You can find an example in 07-first-person-camera.html. The following screenshot shows a still image of this example:

Creating these controls follows the same principles as the ones followed for other controls we've seen until now. The example we've just shown uses the following configuration:

```
var camControls = new THREE.FirstPersonControls(camera);
camControls.lookSpeed = 0.4;
camControls.movementSpeed = 20;
camControls.noFly = true;
camControls.lookVertical = true;
camControls.constrainVertical = true;
camControls.verticalMin = 1.0;
camControls.verticalMax = 2.0;
camControls.lon = -150;
camControls.lat = 120;
```

The only properties that you should carefully look at when using this control for yourself are the last two: the `lon` and `lat` properties. These two properties define where the camera is pointed at when the scene is rendered for the first time.

The controls for this control are pretty straightforward:

Control	Action
Mouse movement	Look around
Left, right, up, and down arrows	Move left, right, forward, and backwards
W	Move forward
A	Move left
S	Move backwards
D	Move right
R	Move up
F	Move down
Q	Stop all movement

For the next control, we'll move on from this first-person perspective to the perspective from space.

OrbitControl

The `OrbitControl` control is a great way to rotate and pan around an object in the center of the scene. With `08-controls-orbit.html`, we've included an example that shows how this control works. The following screenshot shows a still image of this example:

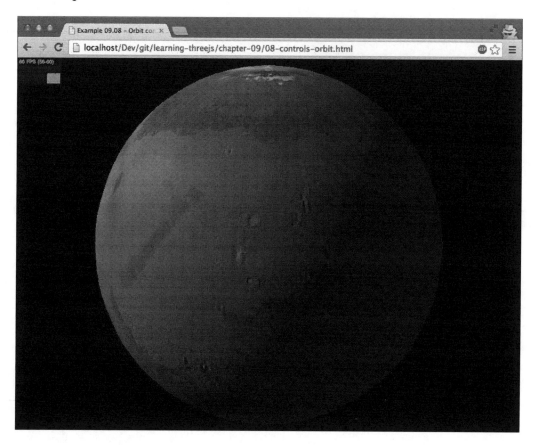

Using `OrbitControl` is just as simple as using the other controls. Include the correct JavaScript file, set up the control with the camera, and use `THREE.Clock` again to update the control:

```
<script type="text/javascript" src="../libs/OrbitControls.js">
  </script>
...
var orbitControls = new THREE.OrbitControls(camera);
orbitControls.autoRotate = true;
var clock = new THREE.Clock();
...
var delta = clock.getDelta();
orbitControls.update(delta);
```

The controls for `THREE.OrbitControls` are focused on using the mouse, as shown in the following table:

Control	Action
Left mouse click + move	Rotate the camera around the center of the scene
Scroll wheel or middle mouse click + move	Zoom in and zoom out
Right mouse click + move	Pan around the scene
Left, right, up, and down arrows	Pan around the scene

That's it for the camera and moving it around. In this part, we've seen a lot of controls that allow you to create interesting camera actions. In the next section, we'll look at a more advanced way of animation: morphing and skinning.

Morphing and skeletal animation

When you create animations in external programs (for instance, Blender), you usually have two main options to define animations:

- **Morph targets**: With morph targets, you define a deformed version, that is, a key position, of the mesh. For this deformed target, all vertex positions are stored. All you need to do to animate the shape is move all the vertices from one position to another key position and repeat that process. The following screenshot shows various morph targets used to show facial expressions (the following image has been provided by the Blender foundation):

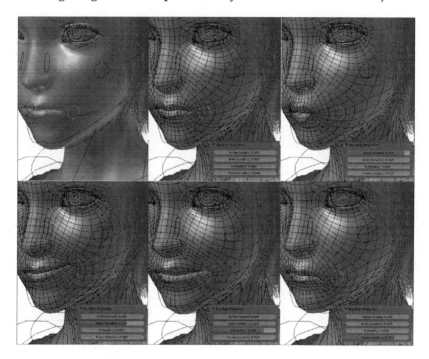

- **Skeletal animation**: An alternative is using skeletal animation. With skeletal animation, you define the skeleton, that is, the bones, of the mesh and attach vertices to the specific bones. Now, when you move a bone, any connected bone is also moved appropriately, and the attached vertices are moved and deformed based on the position, movement, and scaling of the bone. The following screenshot, once again provided by the Blender foundation, shows an example of how bones can be used to move and deform an object:

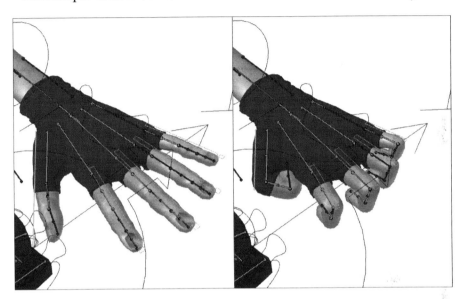

Three.js supports both modes, but generally you'll probably get better results with morph targets. The main problem with skeletal animation is getting a good export from a 3D program like Blender that can be animated in Three.js. It's much easier to get a good working model with morph targets than it is with bones and skins.

In this section, we'll look at both options and additionally look at a couple of external formats supported by Three.js in which animations can be defined.

Animation with morph targets

Morph targets are the most straightforward way of defining an animation. You define all the vertices for each important position (also called key frames) and tell Three.js to move the vertices from one position to the other. The disadvantage of this approach, though, is that for large meshes and large animations, the model files will become very large. The reason is that for each key position, all the vertex positions are repeated.

We'll show you how to work with morph targets using two examples. In the first example, we'll let Three.js handle the transition between the various key frames (or morph targets as we'll call them from now on), and in the second one, we'll do this manually.

Animation with MorphAnimMesh

For our first morphing example, we'll use a model that is also available from the Three.js distribution—the horse. The easiest way to understand how a morph-targets-based animation works is by opening up the `10-morph-targets.html` example. The following screenshot shows a still image of this example:

In this example, the horse on the right-hand side is animated and running, and the horse on the left-hand side is standing still. This second horse (the left-hand side one) is rendered from the basic model, that is, the original set of vertices. With the menu in the top-right corner, you can browse through all the morph targets that are available and see the different positions the left-hand side horse can take.

Three.js provides a way to move from one position to the next, but this would mean we have to manually keep track of the current position we're in and the target we want to morph into, and once we've reached the target position, repeat this for the other positions. Luckily, Three.js also provides a specific mesh, that is, THREE. MorphAnimMesh, that takes care of the details for us. Before we continue, here's a quick note on another animation-related mesh provided by Three.js called THREE. MorphBlendMesh. If you look through the objects provided by Three.js, you might notice this object. With this specific mesh, you can do pretty much the same things you can do with THREE.MorphAnimMesh, and when you look at the source code, you can even see that much of it is duplicated between these two objects. THREE. MorphBlendMesh, however, seems to be deprecated and isn't used in any of the official Three.js examples. Everything you could do with THREE.MorhpBlendMesh can be done with THREE.MorphAnimMesh, so use THREE.MorphAnimMesh for this kind of functionality. The following piece of code shows you how to load the model and create THREE.MorphAnimMesh from it:

```
var loader = new THREE.JSONLoader();
loader.load('../assets/models/horse.js', function(geometry, mat) {

  var mat = new THREE.MeshLambertMaterial({ morphTargets: true,
    vertexColors: THREE.FaceColors});

  morphColorsToFaceColors(geometry);
  geometry.computeMorphNormals();
  meshAnim = new THREE.MorphAnimMesh(geometry, mat );
  scene.add(meshAnim);

},'../assets/models' );


function morphColorsToFaceColors(geometry) {

  if (geometry.morphColors && geometry.morphColors.length) {

    var colorMap = geometry.morphColors[ 0 ];
    for (var i = 0; i < colorMap.colors.length; i++) {
```

```
        geometry.faces[ i ].color = colorMap.colors[ i ];
        geometry.faces[ i ].color.offsetHSL(0, 0.3, 0);
    }
  }
}
```

This is the same approach we saw when loading other models. This time, however, the external model also contains the morph targets. Instead of creating a normal THREE.Mesh object, we create THREE.MorphAnimMesh. There are a couple of things you need to take into account when loading animations:

- Make sure the material you use has THREE.morphTargets set to true. If it's not set, your mesh won't animate.

- Before creating THREE.MorphAnimMesh, make sure to call computeMorphNormals on the geometry so that all the normal vectors for the morph targets are calculated. This is required for correct lighting and shadow effects.

- It's also possible to define colors for faces of a specific morph target. These are available from the morphColors property. You can use this to morph not just the shape of a geometry, but also the colors of the individual faces. With the morphColorsToFaceColors helper method, we just fix the colors of the faces to the first set of colors in the morphColors array.

- The default setting is to play the complete animation in one go. If there are multiple animations defined for the same geometry, you can use the parseAnimations() function together with playAnimation(name, fps) to play one of the defined animations. We'll use this approach in the last section of this chapter, where we load animations from an MD2 model.

All that is left to do is update the animation in the render loop. For this, we once again use THREE.Clock to calculate the delta and use it to update the animation, as follows:

```
function render() {

  var delta = clock.getDelta();
  webGLRenderer.clear();
  if (meshAnim) {
    meshAnim.updateAnimation(delta *1000);
    meshAnim.rotation.y += 0.01;
  }

  // render using requestAnimationFrame
  requestAnimationFrame(render);
  webGLRenderer.render(scene, camera);
}
```

This approach is the easiest and allows you to quickly set up an animation from a model that has morph targets defined. An alternative approach is to set up the animation manually as we show in the next section.

Creating an animation by setting the morphTargetInfluence property

We'll create a very simple example where we morph a cube from one shape to another. This time, we'll manually control which target we will morph to. You can find the example in `11-morph-targets-manually.html`. The following screenshot shows a still image of this example:

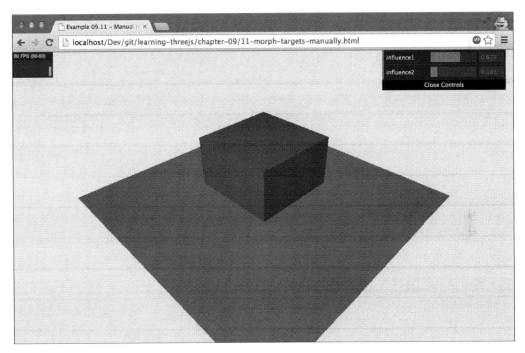

In this example, we've manually created two morph targets for a simple cube, as follows:

```
// create a cube
var cubeGeometry = new THREE.BoxGeometry(4, 4, 4);
var cubeMaterial = new THREE.MeshLambertMaterial({morphTargets:
   true, color: 0xff0000});
```

```
// define morphtargets, we'll use the vertices from these
   geometries
var cubeTarget1 = new THREE.CubeGeometry(2, 10, 2);
var cubeTarget2 = new THREE.CubeGeometry(8, 2, 8);

// define morphtargets and compute the morphnormal
cubeGeometry.morphTargets[0] = {name: 'mt1', vertices:
   cubeTarget2.vertices};
cubeGeometry.morphTargets[1] = {name: 'mt2', vertices:
   cubeTarget1.vertices};
cubeGeometry.computeMorphNormals();

var cube = new THREE.Mesh(cubeGeometry, cubeMaterial);
```

As you open up this example, you'll see a simple cube. With the sliders in the top-right corner, you can set morphTargetInfluences. In other words, you can determine how much the initial cube should morph into the cube specified as mt1 and how much it should morph into mt2. When you create your morph targets by hand, you need to take into account the fact that the morph target has the same number of vertices as the source geometry. You can set the influence using the morphTargetInfluences **property of the mesh:**

```
var controls = new function () {
  // set to 0.01 to make sure dat.gui shows correct output
  this.influence1 = 0.01;
  this.influence2 = 0.01;

  this.update = function () {
    cube.morphTargetInfluences[0] = controls.influence1;
    cube.morphTargetInfluences[1] = controls.influence2;
  };
}
```

Note that the initial geometry can be influenced by multiple morph targets at the same time. These two examples show the most important concepts behind morph target animations. In the next section, we'll have a quick look at animation using bones and skinning.

Animation using bones and skinning

Morph animations are very straightforward. Three.js knows all the target vertex positions and only needs to transition each vertex from one position to the next. For bones and skinning, it becomes a bit more complex. When you use bones for animation, you move the bone, and Three.js has to determine how to translate the attached skin (a set of vertices) accordingly. For this example, we use a model that was exported from Blender to the Three.js format (`hand-1.js` in the `models` folder). This is a model of a hand, complete with a set of bones. By moving the bones around, we can animate the complete model. Let's first look at how we loaded the model:

```
var loader = new THREE.JSONLoader();
loader.load('../assets/models/hand-1.js', function (geometry, mat)
  {
  var mat = new THREE.MeshLambertMaterial({color: 0xF0C8C9,
    skinning: true});
  mesh = new THREE.SkinnedMesh(geometry, mat);

  // rotate the complete hand
  mesh.rotation.x = 0.5 * Math.PI;
  mesh.rotation.z = 0.7 * Math.PI;

  // add the mesh
  scene.add(mesh);

  // and start the animation
  tween.start();

}, '../assets/models');
```

Loading a model for bone animation isn't that different from any of the other models. We just specify the model file, which contains the definition of vertices, faces, and also bones, and based on that geometry, we create a mesh. Three.js also provides a specific mesh for skinned geometries like this called `THREE.SkinnedMesh`. The one thing you need to specify to make sure the model is updated is set the `skinning` property of the material you use to `true`. If you don't set this to `true`, you won't see any bone movement. The last thing we do here is that we set the `useQuaternion` property of all the bones to `false`. In this example, we'll use a `tween` object to handle the animation. This `tween` instance is defined like this:

```
var tween = new TWEEN.Tween({pos: -1}).to({pos: 0},
  3000).easing(TWEEN.Easing.Cubic.InOut).yoyo(true)
  .repeat(Infinity).onUpdate(onUpdate);
```

With this tween, we transition the pos variable from -1 to 0. We've also set the yoyo property to true, which causes our animation to run in reverse the next time it is run. To make sure our animation keeps running, we set repeat to Infinity. You can also see that we specify an onUpdate method. This method is used to position the individual bones, and we'll look at this next.

Before we move the bones, let's look at the 12-bones-manually.html example. The following screenshot shows a still image of this example:

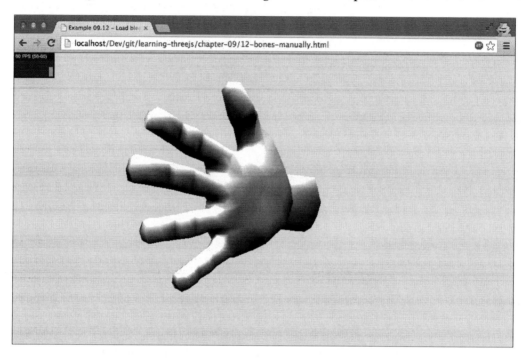

When you open this example, you see the hand making a grab-like motion. We did this by setting the z rotation of the finger bones in the onUpdate method that is called from our tween animation, as follows:

```
var onUpdate = function () {
  var pos = this.pos;

  // rotate the fingers
  mesh.skeleton.bones[5].rotation.set(0, 0, pos);
  mesh.skeleton.bones[6].rotation.set(0, 0, pos);
  mesh.skeleton.bones[10].rotation.set(0, 0, pos);
  mesh.skeleton.bones[11].rotation.set(0, 0, pos);
  mesh.skeleton.bones[15].rotation.set(0, 0, pos);
```

```
mesh.skeleton.bones[16].rotation.set(0, 0, pos);
mesh.skeleton.bones[20].rotation.set(0, 0, pos);
mesh.skeleton.bones[21].rotation.set(0, 0, pos);

// rotate the wrist
mesh.skeleton.bones[1].rotation.set(pos, 0, 0);
};
```

Whenever this update method is called, the relevant bones are set to the `pos` position. To determine which bone you need to move, it is a good idea to print out the `mesh.skeleton` property to the console. This will list all the bones and their names.

> Three.js provides a simple helper you can use to show the bones of the models. Add the following to the code:
>
> ```
> helper = new THREE.SkeletonHelper( mesh );
> helper.material.linewidth = 2;
> helper.visible = false;
> scene.add( helper );
> ```
>
> The bones are highlighted. You can see an example of this by enabling the `showHelper` property shown in the `12-bones-manually.html` example.

As you can see, working with bones takes a bit more effort but is much more flexible than the fixed morph targets. In this example, we've only moved the rotation of the bones; you can also move the position or change the scale. In the next section, we look at loading animations from external models. In that section, we'll revisit this example, but now, we'll run a predefined animation from the model instead of manually moving the bones around.

Creating animations using external models

In *Chapter 8, Creating and Loading Advanced Meshes and Geometries*, we looked at a number of 3D formats that are supported by Three.js. A couple of those formats also support animations. In this chapter, we'll look at the following examples:

- **Blender with the JSON exporter**: We'll start with an animation created in Blender and exported to the Three.js JSON format.

- **Collada model**: The Collada format has support for animations. For this example, we'll load an animation from a Collada file and render it with Three.js.

- **MD2 model**: The MD2 model is a simple format used in the older Quake engines. Even though the format is a bit dated, it is still a very good format for storing character animations.

We'll start with the Blender model.

Creating a bones animation using Blender

To get started with animations from Blender, you can load the example we've included in the models folder. You can find the hand.blend file there, which you can load into Blender. The following screenshot shows a still image of this example:

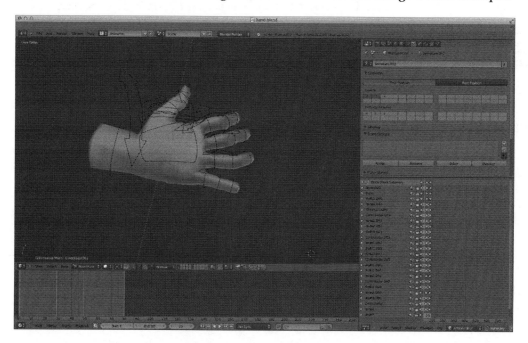

There isn't room in this book to go into much detail on how to create animations in Blender, but there are a couple of things you need to keep in mind:

- Every vertex from your model must at least be assigned to a vertex group.

- The name of the vertex groups you use in Blender must correspond to the name of the bone that controls it. That way, Three.js can determine which vertices it needs to modify when moving the bones.

- Only the first "action" is exported. So make sure the animation you want to export is the first one.

- When creating key frames, it is a good idea to select all the bones even if they don't change.

- When exporting the model, make sure the model is in its rest pose. If this is not the case, you'll see a very deformed animation.

For more information on creating and exporting animations from Blender and the reasons for the aforementioned pointers, you can look at the following great resource: `http://devmatrix.wordpress.com/2013/02/27/creating-skeletal-animation-in-blender-and-exporting-it-to-three-js/`.

When you've created the animation in Blender, you can export the file using the Three.js exporter we used in the previous chapter. When exporting the file using the Three.js exporter, you have to make sure that the following properties are checked:

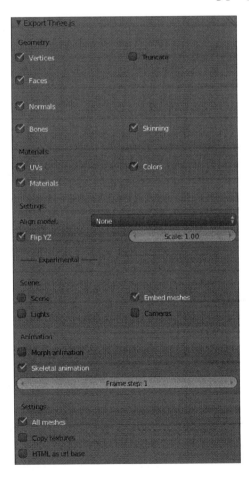

This will export the animation you've specified in Blender as a skeletal animation instead of a morph animation. With a skeletal animation, the movements of the bones are exported, which we can replay in Three.js.

Loading the model in Three.js is the same as we did for our previous example; however, now that the model is loaded, we will also create an animation, as follows:

```
var loader = new THREE.JSONLoader();
loader.load('../assets/models/hand-2.js', function (model, mat) {

    var mat = new THREE.MeshLambertMaterial({color: 0xF0C8C9,
        skinning: true});
    mesh = new THREE.SkinnedMesh(model, mat);

    var animation = new THREE.Animation(mesh, model.animation);

    mesh.rotation.x = 0.5 * Math.PI;
    mesh.rotation.z = 0.7 * Math.PI;
    scene.add(mesh);

    // start the animation
    animation.play();

}, '../assets/models');
```

To run this animation, all we have to do is create a THREE.Animation instance and call the play method on this animation. Before we see the animation, we still need to take one additional step. In our render loop, we call the THREE.AnimationHandler. update(clock.getDelta()) function to update the animation, and Three.js will use the bones to set the model in the correct position. The result of this example (13-animation-from-blender.html) is a simple waving hand.

The following screenshot shows a still image of this example:

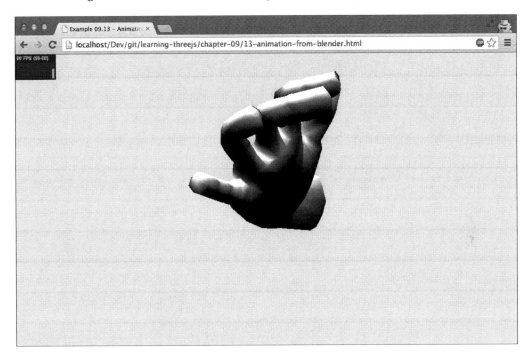

Besides Three.js' own format, we can use a couple of other formats to define animations. The first one we'll look at is loading a Collada model.

Loading an animation from a Collada model

Loading a model from a Collada file works in the same manner as for the other formats. First, you have to include the correct loader JavaScript file:

```
<script type="text/javascript" src="../libs/ColladaLoader.js">
  </script>
```

Next, we create a loader and use it to load the model file:

```
var loader = new THREE.ColladaLoader();
loader.load('../assets/models/monster.dae', function (collada) {

    var child = collada.skins[0];
    scene.add(child);

    var animation = new THREE.Animation(child, child.
      geometry.animation);
    animation.play();

    // position the mesh
    child.scale.set(0.15, 0.15, 0.15);
    child.rotation.x = -0.5 * Math.PI;
    child.position.x = -100;
    child.position.y = -60;
});
```

A Collada file can contain much more than just a single mode; it can store complete scenes, including cameras, lights, animations, and more. A good way to work with a Collada model is to print out the result from the `loader.load` function to the console and determine which components you want to use. In this case, there was a single `THREE.SkinnedMesh` in the scene (`child`). To render and animate this model, all we have to do is set up the animation just like we did for the Blender-based model; even the render loop stays the same. Here's how we render and animate the model:

```
function render() {
  ...
  meshAnim.updateAnimation( delta *1000 );
  ...
}
```

And the result for this specific Collada file looks like this:

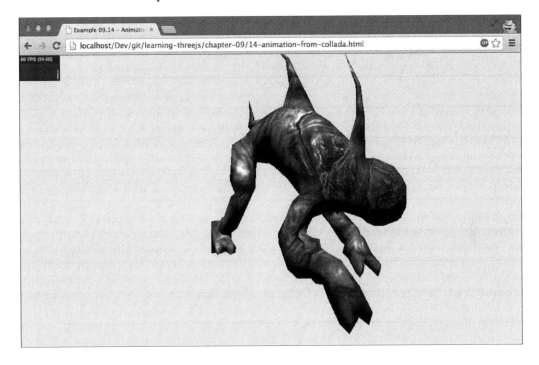

Another example of an external model, one that uses morph targets, is the MD2 file format.

Animation loaded from a Quake model

The MD2 format was created to model characters from Quake, a great game from 1996. Even though the newer engines use a different format, you can still find a lot of interesting models in the MD2 format. To use files in this format, we first have to convert them to the Three.js JavaScript format. You can do this online using the following site:

```
http://oos.moxiecode.com/js_webgl/md2_converter/
```

After conversion, you'll get a JavaScript file in the Three.js format that you can load and render using `MorphAnimMesh`. Since we've already seen how to do this in the previous sections, we'll skip the code where the model is loaded. One interesting thing though is happening in the code. Instead of playing the complete animation, we provide the name of the animation that needs to be played:

```
mesh.playAnimation('crattack', 10);
```

The reason is that an MD2 file usually contains a number of different character animations. Luckily, though, Three.js provides functionality to determine the available animations and play them using the `playAnimation` function. The first thing we need to do is tell Three.js to parse the animations:

```
mesh.parseAnimations();
```

This results in a list of names for the animations that can be played using the `playAnimation` function. In our example, you can select the name of the animation from the menu in the top-right corner. The available animations are determined like this:

```
mesh.parseAnimations();

var animLabels = [];
for (var key in mesh.geometry.animations) {
    if (key === 'length' || !mesh.geometry.animations.
      hasOwnProperty(key)) continue;
    animLabels.push(key);
}

gui.add(controls,'animations',animLabels).onChange(function(e) {
    mesh.playAnimation(controls.animations,controls.fps);
});
```

Whenever an animation from the menu is selected, the `mesh.playAnimation` function is called with the specified animation name. The example that demonstrates this can be found in `15-animation-from-md2.html`. The following screenshot shows us a still image of this example:

Summary

In this chapter, we looked at different ways that you can animate your scene. We started with some basic animation tricks, moved on to camera movement and control, and ended with animation models using morph targets and skeleton/bones animations. When you have the render loop in place, adding animations is very easy. Just change a property of the mesh, and in the next rendering step, Three.js will render the updated mesh.

In previous chapters, we looked at the various materials you can use to skin your objects. For instance, we saw how you can change the color, shininess, and opacity of these materials. What we haven't discussed in detail yet, however, is how you can use external images (also called textures) together with these materials. With textures, you can easily create objects that look like they are made of wood, metal, stone, and much more. In the next chapter, we'll explore all the different aspects of textures and how they are used in Three.js.

10
Loading and Working with Textures

In *Chapter 4, Working with Three.js Materials*, we introduced you to the various materials that are available in Three.js. In that chapter, however, we didn't talk about applying textures to meshes. In this chapter, we'll look at that subject. More specifically, in this chapter, we'll discuss the following topics:

- Loading textures in Three.js and applying them to a mesh
- Using bump and normal maps to apply depth and detail to a mesh
- Creating fake shadows using a light map
- Adding detailed reflection to a material using an environment map
- Using a specular map to set the *shininess* of specific parts of a mesh
- Fine-tuning and customizing the UV mapping of a mesh
- Using the HTML5 canvas and video element as input for a texture

Let's start with the most basic example, where we show you how to load and apply a texture.

Using textures in materials

There are different ways textures are used in Three.js. You can use them to define the colors of the mesh, but you can also use them to define shininess, bumps, and reflections. The first example we look at, though, is the most basic approach, where we use a texture to define the colors of the individual pixels of a mesh.

Loading a texture and applying it to a mesh

The most basic usage of a texture is when it's set as a map on a material. When you use this material to create a mesh, the mesh will be colored based on the supplied texture.

Loading a texture and using it on a mesh can be done in the following manner:

```
function createMesh(geom, imageFile) {
  var texture = THREE.ImageUtils.loadTexture("../assets/
   textures/general/" + imageFile)

  var mat = new THREE.MeshPhongMaterial();
  mat.map = texture;

  var mesh = new THREE.Mesh(geom, mat);
  return mesh;
}
```

In this code sample, we use the `THREE.ImageUtils.loadTexture` function to load an image file from a specific location. You can use PNG, GIF, or JPEG images as input for a texture. Note that loading textures is done asynchronously. In our scenario, this isn't an issue as we have a `render` loop where we render the scene around 60 times per second. If you want to wait until a texture is loaded, you could use the following approach:

```
texture = THREE.ImageUtils.loadTexture('texture.png', {},
  function() { renderer.render(scene); });
```

In this example, we supply a callback function to `loadTexture`. This callback is called when the texture is loaded. In our examples, we don't use the callback and rely on the `render` loop to eventually show the texture when it's loaded.

You can use pretty much any image you'd like as a texture. The best results, however, are when you use a square texture whose dimensions are a power of 2. So dimensions such as 256 x 256, 512 x 512, 1024 x 1024, and so on work the best. The following image is an example of a square texture:

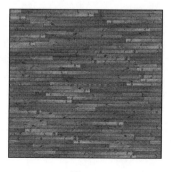

Since the pixels of a texture (also called **texels**) usually don't map one-to-one on the pixels of the face, the texture needs to be magnified or minified. For this purpose, WebGL and Three.js offer a couple of different options. You can specify how the texture is magnified by setting the magFilter property and how it is minified with the minFilter property. These properties can be set to the following two basic values:

Name	Description
THREE.NearestFilter	This filter uses the color of the nearest texel that it can find. When used for magnification, this will result in blockiness, and when used for minification, the result will lose much detail.
THREE.LinearFilter	This filter is more advanced and uses the color value of the four neighboring texels to determine the correct color. You'll still lose much detail in minification, but the magnification will be much smoother and less blocky.

Besides these basic values, we can also use a mipmap. A **mipmap** is a set of texture images, each half the size of the previous one. These are created when you load the texture and allow much smoother filtering. So, when you've got a square texture (as a power of 2), you can use a couple of additional approaches for better filtering. The properties can be set using the following values:

Name	Description
THREE.NearestMipMapNearestFilter	This property selects the mipmap that best maps the required resolution and applies the nearest filter principle that we discussed in the previous table. Magnification is still blocky, but minification looks much better.
THREE.NearestMipMapLinearFilter	This property selects not just a single mipmap but the two nearest mipmap levels. On both these levels, a nearest filter is applied to get two intermediate results. These two results are passed through a linear filter to get the final result.
THREE.LinearMipMapNearestFilter	This property selects the mipmap that best maps the required resolution and applies the linear filter principle we discussed in the previous table.

Name	Description
THREE.LinearMipMapLinearFilter	This property selects not a single mipmap but the two nearest mipmap levels. On both these levels, a linear filter is applied to get two intermediate results. These two results are passed through a linear filter to get the final result.

If you don't specify the `magFilter` and `minFilter` properties explicitly, Three.js uses `THREE.LinearFilter` as the default for the `magFilter` property and `THREE.LinearMipMapLinearFilter` as the default for the `minFilter` property. In our examples, we'll just use these default properties. An example for the basic texture can be found in `01-basic-texture.html`. The following screenshot shows this example:

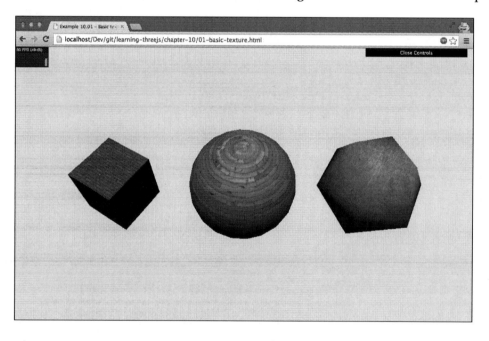

In this example, we load a couple of textures (using the code you saw earlier) and apply them to various shapes. In this example, you can see that the textures nicely wrap around the shapes. When you create geometries in Three.js, it makes sure that any texture that is used is applied correctly. This is done by something called **UV mapping** (more on this later in this chapter). With UV mapping, we tell the renderer which part of a texture should be applied to a specific face. The easiest example for this is the cube. The UV mapping for one of the faces looks like this:

```
(0,1),(0,0),(1,0),(1,1)
```

This means that we use the complete texture (UV values range from 0 to 1) for this face.

Besides the standard image formats we can load with `THREE.ImageUtils.loadTexture`, Three.js also provides a couple of custom loaders you can use to load textures provided in different formats. The following table shows the additional loaders you can use:

Name	Description
`THREE.DDSLoader`	With this loader, you can load textures that are provided in the DirectDraw Surface format. This format is a proprietary Microsoft format to store compressed textures. Using this loader is very easy. First, include the `DDSLoader.js` file in your HTML page and then use the following to use a texture: ```var loader = new THREE.DDSLoader();\nvar texture = loader.load('../assets/\n textures/ seafloor.dds');\n\nvar mat = new THREE.MeshPhongMaterial();\nmat.map = texture;``` You can see an example of this loader in the sources for this chapter in `01-basic-texture-dds.html`. Internally, this loader uses `THREE.CompressedTextureLoader`.
`THREE.PVRLoader`	Power VR is another proprietary file format to store compressed textures. Three.js supports the Power VR 3.0 file format and can use textures provided in this format. To use this loader, include the `PVRLoader.js` file in your HTML page and then use the following to use a texture: ```var loader = new THREE.DDSLoader();\nvar texture = loader.load('../assets/\n textures/ seafloor.dds');\n\nvar mat = new THREE.MeshPhongMaterial();\nmat.map = texture;``` You can see an example of this loader in the sources for this chapter: `01-basic-texture-pvr.html`. Note that not all WebGL implementations support textures in this format. So when you use this and don't see a texture, check the console for errors. Internally, this loader also uses `THREE.CompressedTextureLoader`.

Name	Description
THREE.TGALoader	Targa is a raster graphics file format that is still used by a large number of 3D software programs. With the THREE.TGALoader object, you can use textures provided in this format with your 3D models. To use these image files, you first have to include the TGALoader.js file in your HTML, and then you can use the following to load a TGA texture: ```var loader = new THREE.TGALoader();
var texture = loader.load('../assets/
    textures/crate_color8.tga');

var mat = new THREE.MeshPhongMaterial();
mat.map = texture;```

An example of this loader is provided in the sources of this chapter. You can view this example by opening 01-basic-texture-tga.html in your browser. |

In these examples, we've used textures to define the color of the pixels of our mesh. We can also use textures for other purposes. The following two examples are used to define how shading is applied to a material. You use this to create bumps and wrinkles on the surface of a mesh.

Using a bump map to create wrinkles

A **bump map** is used to add more depth to a material. You can see this in action by opening up the 02-bump-map.html example. Refer to the following screenshot to see the example:

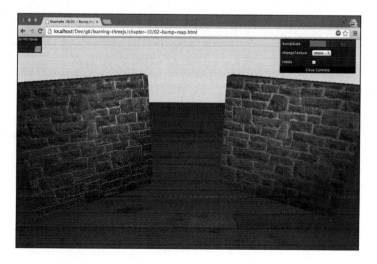

In this example, you can see that the left-hand side wall looks much more detailed and seems to have much more depth when you compare it with the wall on the right-hand side. This is done by setting an additional texture, a so-called bump map, on the material:

```
function createMesh(geom, imageFile, bump) {
  var texture = THREE.ImageUtils.loadTexture("../assets/textures/
    general/" + imageFile)
  var mat = new THREE.MeshPhongMaterial();
  mat.map = texture;

  var bump = THREE.ImageUtils.loadTexture(
    "../assets/textures/general/" + bump)
  mat.bumpMap = bump;
  mat.bumpScale = 0.2;


  var mesh = new THREE.Mesh(geom, mat);
  return mesh;
}
```

You can see in this code that besides setting the `map` property, we also set the `bumpMap` property to a texture. Additionally, with the `bumpScale` property, we can set the height (or depth if set to a negative value) of the bumps. The textures used in this example are shown here:

The bump map is a grayscale image, but you can also use a color image. The intensity of the pixel defines the height of the bump. A bump map only contains the relative height of a pixel. It doesn't say anything about the direction of the slope. So the level of detail and perception of depth that you can reach with a bump map is limited. For more details, you can use a normal map.

Achieving more detailed bumps and wrinkles with a normal map

In a normal map, the height (displacement) is not stored, but the direction of the normal for each picture is stored. Without going into too much detail, with normal maps, you can create very detailed-looking models that still only use a small number of vertices and faces. For instance, have a look at the 03-normal-map.html example. The following screenshot depicts this example:

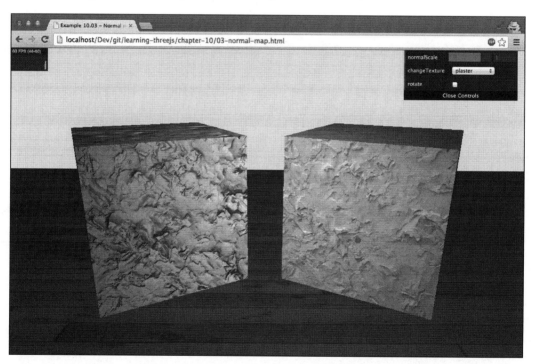

In this screenshot, you can see a very detailed plastered cube to the left. The light source moves around the cubes, and you can see that the texture responds naturally to the light source. This provides a very realistic-looking model and only requires a very simple model and a couple of textures. The following code fragment shows how to use a normal map in Three.js:

```
function createMesh(geom, imageFile, normal) {
  var t = THREE.ImageUtils.loadTexture("../assets/textures
    /general/" + imageFile);
  var m = THREE.ImageUtils.loadTexture("../assets/textures
    /general/" + normal);

  var mat2 = new THREE.MeshPhongMaterial();
  mat2.map = t;
  mat2.normalMap = m;

  var mesh = new THREE.Mesh(geom, mat2);
  return mesh;
}
```

The same approach is used here as was done for the bump map. This time, though, we set the `normalMap` property to the normal texture. We can also define how pronounced the bumps look by setting the `normalScale` property `mat.normalScale.set(1,1)`. With these two properties, you can scale along the *x* and *y* axes. The best approach, though, is to keep these values the same for the best effect. Note that once again, when these values are below zero, the heights inverse. The following screenshot shows both the texture (on the left-hand side) and the normal map (on the right-hand side):

The problem with normal maps, however, is that they aren't very easy to create. You need to use specialized tools, such as Blender or Photoshop. They can use high-resolution renderings or textures as input and create normal maps from them.

Three.js also provides a way to do this during runtime. The THREE.ImageUtils object has a function called getNormalMap, which takes a JavaScript/DOM Image as input and converts it into a normal map.

Creating fake shadows using a light map

In the previous examples, we used specific maps to create real-looking shadows that react to the lighting in the room. There is an alternative option to create fake shadows. In this section, we'll use a light map. A **light map** is a pre-rendered shadow (also called a prebaked shadow) that you can use to create the illusion of a real shadow. The following screenshot, from the 04-light-map.html example, shows how this looks:

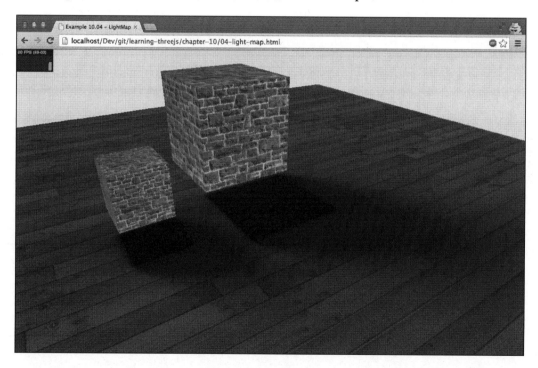

If you look at the previous example, it shows a couple of very nice shadows, which seem to be cast by the two cubes. These shadows, however, are based on a light map texture that looks like the following:

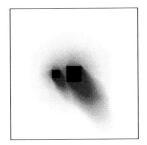

As you can see, the shadows, as specified in the light map, are also shown as the shadows on the ground plane, creating the illusion of real shadows. You can use this technique to create high-resolution shadows, without incurring a heavy rendering penalty. This, of course, only works for static scenes. Using a light map is pretty much the same as using other textures with a couple of small differences. This is how we go about using a light map:

```
var lm = THREE.ImageUtils.loadTexture('../assets/textures/
    lightmap/lm-1.png');
var wood = THREE.ImageUtils.loadTexture('../assets/textures/
    general/floor-wood.jpg');
var groundMaterial = new THREE.MeshBasicMaterial
    ({lightMap: lm, map: wood});
groundGeom.faceVertexUvs[1] = groundGeom.faceVertexUvs[0];
```

To apply a light map, we just need to set the `lightMap` property of the material to the light map we just showed. There is, however, an additional step required to get the light map to show up. We need to explicitly define the UV mapping (what part of the texture is shown on a face) for the light map. This needs to be done so that you can apply and map the light map independently of the other textures. In our example, we just use the basic UV mapping, automatically created by Three.js when we created the ground plane. More information and a background of why an explicit UV mapping is required can be found at http://stackoverflow.com/questions/15137695/three-js-lightmap-causes-an-error-webglrenderingcontext-gl-error-gl-invalid-op.

When the shadow map is positioned correctly, we need to place the cubes in the correct location so that it looks as though the shadows are being cast by them.

Three.js provides another texture that you can use to fake advanced 3D effects. In the next section, we'll look at using environment maps for fake reflections.

Creating fake reflections using an environment map

Calculating environment reflections is very CPU-intensive and usually requires a ray tracer approach. If you want to use reflections in Three.js, you can still do that, but you'll have to fake it. You can do this by creating a texture of the environment the object is in and apply this to the specific object. First, we'll show you the result we're aiming for (see `05-env-map-static.html`, which is also shown in the following screenshot):

In this screenshot, you can see the sphere and cube reflect the environment. If you move your mouse around, you can also see that the reflection corresponds with the camera angle in relation to the city environment you see. To create this example, we perform the following steps:

1. **Create a CubeMap object**: The first thing we need to do is create a `CubeMap` object. `CubeMap` is a set of six textures that can be applied to each side of a cube.

2. **Create a box with this CubeMap object**: The box with `CubeMap` is the environment you see when you move the camera around. It gives the illusion that you're standing in an environment where you can look around. In reality, you're inside a cube with textures rendered on the inside to give an illusion of space.

3. **Apply the CubeMap object as a texture**: The same `CubeMap` object we used to simulate the environment can be used as a texture on the meshes. Three.js will make sure it looks like a reflection of the environment.

Creating `CubeMap` is pretty easy once you've got the source material. What you need are six images that together make up a complete environment. So you need the following pictures: looking forward (`posz`), looking backward (`negz`), looking up (`posy`), looking down (`negy`), looking right (`posx`), and looking left (`negx`). Three.js will patch these together to create a seamless environment map. There are a couple of sites where you can download these pictures. The ones used in this example are from `http://www.humus.name/index.php?page=Textures`.

Once you've got the six separate pictures, you can load them as shown in the following code fragment:

```
function createCubeMap() {

    var path = "../assets/textures/cubemap/parliament/";
    var format = '.jpg';
    var urls = [
      path + 'posx' + format, path + 'negx' + format,
      path + 'posy' + format, path + 'negy' + format,
      path + 'posz' + format, path + 'negz' + format
    ];

    var textureCube = THREE.ImageUtils.loadTextureCube( urls );
    return textureCube;
}
```

We again use the `THREE.ImageUtils` JavaScript object, but this time, we pass in an array of textures and create the `CubeMap` object using the `loadTextureCube` function. If you've already got a 360-degree panoramic image, you can also convert that into a set of images you can use to create `CubeMap`. Just go to `http://gonchar.me/panorama/` to convert an image, and you end up with six images with names like `right.png`, `left.png`, `top.png`, `bottom.png`, `front.png`, and `back.png`. You can use these by creating the `urls` variable like this:

```
var urls = [
  'right.png',
```

```
    'left.png',
    'top.png',
    'bottom.png',
    'front.png',
    'back.png'
];
```

Alternatively, you can also let Three.js handle the conversion when you load the scene by creating `textureCube` like this:

```
var textureCube = THREE.ImageUtils.loadTexture("360-degrees.png",
    new THREE.UVMapping());
```

With `CubeMap`, we first create a box, which can be created like this:

```
var textureCube = createCubeMap();
var shader = THREE.ShaderLib[ "cube" ];
shader.uniforms[ "tCube" ].value = textureCube;
var material = new THREE.ShaderMaterial( {
    fragmentShader: shader.fragmentShader,
    vertexShader: shader.vertexShader,
    uniforms: shader.uniforms,
    depthWrite: false,
    side: THREE.BackSide
});
cubeMesh = new THREE.Mesh(new THREE.BoxGeometry(100, 100, 100),
    material);
```

Three.js provides a specific shader that we can use with `THREE.ShaderMaterial` to create an environment based on `CubeMap` (`var shader = THREE.ShaderLib[ "cube" ];`). We configure this shader with `CubeMap`, create a mesh, and add it to the scene. This mesh, if seen from the inside, represents the fake environment we're standing in.

This same `CubeMap` object should be applied to the meshes we want to render to create the fake reflection:

```
var sphere1 = createMesh(new THREE.SphereGeometry(10, 15, 15),
    "plaster.jpg");
sphere1.material.envMap = textureCube;
sphere1.rotation.y = -0.5;
sphere1.position.x = 12;
sphere1.position.y = 5;
scene.add(sphere1);
```

```
var cube = createMesh(new THREE.CubeGeometry(10, 15, 15),
    "plaster.jpg","plaster-normal.jpg");
sphere2.material.envMap = textureCube;
sphere2.rotation.y = 0.5;
sphere2.position.x = -12;
sphere2.position.y = 5;
scene.add(cube);
```

As you can see, we set the envMap property of the material to the cubeMap object we created. The result is a scene where it looks like we're standing in a wide, outdoors environment, where the meshes reflect this environment. If you use the sliders, you can set the reflectivity property of the material, and, as the name implies, this determines how much of the environment is reflected by the material.

Besides reflection, Three.js also allows you to use a CubeMap object for refraction (glass-like objects). The following screenshot shows this:

To get this effect, we just need to change the loading of the textures to this:

```
var textureCube = THREE.ImageUtils.loadTextureCube( urls, new
    THREE.CubeRefractionMapping());
```

You can control the `refraction` ratio with the `refraction` property on the material, just as with the `reflection` property. In this example, we've used a static environment map for the meshes. In other words, we only saw the environment reflection and not the other meshes in this environment. In the following screenshot (which you can see in action by opening `05-env-map-dynamic.html` in your browser), we'll show you how you can create a reflection that also shows the other objects in the scene:

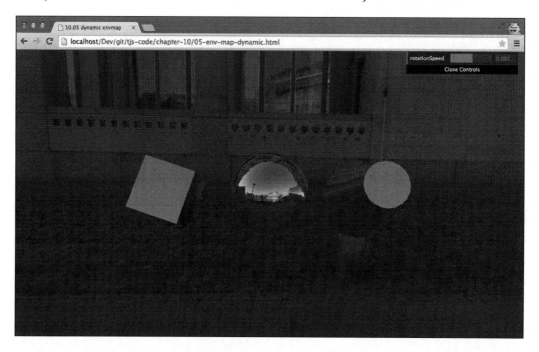

To also show reflections from the other objects in the scene, we need to use some other Three.js components. The first thing we need is an additional camera called `THREE.CubeCamera`:

```
Var cubeCamera = new THREE.CubeCamera(0.1, 20000, 256);
scene.add(cubeCamera);
```

We will use `THREE.CubeCamera` to take a snapshot of the scene with all the objects rendered, and use that to set up `CubeMap`. You need to make sure you position this camera at the exact location of `THREE.Mesh` on which you want to show the dynamic reflections. For this example, we'll only show reflections on the center sphere (as you can see in the previous screenshot). This sphere is located at the position 0, 0, 0, so for this example, we don't need to explicitly position `THREE.CubeCamera`.

We only apply the dynamic reflections to the sphere, so we're going to need two different materials:

```
var dynamicEnvMaterial = new THREE.MeshBasicMaterial({envMap:
    cubeCamera.renderTarget });
var envMaterial = new THREE.MeshBasicMaterial({envMap: textureCube
    });
```

The main difference with our previous example is that for the dynamic reflections, we set the `envMap` property to `cubeCamera.renderTarget` instead of to `textureCube`, which we created earlier. For this example, we use `dynamicEnvMaterial` on the central sphere and `envMaterial` for the other two objects:

```
sphere = new THREE.Mesh(sphereGeometry, dynamicEnvMaterial);
sphere.name = 'sphere';
scene.add(sphere);

var cylinder = new THREE.Mesh(cylinderGeometry, envMaterial);
cylinder.name = 'cylinder';
scene.add(cylinder);
cylinder.position.set(10, 0, 0);

var cube = new THREE.Mesh(boxGeometry, envMaterial);
cube.name = 'cube';
scene.add(cube);
cube.position.set(-10, 0, 0);
```

All that is left to do is make sure `cubeCamera` renders the scene, so we can use that output as input for the center sphere. To do this, we update the `render` loop like this:

```
function render() {
    sphere.visible = false;
    cubeCamera.updateCubeMap( renderer, scene );
    sphere.visible = true;
    renderer.render(scene, camera);
    ...
    requestAnimationFrame(render);
}
```

As you can see, we first disable the visibility of `sphere`. We do this because we only want to see reflections from the other two objects. Next, we render the scene using `cubeCamera` by calling the `updateCubeMap` function. After that, we make `sphere` visible again and render the scene as normal. The result is that in the reflection of the sphere, you can see the reflections of the cube and the cylinder.

The last of the basic materials we'll look at is the specular map.

Specular map

With a **specular map**, you can specify a map that defines the shininess and the highlight color of a material. For instance, in the following screenshot, we've used a specular map together with a normal map to render a globe. You can see this example if you open `06-specular-map.html` in your browser. The result of this is also shown in the following screenshot:

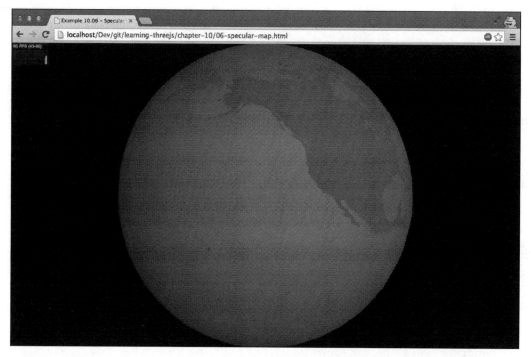

In this screenshot, you can see that the oceans are highlighted and reflect light. The continents, on the other hand, are very dark and don't reflect (much) light. For this effect, we didn't use any specific normal textures, but only a normal map to show heights and the following specular map to highlight the oceans:

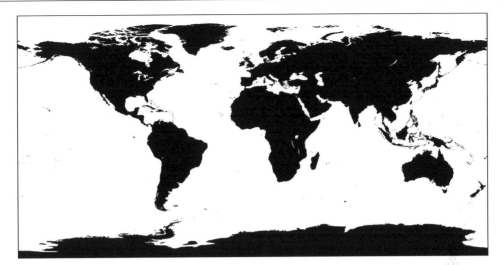

Basically, what happens is that the higher the value of the pixel (from black to white), the shinier the surface will appear. A specular map is usually used together with the `specular` property that you can use to determine the color of the reflection. In this case, it is set to red:

```
var specularTexture=THREE.ImageUtils.loadTexture("../assets/
    textures/planets/EarthSpec.png");
var normalTexture=THREE.ImageUtils.loadTexture("../assets/
    textures/planets/EarthNormal.png");

var planetMaterial = new THREE.MeshPhongMaterial();
planetMaterial.specularMap = specularTexture;
planetMaterial.specular = new THREE.Color( 0xff0000 );
planetMaterial.shininess = 1;

planetMaterial.normalMap = normalTexture;
```

Also note that the best effects are usually realized with low shininess, but depending on the lighting and the specular map you use, you might need to experiment to get the desired effect.

Advanced usage of textures

In the previous section, we saw some basic texture usages. Three.js also provides options for more advanced texture usage. In this section, we'll look at a couple of options that Three.js provides.

Custom UV mapping

We'll start off with a deeper look at UV mappings. We explained earlier that with UV mapping, you can specify what part of a texture is shown on a specific face. When you create a geometry in Three.js, these mappings will also be automatically created based on the type of geometry you created. In most cases, you don't really need to change this default UV mapping. A good way to understand how UV mapping works is to look at an example from Blender, which is shown in the following screenshot:

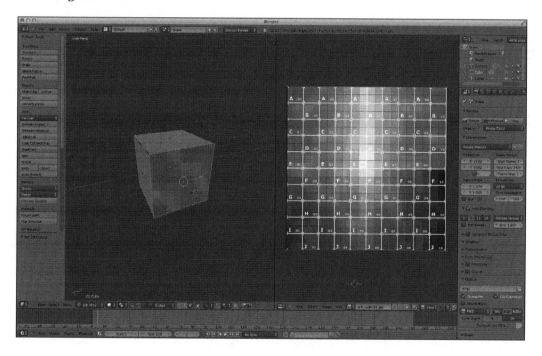

In this example, you see two windows. The window on the left-hand side contains a cube geometry. The window on the right-hand side is the UV mapping, where we've loaded an example texture to show how the mapping is. In this example, we've selected a single face for the window on the left-hand side and the window on the right-hand side shows the UV mapping for this face. As you can see, each vertex of the face is positioned in one of the corners of the UV mapping on the right (the small circles). This means that the complete texture will be used for that face. All the other faces of this cube are mapped in the same manner, so the result will show a cube where each face shows the complete texture; see `07-uv-mapping.html`, which is also shown in the following screenshot:

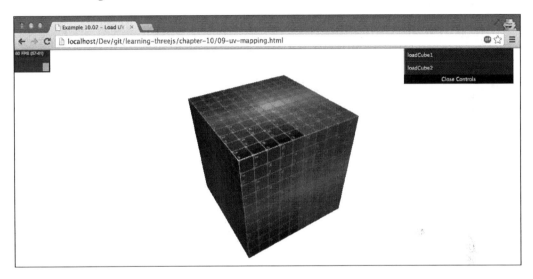

This is the default for a cube in Blender (also in Three.js). Let's change the UV by selecting only two-thirds of the texture (see the selected area in the following screenshot):

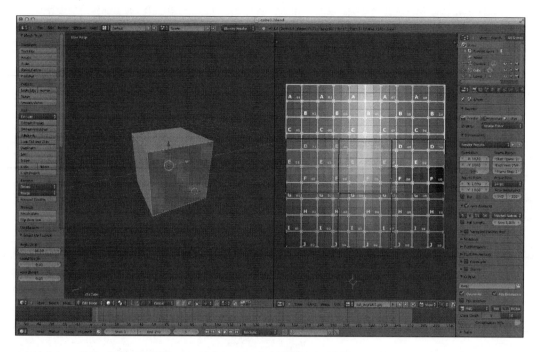

If we now show this in Three.js, you can see that the texture is applied differently, as shown in the following screenshot:

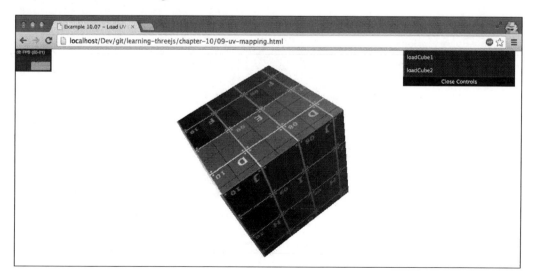

Customizing UV mappings is normally done from programs such as Blender, especially when the models become more complex. The most important part to remember here is that UV mappings run in two dimensions, u and v, from 0 to 1. To customize the UV mapping, you need to define, for each face, what part of the texture should be shown. You do this by defining the u and v coordinates for each of the vertices that make up the face. You can use the following code to set the u and v values:

```
geom.faceVertexUvs[0][0][0].x = 0.5;
geom.faceVertexUvs[0][0][0].y = 0.7;
geom.faceVertexUvs[0][0][1].x = 0.4;
geom.faceVertexUvs[0][0][1].y = 0.1;
geom.faceVertexUvs[0][0][2].x = 0.4;
geom.faceVertexUvs[0][0][2].y = 0.5;
```

This code snippet will set the uv properties of the first face to the specified value. Remember that each face is defined by three vertices, so to set all the uv values for a face, we need to set six properties. If you open the `07-uv-mapping-manual.html`, example you can see what happens when you change the uv mappings manually. The following screenshot shows the example:

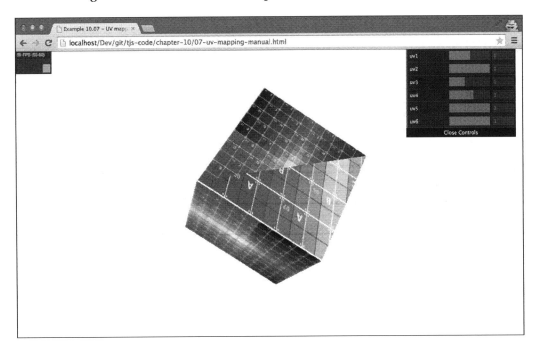

Next, we'll look at how textures can be repeated, which is done by some internal UV mapping tricks.

Repeat wrapping

When you apply a texture to a geometry created by Three.js, Three.js will try to apply the texture as optimally as possible. For instance, for cubes, this means each side will show the complete texture, and for spheres, the complete texture is wrapped around the sphere. There are, however, situations where you don't want the texture to spread around a complete face or the complete geometry, but have the texture repeat itself. Three.js provides detailed functionality that allows you to control this. An example where you can play around with the repeat properties is provided in the `08-repeat-wrapping.html` example. The following screenshot shows this example:

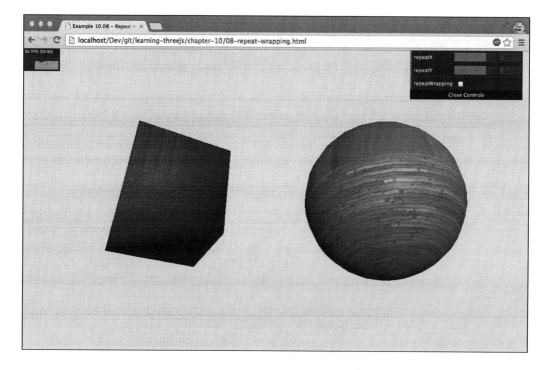

In this example, you can set the property that controls how a texture repeats itself.

Before this property has the desired effect, you need to make sure you set the wrapping of the texture to THREE.RepeatWrapping, as shown in the following code snippet:

```
cube.material.map.wrapS = THREE.RepeatWrapping;
cube.material.map.wrapT = THREE.RepeatWrapping;
```

The `wrapS` property defines how you want the texture to behave along its *x* axis and the `wrapT` property defines how the texture should behave along its *y* axis. Three.js provides two options for this, which are as follows:

- `THREE.RepeatWrapping` allows the texture to repeat itself.
- `THREE.ClampToEdgeWrapping` is a default setting. With `THREE. ClampToEdgeWrapping,` the texture doesn't repeat as a whole, but only the pixels at the edge are repeated.

If you disable the **repeatWrapping** menu option, the `THREE.ClampToEdgeWrapping` option is used, as follows:

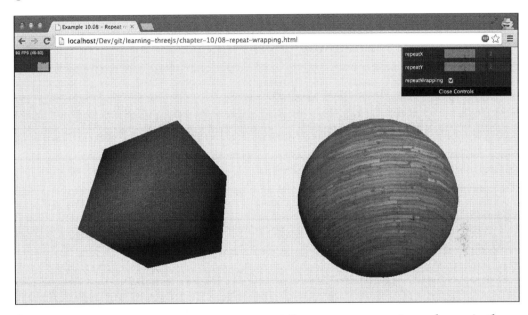

If we use `THREE.RepeatWrapping`, we can set the `repeat` property as shown in the following code fragment:

```
cube.material.map.repeat.set(repeatX, repeatY);
```

The `repeatX` variable defines how often the texture is repeated along its *x* axis and the `repeatY` variable defines the same for the *y* axis. If these values are set to 1, the texture won't repeat itself; if they are set to a higher value, you'll see that the texture will start repeating. You can also use values less than 1. In that case, you can see that you'll zoom in on the texture. If you set the repeat value to a negative value, the texture will be mirrored.

When you change the `repeat` property, Three.js will automatically update the textures and render with this new setting. If you change from `THREE.RepeatWrapping` to `THREE.ClampToEdgeWrapping`, you need to explicitly update the texture:

```
cube.material.map.needsUpdate = true;
```

Until now, we've only used static images for our textures. Three.js, however, also has the option to use the HTML5 canvas as a texture.

Rendering to canvas and using it as a texture

In this section, we're going to look at two different examples. First, we're going to look at how you can use the canvas to create a simple texture and apply it to a mesh, and after that, we'll go one step further and create a canvas that can be used as a bump map using a randomly generated pattern.

Using the canvas as a texture

In the first example, we will use the **Literally** library (from `http://literallycanvas.com/`) to create an interactive canvas that you can draw on; see the bottom-left corner in the following screenshot. You can view this example at `09-canvas-texture`. The ensuing screenshot shows this example:

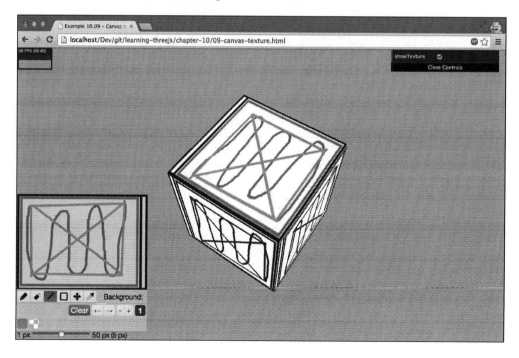

Anything you draw on this canvas is directly rendered on the cube as a texture. Accomplishing this in Three.js is really simple and only takes a couple of steps. The first thing we need to do is create a canvas element and, for this specific example, configure it to be used with the `Literally` library, as follows:

```
<div class="fs-container">
  <div id="canvas-output" style="float:left">
  </div>
</div>
...
var canvas = document.createElement("canvas");
$('#canvas-output')[0].appendChild(canvas);
$('#canvas-output').literallycanvas(
  {imageURLPrefix: '../libs/literally/img'});
```

We just create a `canvas` element from JavaScript and add it to a specific `div` element. With the `literallycanvas` call, we can create the drawing tools that you can use to directly draw on the canvas. Next, we need to create a texture that uses the canvas drawing as its input:

```
function createMesh(geom) {

  var canvasMap = new THREE.Texture(canvas);
  var mat = new THREE.MeshPhongMaterial();
  mat.map = canvasMap;
  var mesh = new THREE.Mesh(geom, mat);

  return mesh;
}
```

As the code shows, the only thing you need to do to is pass in the reference to the canvas element when you create a new texture, `new THREE.Texture(canvas)`. This will create a texture that uses the canvas element as its material. All that is left is to update the material whenever we render so that the latest version of the canvas drawing is shown on the cube, as follows:

```
function render() {
  stats.update();

  cube.rotation.y += 0.01;
  cube.rotation.x += 0.01;

  cube.material.map.needsUpdate = true;
  requestAnimationFrame(render);
  webGLRenderer.render(scene, camera);
}
```

To inform Three.js that we want to update the texture, we just set the `needsUpdate` property of the texture to `true`. In this example, we've used the canvas element as input for the most simple of textures. We can, of course, use this same idea for all the different types of maps we've seen so far. In the next example, we'll use it as a bump map.

Using the canvas as a bump map

As we've seen earlier in this chapter, we can create a simple wrinkled texture with a bump map. The higher the intensity of a pixel in this map, the higher the wrinkling. Since a bump map is just a simple black-and-white image, nothing keeps us from creating this on a canvas and using that canvas as an input for the bump map.

In the following example, we use a canvas to generate a random grayscale image, and we use that image as an input for the bump map we apply to the cube. See the `09-canvas-texture-bumpmap.html` example. The following screenshot shows this example:

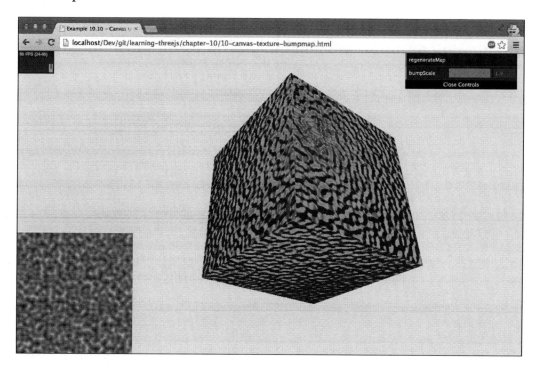

The JavaScript code required for this is not that different from the previous example we explained. We need to create a canvas element and fill this canvas with some random noise. For the noise, we use **Perlin noise**. Perlin noise (http://en.wikipedia.org/wiki/Perlin_noise) generates a very natural-looking random texture as you can see in the preceding screenshot. We use the Perlin noise function from https://github.com/wwwtyro/perlin.js for this:

```
var ctx = canvas.getContext("2d");
function fillWithPerlin(perlin, ctx) {

  for (var x = 0; x < 512; x++) {
    for (var y = 0; y < 512; y++) {
      var base = new THREE.Color(0xffffff);
      var value = perlin.noise(x / 10, y / 10, 0);
      base.multiplyScalar(value);
      ctx.fillStyle = "#" + base.getHexString();
      ctx.fillRect(x, y, 1, 1);
    }
  }
}
```

We use the `perlin.noise` function to create a value from 0 to 1 based on the *x* and *y* coordinates of the canvas element. This value is used to draw a single pixel on the canvas element. Doing this for all the pixels creates the random map you can also see in the bottom-left corner of the previous screenshot. This map can then be easily used as a bump map. Here's how the random map can be created:

```
var bumpMap = new THREE.Texture(canvas);

var mat = new THREE.MeshPhongMaterial();
mat.color = new THREE.Color(0x77ff77);
mat.bumpMap = bumpMap;
bumpMap.needsUpdate = true;

var mesh = new THREE.Mesh(geom, mat);
return mesh;
```

In this example, we've rendered Perlin noise using an HTML canvas element. Three.js also provides an alternative way to dynamically create a texture. The `THREE.ImageUtils` object has a `generateDataTexture` function, which you can use to create a `THREE.DataTexture` texture of a specific size. This texture contains `Uint8Array` in the `image.data` property, which you can use to directly set the RGB values of this texture.

The final input we use for the texture is another HTML element: the HTML5 video element.

Using the output from a video as a texture

If you've read the previous paragraph on rendering to canvas, you might have thought about rendering video to canvas and using that as input for a texture. That is an option, but Three.js (through WebGL) already has direct support to use the HTML5 video element. Check out 11-video-texture.html. Refer to the following screenshot for a still image of this example:

Using video as input for a texture is, just like using the canvas element, very easy. First off, we need to have a video element to play the video:

```
<video  id="video"
  style="display: none;
  position: absolute; left: 15px; top: 75px;"
  src="../assets/movies/Big_Buck_Bunny_small.ogv"
  controls="true" autoplay="true">
</video>
```

This was just a basic HTML5 video element that we set to automatically play. Next, we can configure Three.js to use this video as an input for a texture, as follows:

```
var video  = document.getElementById('video');
texture = new THREE.Texture(video);
texture.minFilter = THREE.LinearFilter;
texture.magFilter = THREE.LinearFilter;
texture.generateMipmaps = false;
```

Since our video isn't square, we need to make sure we disable the mipmap generation on the material. We also set some simple high-performance filters as the material changes very often. All that is left to do now is create a mesh and set the texture. In this example, we've used `MeshFaceMaterial` together with `MeshBasicMaterial`:

```
var materialArray = [];
materialArray.push(new THREE.MeshBasicMaterial({color:
   0x0051ba}));
materialArray.push(new THREE.MeshBasicMaterial({color:
   0x0051ba}));
materialArray.push(new THREE.MeshBasicMaterial({color:
   0x0051ba}));
materialArray.push(new THREE.MeshBasicMaterial({color:
   0x0051ba}));
materialArray.push(new THREE.MeshBasicMaterial({map: texture }));
materialArray.push(new THREE.MeshBasicMaterial({color:
   0xff51ba}));

var faceMaterial = new THREE.MeshFaceMaterial(materialArray);
var mesh = new THREE.Mesh(geom,faceMaterial);
```

All that is left to do is make sure that in our `render` loop, we update the texture, as follows:

```
if ( video.readyState === video.HAVE_ENOUGH_DATA ) {
  if (texture) texture.needsUpdate = true;
}
```

In this example, we just rendered the video to one side of the cube, but since this is a normal texture, we could do anything we want with it. We could, for instance, divide it along the sides of a cube using custom UV mapping, or we could even use video input as input for a bump map or a normal map.

In Three.js version r69, a texture specifically for dealing with videos was introduced. This texture (THREE.VideoTexture) wraps the code you've seen in this section, and you can use the THREE.VideoTexture approach as an alternative. The following code fragment shows how to use THREE.VideoTexture to create a texture (you can see this in action by looking at the 11-video-texture.html example):

```
var video = document.getElementById('video');
texture = new THREE.VideoTexture(video);
```

Summary

And so we end this chapter on textures. As you've seen, there are lots of different kinds of textures available in Three.js, each with their different uses. You can use any image in the PNG, JPG, GIF, TGA, DDS, or PVR format as a texture. Loading these images is done asynchronously, so remember to either use a rendering loop or add a callback when you load the texture. With textures, you can create great-looking objects from low-poly models and even add fake detailed depth using bump maps and normal maps. With Three.js, it is also easy to create dynamic textures using either the HTML5 canvas element or the video element. Just define a texture with these elements as the input and set the needsUpdate property to true whenever you want the texture to be updated.

With this chapter out of the way, we've pretty much covered all the important concepts of Three.js. We haven't, however, looked at an interesting feature Three.js offers—**postprocessing**. With postprocessing, you can add effects to your scene after it is rendered. You could, for instance, blur or colorize your scene or add a TV-like effect using scan lines. In the next chapter, we'll look at postprocessing and how you can apply it to your scene.

11
Custom Shaders and Render Postprocessing

We're getting to the end of the book, and in this chapter, we'll look at the one main feature of Three.js we haven't touched upon: render postprocessing. Besides that, in this chapter, we'll also introduce you to how you can create custom shaders. The main points we'll discuss in this chapter are the following:

- Setting up Three.js for postprocessing
- Discussing the basic postprocessing passes provided by Three.js, such as THREE.BloomPass and THREE.FilmPass
- Applying effects to part of the scene using masks
- Using THREE.TexturePass to store rendering results
- Using THREE.ShaderPass to add even more basic postprocessing effects, such as sepia filters, mirror effects, and color adjustments
- Using THREE.ShaderPass for various blurring effects and more advanced filters
- Creating a custom postprocessing effect by writing a simple shader

In the *Introducing requestAnimationFrame* section of *Chapter 1, Creating Your First 3D Scene with Three.js*, we set up a rendering loop that we've used throughout the book to render and animate our scene. For postprocessing, we need to make a couple of changes to this setup to allow Three.js to postprocess the final rendering. In the first section, we'll look at how to do this.

Setting up Three.js for postprocessing

To set up Three.js for postprocessing, we need to make a couple of changes in our current setup. We need to take the following steps:

1. Create THREE.EffectComposer, which we can use to add postprocessing passes.

2. Configure THREE.EffectComposer so that it renders our scene and applies any additional postprocessing steps.

3. In the render loop, use THREE.EffectComposer to render the scene, apply the passes, and show the output.

As always, we have an example that you can use to experiment with and adopt for your own uses. The first example for this chapter can be accessed from 01-basic-effect-composer.html. You can use the menu in the top-right corner to modify the properties of the postprocessing step used in this example. In this example, we render a simple globe and add an old-television-like effect to it. This television effect is added after the scene is rendered using THREE.EffectComposer. The following screenshot shows this example:

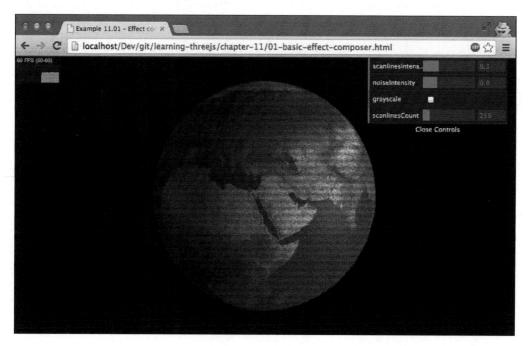

Creating THREE.EffectComposer

Let's first look at the additional JavaScript files you need to include. These files can be found in the Three.js distribution in the examples/js/postprocessing and examples/js/shaders directories.

The minimal setup you need to get THREE.EffectComposer working is the following:

```
<script type="text/javascript" src="../libs/postprocessing/
  EffectComposer.js"></script>
<script type="text/javascript" src="../libs/postprocessing/
  MaskPass.js"></script>
<script type="text/javascript" src="../libs/postprocessing/
  RenderPass.js"></script>
<script type="text/javascript" src="../libs/shaders/
  CopyShader.js"></script>
<script type="text/javascript" src="../libs/postprocessing/
  ShaderPass.js"></script>
```

The EffectComposer.js file provides the THREE.EffectComposer object that allows us to add postprocessing steps. MaskPass.js, ShaderPass.js, and CopyShader.js are used internally by THREE.EffectComposer, and RenderPass.js allows us to add a rendering pass to THREE.EffectComposer. Without that pass, our scene won't be rendered at all.

For this example, we add two additional JavaScript files to add a film-like effect to our scene:

```
<script type="text/javascript" src="../libs/postprocessing/
  FilmPass.js"></script>
<script type="text/javascript" src="../libs/shaders/
  FilmShader.js"></script>
```

The first thing we need to do is create THREE.EffectComposer. You can do this by passing in THREE.WebGLRenderer to its constructor:

```
var webGLRenderer = new THREE.WebGLRenderer();
var composer = new THREE.EffectComposer(webGLRenderer);
```

Next, we add various *passes* to this composer.

Configuring THREE.EffectComposer for postprocessing

Each pass is executed in the sequence it is added to THREE.EffectComposer. The first pass we add is THREE.RenderPass. The following pass renders our scene but doesn't output it to the screen yet:

```
var renderPass = new THREE.RenderPass(scene, camera);
composer.addPass(renderPass);
```

To create THREE.RenderPass, we pass in the scene we want to render and the camera that we want to use. With the addPass function, we add THREE.RenderPass to THREE.EffectComposer. The next step is to add another pass that will output its result to the screen. Not all the available passes allow this—more on that later—but THREE.FilmPass, which is used in this example, allows us to output the result of its pass to the screen. To add THREE.FilmPass, we first need to create it and add it to the composer. The resulting code looks like this:

```
var renderPass = new THREE.RenderPass(scene,camera);
var effectFilm = new THREE.FilmPass(0.8, 0.325, 256, false);
effectFilm.renderToScreen = true;

var composer = new THREE.EffectComposer(webGLRenderer);
composer.addPass(renderPass);
composer.addPass(effectFilm);
```

As you can see, we created THREE.FilmPass and set the renderToScreen property to true. This pass is added to THREE.EffectComposer after renderPass, so when this composer is used, first the scene is rendered, and through THREE.FilmPass, we can also see the output on screen.

Updating the render loop

Now we just need to make a small modification to our render loop to use the composer instead of THREE.WebGLRenderer:

```
var clock = new THREE.Clock();
function render() {
  stats.update();

  var delta = clock.getDelta();
  orbitControls.update(delta);

  sphere.rotation.y += 0.002;

  requestAnimationFrame(render);
  composer.render(delta);
}
```

The only modification we made is we removed `webGLRenderer.render(scene, camera)` and replaced it with `composer.render(delta)`. This will call the render function on `EffectComposer`, which in turn uses the passed-in `THREE.WebGLRenderer`, and since we set `renderToScreen` of `FilmPass` to `true`, the result from `FilmPass` is shown on screen.

With this basic setup, we'll look at the available postprocessing passes in the next couple of sections.

Postprocessing passes

Three.js comes with a number of postprocessing passes you can use directly with `THREE.EffectComposer`. Note that it's best to play around with the examples in this chapter to see the result of these passes and understand what is happening. The following table gives an overview of the passes that are available:

Pass name	Description
THREE.BloomPass	This is an effect that makes light areas bleed into darker areas. This simulates an effect where the camera is overwhelmed by extremely bright light.
THREE.DotScreenPass	This applies a layer of black dots representing the original image across the screen.
THREE.FilmPass	This simulates a TV screen by applying scanlines and distortions.
THREE.GlitchPass	This shows an electronic glitch on the screen at a random time interval.
THREE.MaskPass	This allows you to apply a mask to the current image. Subsequent passes are only applied to the masked area.
THREE.RenderPass	This renders a scene based on the supplied scene and camera.
THREE.SavePass	When this pass is executed, it makes a copy of the current rendering step that you can use later. This pass isn't that useful in practice, and we won't use it in any of our examples.
THREE.ShaderPass	This allows you to pass in custom shaders for advanced or custom postprocessing passes.
THREE.TexturePass	This stores the current state of the composer in a texture that you can use as input for other `EffectComposer` instance.

Let's start with a number of simple passes.

Simple postprocessing passes

For simple passes, we'll look at what we can do with THREE.FilmPass, THREE.BloomPass, and THREE.DotScreenPass. For these passes, an example is available, 02-post-processing-simple, that allows you to experiment with these passes and see how they affect the original output differently. The following screenshot shows this example:

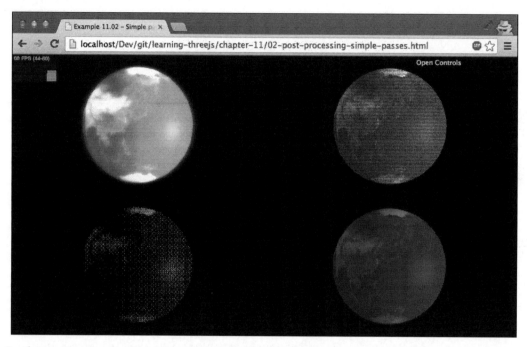

In this example, we show four scenes at the same time, and on each scene, a different postprocessing pass is added. The one in the top-left corner shows THREE.BloomPass, the one in the top-right corner shows THREE.FilmPass, the one in the bottom-left corner shows THREE.DotScreenPass, and the one in the bottom-right corner shows the original render.

In this example, we also use THREE.ShaderPass and THREE.TexturePass to reuse the output from the original rendering as input for the other three scenes. So, before we look at the individual passes, let's look at these two passes first:

```
var renderPass = new THREE.RenderPass(scene, camera);
var effectCopy = new THREE.ShaderPass(THREE.CopyShader);
effectCopy.renderToScreen = true;
```

```
var composer = new THREE.EffectComposer(webGLRenderer);
composer.addPass(renderPass);
composer.addPass(effectCopy);

var renderScene = new THREE.TexturePass(composer.renderTarget2);
```

In this piece of code, we set up THREE.EffectComposer, which will output the default scene (the one in the bottom-right corner). This composer has two passes. THREE.RenderPass renders the scene, and THREE.ShaderPass, when configured with THREE.CopyShader, renders the output, without any further postprocessing to the screen if we set the renderToScreen property to true. If you look at the example, you can see that we show the same scene four times but with a different effect applied each time. We could render the scene from scratch using THREE.RenderPass four times, but that would be a bit of a waste since we can just reuse the output from this first composer. To do this, we create THREE.TexturePass and pass in the composer.renderTarget2 value. We can now use the renderScene variable as input for our other composers without having to render the scene from scratch. Let's revisit THREE.FilmPass first and see how we can use THREE.TexturePass as input.

Using THREE.FilmPass to create a TV-like effect

We already looked at how to create THREE.FilmPass in the first section of this chapter, so let's see how to use this effect together with THREE.TexturePass from the previous section:

```
var effectFilm = new THREE.FilmPass(0.8, 0.325, 256, false);
effectFilm.renderToScreen = true;

var composer4 = new THREE.EffectComposer(webGLRenderer);
composer4.addPass(renderScene);
composer4.addPass(effectFilm);
```

The only step you need to take to use THREE.TexturePass is to add it as the first pass in your composer. Next, we can just add THREE.FilmPass, and the effect is applied. THREE.FilmPass itself takes four parameters:

Property	Description
noiseIntensity	This property allows you to control how grainy the scene looks.
scanlinesIntensity	THREE.FilmPass adds a number of scanlines to the scene. With this property, you can define how prominently these scanlines are shown.

Property	Description
scanLinesCount	The number of scanlines that are shown can be controlled with this property.
grayscale	If this is set to `true`, the output will be converted to grayscale.

There are actually two ways you can pass in these parameters. In this example, we passed them in as arguments to the constructor, but you can also set them directly, as follows:

```
effectFilm.uniforms.grayscale.value = controls.grayscale;
effectFilm.uniforms.nIntensity.value = controls.noiseIntensity;
effectFilm.uniforms.sIntensity.value = controls.scanlines
    Intensity;
effectFilm.uniforms.sCount.value = controls.scanlinesCount;
```

In this approach, we use the `uniforms` property, which is used to communicate directly with WebGL. In the section where we talk about creating a custom shader later in this chapter, we'll go a bit deeper into `uniforms`; for now, all you need to know is that this way, you can directly update the configuration of postprocessing passes and shaders and directly see the results.

Adding a bloom effect to the scene with THREE.BloomPass

The effect you see in the upper-left corner is called the bloom effect. When you apply the bloom effect, the bright areas of a scene will be made more prominent and *bleed* into the darker areas. The code to create `THREE.BloomPass` is shown here:

```
var effectCopy = new THREE.ShaderPass(THREE.CopyShader);
effectCopy.renderToScreen = true;
...
var bloomPass = new THREE.BloomPass(3, 25, 5, 256);
var composer3 = new THREE.EffectComposer(webGLRenderer);
composer3.addPass(renderScene);
composer3.addPass(bloomPass);
composer3.addPass(effectCopy);
```

If you compare this with `THREE.EffectComposer`, which we used with `THREE.FilmPass`, you'll notice that we add an additional pass, `effectCopy`. This step, which we also used for the normal output, doesn't add any special effect but just copies the output from the last pass to the screen. We need to add this step since `THREE.BloomPass` can't render directly to the screen.

The following table lists the properties you can set on `THREE.BloomPass`:

Property	Description
Strength	This is the strength of the bloom effect. The higher this is, the more bright the brighter areas are and the more they "bleed" to the darker areas.
kernelSize	This property controls the offset of the bloom effect.
sigma	With the `sigma` property, you can control the sharpness of the bloom effect. The higher the value, the more blurred the bloom effect looks.
Resolution	The `Resolution` property defines how precisely the bloom effect is created. If you make this too low, the result will look blocky.

A better way to understand these properties is to just experiment with them using the previously mentioned example, `02-post-processing-simple`. The following screenshot shows the bloom effect with a high kernel and sigma size and low strength:

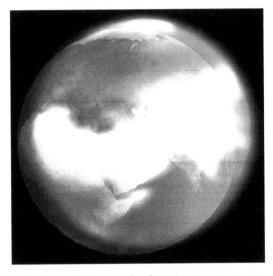

The last of the simple effects we'll have a look at is `THREE.DotScreenPass`.

Output the scene as a set of dots

Using THREE.DotScreenPass is very similar to using THREE.BloomPass. We just saw THREE.BloomPass in action. Now let's see the code for THREE.DotScreenPass:

```
var dotScreenPass = new THREE.DotScreenPass();
var composer1 = new THREE.EffectComposer(webGLRenderer);
composer1.addPass(renderScene);
composer1.addPass(dotScreenPass);
composer1.addPass(effectCopy);
```

With this effect, we once again have to add effectCopy to output the result to the screen. THREE.DotScreenPass can also be configured with a number of properties, as follows:

Property	Description
center	With the center property, you can fine-tune the way the dots are offset.
angle	The dots are aligned in a certain manner. With the angle properties, you can change this alignment.
Scale	With this, we can set the size of the dots to use. The lower the scale, the larger the dots.

What applies to the other shaders also applies to this shader. It's much easier to get the right settings with experimentation.

Showing the output of multiple renderers on the same screen

This section doesn't go into the details of how to use postprocessing effects, but explains how to get the output of all four THREE.EffectComposer instances on the same screen. First, let's look at the render loop used for this example:

```
function render() {
  stats.update();

  var delta = clock.getDelta();
  orbitControls.update(delta);

  sphere.rotation.y += 0.002;

  requestAnimationFrame(render);

  webGLRenderer.autoClear = false;
  webGLRenderer.clear();

  webGLRenderer.setViewport(0, 0, 2 * halfWidth, 2 * halfHeight);
  composer.render(delta);

  webGLRenderer.setViewport(0, 0, halfWidth, halfHeight);
  composer1.render(delta);

  webGLRenderer.setViewport(halfWidth, 0, halfWidth, halfHeight);
  composer2.render(delta);

  webGLRenderer.setViewport(0, halfHeight, halfWidth, halfHeight);
  composer3.render(delta);

  webGLRenderer.setViewport(halfWidth, halfHeight, halfWidth,
  halfHeight);
  composer4.render(delta);
}
```

The first thing to notice here is that we set the webGLRenderer.autoClear property to false and then explicitly call the clear() function. If we don't do this each time we call the render() function on a composer, the previously rendered scenes will be cleared. With this approach, we only clear everything at the beginning of our render loop.

To avoid all our composers rendering in the same space, we set the viewport of `webGLRenderer`, which is used by our composers, to a different part of the screen. This function takes four arguments: `x`, `y`, `width`, and `height`. As you can see in the code sample, we use this function to divide the screen into four areas and make the composers render to their individual area. Note that you can also use this approach with multiple scenes, cameras, and `WebGLRenderer` if you want.

In the table at the beginning of this section, we also mentioned `THREE.GlitchPass`. With this render pass, you can add a kind of electronic glitch effect to your scenes. This effect is just as easy to use as the other ones you've seen until now. To use it, first include the following two files in your HTML page:

```
<script type="text/javascript" src="../libs/postprocessing/
    GlitchPass.js"></script>
<script type="text/javascript" src="../libs/postprocessing/
    DigitalGlitch.js"></script>
```

Then, create the `THREE.GlitchPass` object, as follows:

```
var effectGlitch = new THREE.GlitchPass(64);
effectGlitch.renderToScreen = true;
```

The result is a scene where the result is rendered normally except that at random intervals, a glitch occurs, as shown in the following screenshot:

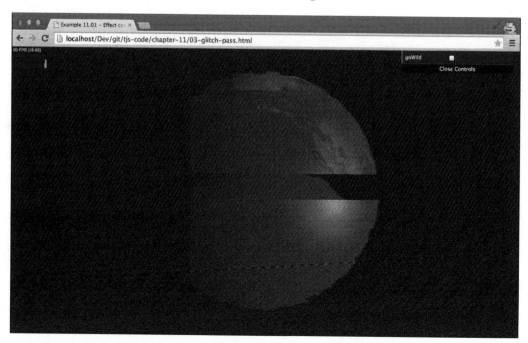

Until now, we've only chained a couple of simple passes. In the next example, we'll configure a more complex THREE.EffectComposer and use masks to apply effects to a part of the screen.

Advanced EffectComposer flows using masks

In the previous examples, we applied the postprocessing pass to the complete screen. Three.js, however, also has the ability to only apply passes to a specific area. In this section, we're going to perform the following steps:

1. Create a scene to serve as a background image.
2. Create a scene containing a sphere that looks like Earth.
3. Create a scene containing a sphere that looks like Mars.
4. Create EffectComposer, which renders these three scenes into a single image.
5. Apply a *colorify* effect to the sphere rendered as Mars.
6. Apply a sepia effect to the sphere rendered as Earth.

This might sound complex, but is actually surprisingly easy to accomplish. First, let's look at the result we're aiming for in the 03-post-processing-masks.html example. The following screenshot shows the result of these steps:

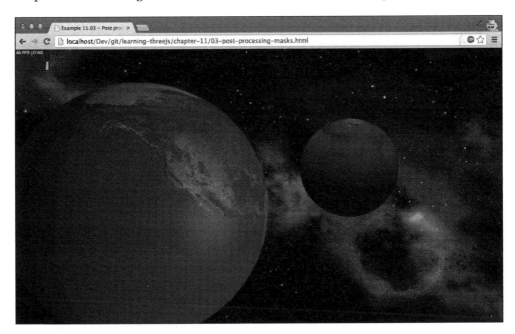

The first thing we need to do is set up the various scenes we'll be rendering, as follows:

```
var sceneEarth = new THREE.Scene();
var sceneMars = new THREE.Scene();
var sceneBG = new THREE.Scene();
```

To create the Earth and Mars spheres, we just create the spheres with the correct material and textures and add them to their specific scenes, as shown in the following code:

```
var sphere = createEarthMesh(new THREE.SphereGeometry(10, 40,
  40));
sphere.position.x = -10;
var sphere2 = createMarshMesh(new THREE.SphereGeometry(5, 40,
  40));
sphere2.position.x = 10;
sceneEarth.add(sphere);
sceneMars.add(sphere2);
```

We also need to add some lights to the scene just as we would for a normal scene, but we won't show that here (see *Chapter 3, Working with the Different Light Sources Available in Three.js,* for more details). The only thing to remember is that a light cannot be added to different scenes, so you need to create separate lights for both scenes. That's all the setting up we need to do for these two scenes.

For the background image, we create THREE.OrthoGraphicCamera. Remember from *Chapter 2, Basic Components That Make Up a Three.js Scene,* that the size of objects in the orthographic projection doesn't depend on the distance from the camera, so this also provides a good way to create fixed backgrounds. Here's how we create THREE.OrthoGraphicCamera:

```
var cameraBG = new THREE.OrthographicCamera(-window.innerWidth,
  window.innerWidth, window.innerHeight, -window.innerHeight, -
  10000, 10000);
cameraBG.position.z = 50;

var materialColor = new THREE.MeshBasicMaterial({ map:
  THREE.ImageUtils.loadTexture("../assets/textures/starry-deep-
  outer-space-galaxy.jpg"), depthTest: false });
var bgPlane = new THREE.Mesh(new THREE.PlaneGeometry(1, 1),
  materialColor);
bgPlane.position.z = -100;
bgPlane.scale.set(window.innerWidth * 2, window.innerHeight * 2,
  1);
sceneBG.add(bgPlane);
```

We won't go into too much detail for this part, but we have to take a couple of steps to create a background image. First, we create a material from our background image, and we apply this material to a simple plane. Next, we add this plane to the scene and scale it to exactly fill the complete screen. So, when we render this scene with this camera, our background image is shown stretched to the width of the screen.

We've now got our three scenes, and we can start to set up our passes and THREE. EffectComposer. Let's start by looking at the complete chain of passes, after which we'll look at the individual passes:

```
var composer = new THREE.EffectComposer(webGLRenderer);
composer.renderTarget1.stencilBuffer = true;
composer.renderTarget2.stencilBuffer = true;

composer.addPass(bgPass);
composer.addPass(renderPass);
composer.addPass(renderPass2);

composer.addPass(marsMask);
composer.addPass(effectColorify1);
composer.addPass(clearMask);

composer.addPass(earthMask);
composer.addPass(effectSepia);
composer.addPass(clearMask);

composer.addPass(effectCopy);
```

To work with masks, we need to create THREE.EffectComposer in a different manner. In this case, we need to create a new THREE.WebGLRenderTarget and set the stencilBuffer property of the internally used render targets to true. A stencil buffer is a special type of buffer and is used to limit the area of rendering. So, by enabling the stencil buffer, we can use our masks. First, let's look at the first three passes that are added. These three passes render the background, the Earth scene, and the Mars scene, as follows:

```
var bgPass = new THREE.RenderPass(sceneBG, cameraBG);
var renderPass = new THREE.RenderPass(sceneEarth, camera);
renderPass.clear = false;
var renderPass2 = new THREE.RenderPass(sceneMars, camera);
renderPass2.clear = false;
```

There's nothing new here except that we set the `clear` property of two of these passes to `false`. If we don't do this, we'll only see the output from `renderPass2` since it will clear everything before it starts rendering. If you look back at the code for `THREE.EffectComposer`, the next three passes are `marsMask`, `effectColorify`, and `clearMask`. First, we'll look at how these three passes are defined:

```
var marsMask = new THREE.MaskPass(sceneMars, camera );
var clearMask = new THREE.ClearMaskPass();
var effectColorify = new THREE.ShaderPass(THREE.ColorifyShader );
effectColorify.uniforms['color'].value.setRGB(0.5, 0.5, 1);
```

The first of these three passes is `THREE.MaskPass`. When creating `THREE.MaskPass`, you pass in a scene and a camera just as you did for `THREE.RenderPass`. `THREE.MaskPass` will render this scene internally, but instead of showing this on screen, it uses this information to create a mask. When `THREE.MaskPass` is added to `THREE.EffectComposer`, all the subsequent passes will only be applied to the mask defined by `THREE.MaskPass`, until `THREE.ClearMaskPass` is encountered. In this example, this means that the `effectColorify` pass, which adds a blue glow, is only applied to the objects rendered in `sceneMars`.

We use the same approach to apply a sepia filter on the Earth object. We first create a mask based on the Earth scene and use this mask in `THREE.EffectComposer`. After `THREE.MaskPass`, we add the effect we want to apply (`effectSepia` in this case), and once we're done with that, we add `THREE.ClearMaskPass` to remove the mask. The last step for this specific `THREE.EffectComposer` is one we've already seen. We need to copy the final result to the screen, and we once again use the `effectCopy` pass for that.

There is one additional property that's interesting when working with `THREE.MaskPass`, and that's the `inverse` property. If this property is set to `true`, the mask is inversed. In other words, the effect is applied to everything but the scene passed into `THREE.MaskPass`. This is shown in the following screenshot:

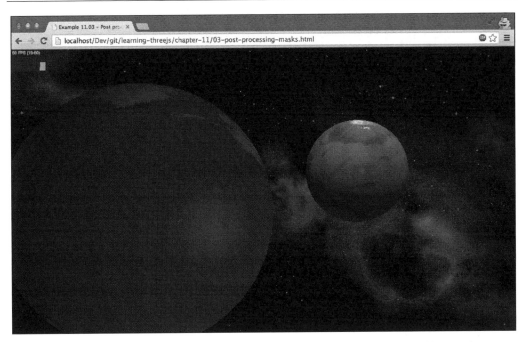

Until now, we've used standard passes provided by Three.js for our effects. Three.js also provides THREE.ShaderPass, which can be used for custom effects and comes with a large number of shaders you can use and experiment with.

Using THREE.ShaderPass for custom effects

With THREE.ShaderPass, we can apply a large number of additional effects to our scene by passing in a custom shader. This section is divided into three parts. First, we'll look at the following set of simple shaders:

Name	Description
THREE.MirrorShader	This creates a mirror effect for part of the screen.
THREE.HueSaturationShader	This allows you to change the *hue* and *saturation* of the colors.
THREE.VignetteShader	This applies a vignette effect. This effect shows dark borders around the center of the image.
THREE.ColorCorrectionShader	With this shader, you can change the color distribution.
THREE.RGBShiftShader	This shader separates the red, green, and blue components of a color.

Name	Description
THREE.BrightnessContrastShader	This changes the brightness and contrast of an image.
THREE.ColorifyShader	This applies a color overlay to the screen.
THREE.SepiaShader	This creates a sepia-like effect on the screen.
THREE.KaleidoShader	This adds a kaleidoscope effect to the scene that provides radial reflection around the center of the scene.
THREE.LuminosityShader	This provides a luminosity effect where the luminosity of the scene is shown.
THREE.TechnicolorShader	This simulates the effect of two-strip technicolor that can be seen in older movies.

Next, we'll look at shaders that provide a couple of blur-related effects:

Name	Description
THREE.HorizontalBlurShader and THREE.VerticalBlurShader	These apply a blur effect to the complete scene.
THREE.HorizontalTiltShiftShader and THREE.VerticalTiltShiftShader	These recreate the *tilt shift* effect. With the tilt shift effect, it is possible to create scenes that look like a miniature by making sure only part of the image is sharp.
THREE.TriangleBlurShader	This applies a blur effect using a triangle-based approach.

And finally, we'll look at a few shaders that provide advanced effects:

Name	Description
THREE.BleachBypassShader	This creates a *bleach bypass* effect. With this effect, a silver-like overlay will be applied to the image.
THREE.EdgeShader	This shader can be used to detect the sharp edges in an image and highlight them.
THREE.FXAAShader	This shader applies an anti-aliasing effect during the postprocessing phase. Use this if applying anti-aliasing during rendering is too expensive.
THREE.FocusShader	This is a simple shader that results in a sharply rendered center area and blurring along its borders.

We won't go into the details of all the shaders since if you've seen how one works, you pretty much know how the others work. In the following sections, we'll highlight a couple of interesting ones. You can experiment with the others using the interactive examples provided for each section.

 Three.js also provides two advanced postprocessing effects that allow you to apply a *bokeh* effect to your scene. A bokeh effect provides a blur effect to part of the scene while rendering your main subject very sharply. Three.js provides `THREE.BrokerPass`, which you can use for this, or `THREE.BokehShader2` and `THREE.DOFMipMapShader`, which you can use together with `THREE.ShaderPass`. An example of these shaders in action can be found on the Three.js website at `http://threejs.org/examples/webgl_postprocessing_dof2.html` and `http://threejs.org/examples/webgl_postprocessing_dof.html`.

We start with a couple of the simple shaders.

Simple shaders

To experiment with the basic shaders, we've created an example where you can play around with the shaders and see the effect directly in the scene. You can find this example in `04-shaderpass-simple.html`. The following screenshot shows this example:

With the menu in the top-right corner, you can select the specific shader you want to apply, and with the various drop-down menus, you can set the properties of the shader you've selected. For instance, the following screenshot shows RGBShiftShader in action:

When you change one of the properties of a shader, the result is updated directly. For this example, we set the changed value directly on the shader. For instance, when values for RGBShiftShader have changed, we update the shader like this:

```
this.changeRGBShifter = function() {
  rgbShift.uniforms.amount.value = controls.rgbAmount;
  rgbShift.uniforms.angle.value = controls.angle;
}
```

Let's look at a couple of other shaders. The following image shows the result of
`VignetteShader`:

`MirrorShader` has the following effect:

With postprocessing, we can also apply extreme effects. A good example of this is THREE.KaleidoShader. If you select this shader from the menu in the top-right corner, you'll see the following effect:

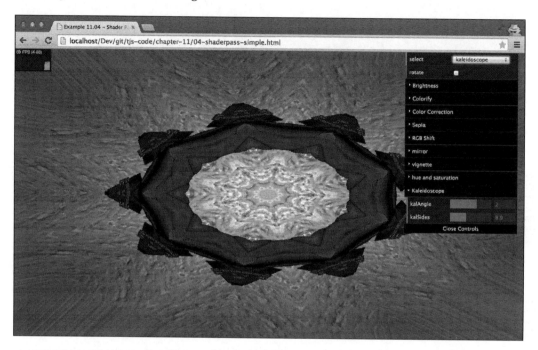

That's enough for the simple shaders. As you can see, they are very versatile and can create very interesting-looking effects. In this example, we applied a single shader each time, but you can add as many THREE.ShaderPass steps to THREE. EffectComposer as you like.

Blurring shaders

In this section, we won't dive into the code; we'll just show you the results from the various blur shaders. You can experiment with these using the 05-shaderpass-blur.html example. The following scene is blurred with HorizontalBlurShader and VerticalBlurShader, both of which you will learn about in the following paragraphs:

The preceding image shows THREE.HorizontalBlurShader and THREE.
VerticalBlurShader. You can see the effect is a blurred scene. Besides
these two blur effects, Three.js provides an additional shader that blurs an
image, THREE.TriangleShader, which is shown here. For instance, you could
use this shader to depict motion blur, as shown in the following screenshot:

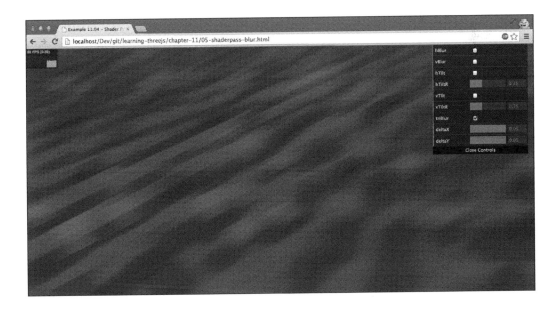

The last blur-like effect is provided by THREE.HorizontalTiltShiftShader and THREE.VerticalTiltShiftShader. This shader doesn't blur the complete scene, but only a small area. This provides an effect called *tilt shift*. This is often used to create miniature-like scenes from normal photographs. The following image shows this effect:

Advanced shaders

For the advanced shaders, we'll do what we did for the previous blur-shaders. We'll just show you the output of the shaders. For details on how to configure them, look at the 06-shaderpass-advanced.html example. The following screenshot shows this example:

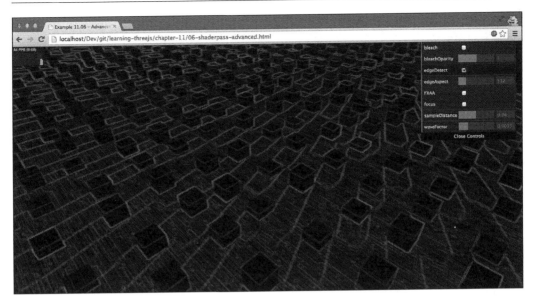

The preceding example shows THREE.EdgeShader. With this shader, you can detect the edges of objects in your scene.

The next shader is THREE.FocusShader. This shader only renders the center of the screen in focus, as shown in the following screenshot:

Until now, we've only used shaders that are provided by Three.js. However, it's also very easy to create shaders yourself.

Creating custom postprocessing shaders

In this section, you'll learn how to create a custom shader that you can use in postprocessing. We'll create two different shaders. The first one will convert the current image into a grayscale image, and the second one will convert the image into an 8-bit image by reducing the number of colors that are available. Note that creating vertex and fragment shaders is a very broad subject. In this section, we only touch the surface of what can be done by these shaders and how they work. For more in-depth information, you can find the WebGL specification at `http://www.khronos.org/webgl/`. An additional good resource full of examples is Shadertoy at `https://www.shadertoy.com/`.

Custom grayscale shader

To create a custom shader for Three.js (and also for other WebGL libraries), you need to implement two components: a vertex shader and a fragment shader. The vertex shader can be used to change the position of individual vertices, and the fragment shader is used to determine the color of individual pixels. For a postprocessing shader, we only need to implement a fragment shader, and we can keep the default vertex shader provided by Three.js. An important point to make before looking at the code is that GPUs usually support multiple shader pipelines. This means that in the vertex shaders step, multiple shaders can run in parallel—something that goes for the fragment shaders step as well.

Let's start by looking at the complete source code for the shader that applies a grayscale effect to our image (`custom-shader.js`):

```
THREE.CustomGrayScaleShader = {

  uniforms: {

    "tDiffuse": { type: "t", value: null },
    "rPower":   { type: "f", value: 0.2126 },
    "gPower":   { type: "f", value: 0.7152 },
    "bPower":   { type: "f", value: 0.0722 }

  },

  vertexShader: [
```

```
    "varying vec2 vUv;",
    "void main() {",
      "vUv = uv;",
      "gl_Position = projectionMatrix * modelViewMatrix * vec4(
        position, 1.0 );",
    "}"
  ].join("\n"),

  fragmentShader: [

    "uniform float rPower;",
    "uniform float gPower;",
    "uniform float bPower;",
    "uniform sampler2D tDiffuse;",

    "varying vec2 vUv;",

    "void main() {",
      "vec4 texel = texture2D( tDiffuse, vUv );",
      "float gray = texel.r*rPower + texel.g*gPower
        + texel.b*bPower;",
      "gl_FragColor = vec4( vec3(gray), texel.w );",
    "}"
  ].join("\n")
};
```

As you can see from the code, this isn't JavaScript. When you write shaders, you write them in the **OpenGL Shading Language (GLSL)**, which looks a lot like the C programming language. More information on GLSL can be found at http://www.khronos.org/opengles/sdk/docs/manglsl/.

Let's first look at this vertex shader:

```
    "varying vec2 vUv;","void main() {",
      "vUv = uv;",
      "gl_Position = projectionMatrix * modelViewMatrix * vec4(
        position, 1.0 );",
      "}"
```

For postprocessing, this shader doesn't really need to do anything. The code you see above is the standard way Three.js implements a vertex shader. It uses `projectionMatrix`, which is the projection from the camera, together with `modelViewMatrix`, which maps an object's position into the world position, to determine where to render an object on screen.

For postprocessing, the only interesting thing in this piece of code is that the uv value, which indicates which texel to read from a texture, is passed on to the fragment shader using the "varying vec2 vUv" variable. We will use the vUV value to get the correct pixel to work on in the fragment shader. Let's look at the fragment shader and see what the code is doing. We start with the following variable declaration:

```
"uniform float rPower;",
"uniform float gPower;",
"uniform float bPower;",
"uniform sampler2D tDiffuse;",

"varying vec2 vUv;",
```

Here, we see four instances of the uniforms property. The instances of the uniforms property have values that are passed in from JavaScript to the shader and which are the same for each fragment that is processed. In this case, we pass in three floats, identified by type f (which are used to determine the ratio of a color to include in the final grayscale image), and a texture (tDiffuse) is passed in, identified by type t. This texture contains the image from the previous pass from THREE.EffectComposer. Three.js makes sure it gets passed correctly to this shader, and we can set the other instances of the uniforms property ourselves from JavaScript. Before we can use these uniforms from JavaScript, we have to define which uniforms property is available for this shader. This is done like this, at the top of the shader file:

```
uniforms: {

  "tDiffuse": { type: "t", value: null },
  "rPower":   { type: "f", value: 0.2126 },
  "gPower":   { type: "f", value: 0.7152 },
  "bPower":   { type: "f", value: 0.0722 }

},
```

At this point, we can receive configuration parameters from Three.js and have received the image we want to modify. Let's look at the code that will convert each pixel to a gray pixel:

```
"void main() {",
  "vec4 texel = texture2D( tDiffuse, vUv );",
  "float gray = texel.r*rPower + texel.g*gPower +
    texel.b*bPower;",
  "gl_FragColor = vec4( vec3(gray), texel.w );"
```

What happens here is that we get the correct pixel from the passed-in texture. We do this by using the `texture2D` function, where we pass in our current image (`tDiffuse`) and the location of the pixel (`vUv`) we want to analyze. The result is a texel (a pixel from a texture) that contains a color and an opacity (`texel.w`).

Next, we use the `r`, `g`, and `b` properties of this texel to calculate a gray value. This gray value is set to the `gl_FragColor` variable, which is eventually shown on screen. And with that, we've got our own custom shader. Using this shader is just like the other shaders. First, we just need to set up `THREE.EffectComposer`:

```
var renderPass = new THREE.RenderPass(scene, camera);

var effectCopy = new THREE.ShaderPass(THREE.CopyShader);
effectCopy.renderToScreen = true;

var shaderPass = new THREE.ShaderPass(THREE.CustomGrayScaleShader);

var composer = new THREE.EffectComposer(webGLRenderer);
composer.addPass(renderPass);
composer.addPass(shaderPass);
composer.addPass(effectCopy);
```

Call `composer.render(delta)` in the render loop. If we want to change the properties of this shader at runtime, we can just update the `uniforms` property we've defined:

```
shaderPass.enabled = controls.grayScale;
shaderPass.uniforms.rPower.value = controls.rPower;
shaderPass.uniforms.gPower.value = controls.gPower;
shaderPass.uniforms.bPower.value = controls.bPower;
```

The result can be seen in `07-shaderpass-custom.html`. The following screenshot shows this example:

Let's create another custom shader. This time, we'll reduce the 24-bit output to a lower bit count.

Creating a custom bit shader

Normally, colors are represented as a 24-bit value, which gives us about 16 million different colors. In the early days of computing, this wasn't possible, and colors where often represented as 8- or 16-bit colors. With this shader, we'll automatically transform our 24-bit output to a color depth of 8 bits (or anything you want).

Since it hasn't changed with regard to our previous example, we'll skip the vertex shader and directly list the instances of the `uniforms` property:

```
uniforms: {

  "tDiffuse": { type: "t", value: null },
  "bitSize":  { type: "i", value: 4 }

}
```

Here's the fragment shader itself:

```
fragmentShader: [

    "uniform int bitSize;",

    "uniform sampler2D tDiffuse;",

    "varying vec2 vUv;",

    "void main() {",

        "vec4 texel = texture2D( tDiffuse, vUv );",
        "float n = pow(float(bitSize),2.0);",
        "float newR = floor(texel.r*n)/n;",
        "float newG = floor(texel.g*n)/n;",
        "float newB = floor(texel.b*n)/n;",

        "gl_FragColor = vec4(newR, newG, newB, texel.w );",

    "}"

].join("\n")
```

We define two instances of the `uniforms` property that can be used to configure this shader. The first one is the one Three.js uses to pass in the current screen, and the second one is defined by us as an integer (`type: "i"`) and serves as the color depth we want to render the result in. The code itself is very straightforward:

- We first get `texel` from the texture and `tDiffuse` based on the passed-in vUv location of the pixel.
- We calculate the number of colors we can have based on the `bitSize` property by calculating 2 to the power of `bitSize` (`pow(float(bitSize),2.0)`).
- Next, we calculate the new value of the color of `texel` by multiplying the value with n, rounding it off, (`floor(texel.r*n)`), and dividing it again by n.
- The result is set to `gl_FragColor` (red, green, and blue values and the opacity) and shown on screen.

You can view the result for this custom shader in the same example as our previous custom shader, `07-shaderpass-custom.html`. The following screenshot shows this example:

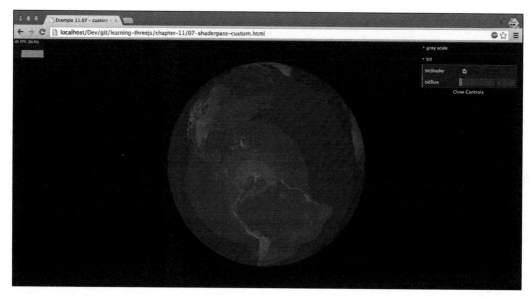

That's it for this chapter on postprocessing.

Summary

We talked about a lot of different postprocessing options in this chapter. As you saw, creating THREE.EffectComposer and chaining passes together is actually very easy. You just have to keep in mind a few things. Not all passes output to the screen. If you want to output to the screen, you can always use THREE.ShaderPass with THREE.CopyShader. The sequence in which you add passes to a composer is important. Effects are applied in that sequence. If you want to reuse the result from a specific THREE.EffectComposer instance, you can do this by using THREE.TexturePass. When you have more than one THREE.RenderPass in your THREE.EffectComposer, make sure to set the `clear` property to `false`. If not, you'll only see the output from the last THREE.RenderPass step. If you only want to apply an effect to a specific object, you can use THREE.MaskPass. When you're done with the mask, clear the mask with THREE.ClearMaskPass. Besides the standard passes provided by Three.js, there are also a large number of standard shaders available. You can use these together with THREE.ShaderPass. Creating custom shaders for postprocessing is very easy using the standard approach from Three.js. You only need to create a fragment shader.

Until now, we pretty much covered everything there is to know about Three.js. For the next chapter, the last one, we'll look at a library called **Physijs** that you can use to extend Three.js with physics and apply collisions, gravity, and constraints.

12
Adding Physics and Sounds to Your Scene

In this final chapter, we'll look at Physijs, another library you can use to extend the basic functionality of Three.js. Physijs is a library that allows you to introduce physics into your 3D scene. By physics, we mean that your objects are subject to gravity, they can collide with each other, can be moved by applying impulse, and can be constrained in their movement through hinges and sliders. This library internally makes use of another well-known physics engine called **ammo.js**. Besides physics, we'll also look at how Three.js can help you with adding spatial sounds to your scene.

In this chapter, we'll discuss the following topics:

- Creating a Physijs scene where your objects are subject to gravity and can collide with each other
- Showing how to change the friction and restitution (bounciness) of the objects in the scene
- Explaining the various shapes supported by Physijs and how to use them
- Showing how to create compound shapes by combining simple shapes together
- Showing how a height field allows you to simulate a complex shape
- Limiting the movement of an object by applying a point, hinge, slider, and cone twist, and the 'degree of freedom' constraint
- Adding sound sources to your scene whose sound volume and direction is based on their distance to the camera.

The first thing we will do is create a Three.js scene that can be used with Physijs. We'll do that in our first example.

Creating a basic Three.js scene

Setting up a Three.js scene for Physijs is very simple and only takes a couple of steps. The first thing we need to do is include the correct JavaScript file, which you can get from the GitHub repository at `http://chandlerprall.github.io/Physijs/`. Add the Physijs library to your HTML page like this:

```
<script type="text/javascript" src="../libs/physi.js"></script>
```

Simulating a scene is rather processor intensive. If we run all the simulation computations on the render thread (since JavaScript is single threaded in nature), it will seriously affect the frame rate of our scene. To compensate for that, Physijs does its calculations in a background thread. This background thread is provided through the "web workers" specification that is implemented by most modern browsers. With this specification, you can run CPU-intensive tasks in a separate thread, thus not affecting the rendering. More information on web workers can be found at `http://www.w3.org/TR/workers/`.

For Physijs, this means we have to configure the JavaScript file that contains this worker task and also tell Physijs where it can find the ammo.js file needed to simulate our scene. The reason we need to include the ammo.js file is that Physijs is a wrapper around ammo.js to make it easy to use. Ammo.js (which you can find at `https://github.com/kripken/ammo.js/`) is the library that implements the physics engine; Physijs just provides an easy-to-use interface to this physics library. Since Physijs is just a wrapper, we can also use other physics engines together with Physijs. On the Physijs repository, you can also find a branch that uses Cannon.js, a different physics engine.

To configure Physijs, we have to set the following two properties:

```
Physijs.scripts.worker = '../libs/physijs_worker.js';
Physijs.scripts.ammo = '../libs/ammo.js';
```

The first property points to the worker tasks we want to execute, and the second property points to the ammo.js library that is used internally. The next step we need to perform is create a scene. Physijs provides a wrapper around the Three.js normal scene, so in your code, you do the following to create a scene:

```
var scene = new Physijs.Scene();
scene.setGravity(new THREE.Vector3(0, -10, 0));
```

This creates a new scene where physics is applied, and we set the gravity. In this case, we set the gravity on the *y* axis to be -10. In other words, objects fall straight down. You can set, or change at runtime, the gravity for the various axes to any value you see fit, and the scene will respond accordingly.

Before we can start simulating the physics in the scene, we need to add some objects. For this, we can use the normal way Three.js specifies objects, but we have to wrap them inside a specific Physijs object so that they can be managed by the Physijs library, as you can see in the following code fragment:

```
var stoneGeom = new THREE.BoxGeometry(0.6,6,2);
var stone = new Physijs.BoxMesh(stoneGeom, new THREE.
  MeshPhongMaterial({color: 0xff0000}));
scene.add(stone);
```

In this example, we create a simple `THREE.BoxGeometry` object. Instead of creating `THREE.Mesh`, we create `Physijs.BoxMesh`, which tells Physijs to treat the shape of the geometry as a box when simulating physics and detecting collisions. Physijs provides a number of meshes you can use for the various shapes. More information on the available shapes can be found later in this chapter.

Now that `THREE.BoxMesh` has been added to the scene, we have all the ingredients for the first Physijs scene. All that is left to do is tell Physijs to simulate the physics and update the position and rotation of the objects in our scene. We can do this by calling the simulate method on the scene we just created. So, for this, we change our basic render loop to the following:

```
render = function() {
  requestAnimationFrame(render);
  renderer.render(scene, camera);
  scene.simulate();
}
```

And with that final step, by calling `scene.simulate()`, we have our basic setup for a Physijs scene. If we would run this example, though, we wouldn't see much. We would just see a single cube in the middle of the screen, which starts falling down as soon as the scene renders. So, let's look at a more complex example, where we'll simulate dominos falling down.

For this example, we're going to create the following scene:

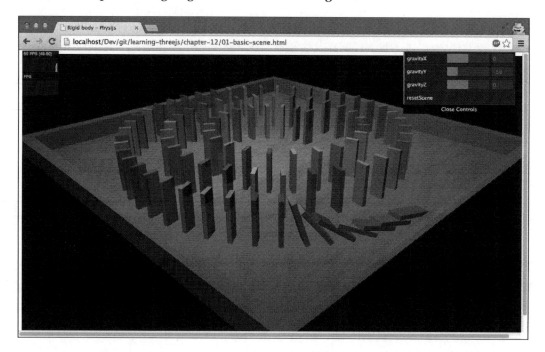

If you open the `01-basic-scene.html` example in your browser, you'll see a set of domino stones that start falling down as soon as the scene is loaded. The first one will tip over the second one, and so on. The complete physics of this scene is managed by Physijs. The only thing we did to start this animation is tip over the first domino. Creating this scene is actually very easy and only takes a few steps, which are as follows:

1. Define a Physijs scene.
2. Define the ground area that holds the stones.
3. Place the stones.
4. Tip over the first stone.

Let's skip this first step since we've already seen how to do this and go directly to the second step, where we define the sandbox that contains all the stones. This sandbox is constructed out of a couple of boxes that are grouped together. The following is the code required to accomplish this:

```
function createGround() {
  var ground_material = Physijs.createMaterial(new
    THREE.MeshPhongMaterial({ map: THREE.ImageUtils.loadTexture(
    '../assets/textures/general/wood-2.jpg' )}),0.9,0.3);

  var ground = new Physijs.BoxMesh(new THREE.BoxGeometry(60, 1,
    60), ground_material, 0);

  var borderLeft = new Physijs.BoxMesh(new THREE.BoxGeometry (2,
    3, 60), ground_material, 0);
  borderLeft.position.x=-31;
  borderLeft.position.y=2;
  ground.add(borderLeft);

  var borderRight = new Physijs.BoxMesh(new THREE. BoxGeometry (2,
    3, 60), ground_material, 0);
  borderRight.position.x=31;
  borderRight.position.y=2;
  ground.add(borderRight);

  var borderBottom = new Physijs.BoxMesh(new THREE. BoxGeometry
    (64, 3, 2), ground_material, 0);
  borderBottom.position.z=30;
  borderBottom.position.y=2;
  ground.add(borderBottom);

  var borderTop = new Physijs.BoxMesh(new THREE.BoxGeometry (64,
    3, 2), ground_material, 0);
  borderTop.position.z=-30;
  borderTop.position.y=2;
  ground.add(borderTop);

  scene.add(ground);
}
```

This code isn't very complicated. First, we create a simple box that serves as the ground plane, and next we add a couple of borders to prevent objects falling off this ground plane. We add these borders to the ground object to create a compound object. This is an object that is treated by Physijs as a single object. There are a couple of other new things in this code that we'll explain in more depth in the following sections. The first one is `ground_material`, which we create. We use the `Physijs.createMaterial` function to create this material. This function wraps a standard Three.js material but allows us to set `friction` and `restitution` (bounciness) of the material. More on this can be found in the next section. Another new aspect is the final parameter we add to the `Physijs.BoxMesh` constructor. For all the `BoxMesh` objects we create in this section, we add `0` as the final parameter. With this parameter, we set the weight of the object. We do this to prevent the ground from being subject to the gravity in the scene so that it doesn't fall down.

Now that we have the ground, we can place the dominos. For this, we create simple `Three.BoxGeometry` instances that we wrap inside `BoxMesh` and place them at a specific position on top of the ground mesh, as follows:

```
var stoneGeom = new THREE.BoxGeometry(0.6,6,2);
var stone = new Physijs.BoxMesh(stoneGeom,
  Physijs.createMaterial(new THREE.MeshPhongMaterial(color:
  scale(Math.random()).hex(),transparent:true, opacity:0.8})));
stone.position.copy(point);
stone.lookAt(scene.position);
stone.__dirtyRotation = true;
stone.position.y=3.5;
scene.add(stone);
```

We don't show the code where the position of each domino is calculated (see the `getPoints()` function in the source code of the example for this); this code just shows how the dominos are positioned. What you can see here is that we once again create `BoxMesh`, which wraps `THREE.BoxGeometry`. To make sure the dominos are aligned correctly, we use the `lookAt` function to set their correct rotation. If we don't do this, they'll all face the same way and won't fall down. We have to make sure that after we manually update the rotation (or the position) of a Physijs wrapped object, we tell Physijs that something has changed so that Physijs can update it's own internal representation of all the objects in the scene. For the rotation, we can do this with the internal `__dirtyRotation` property, and for the position, we set `__dirtyPosition` to `true`.

Now all that is left to do is tip the first domino. We do this by just setting the rotation on the *x* axis to 0.2, which tips it slightly. The gravity in the scene will do the rest and completely tip over the first domino. Here's how we tip the first domino:

```
stones[0].rotation.x=0.2;
stones[0].__dirtyRotation = true;
```

This completes the first example, which already shows a lot of features from Physijs. If you want to play around with the gravity, you can change it through the menu in the top-right corner. The change to the gravity is applied when you push the **resetScene** button:

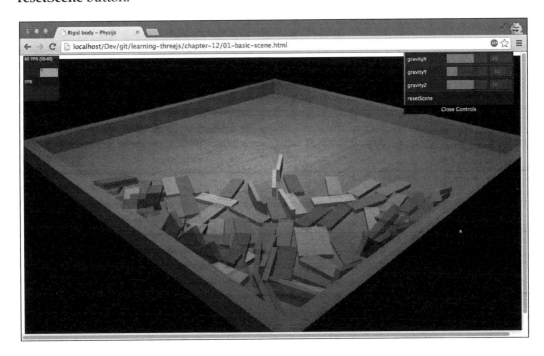

In the next section, we'll have a closer look at how the Physijs material properties affect the objects.

Material properties

Let's begin with an explanation of the example. When you open up the
`02-material-properties.html` example, you'll see an empty box somewhat
similar to the previous example. This box is rotating up and down around its *x*
axis. In the menu in the top-right corner, you have several sliders that can be used
to change some of the material properties of Physijs. These properties apply to
the cubes and spheres you can add with the **addCubes** and **addSpheres** buttons.
When you press the **addSpheres** button, five spheres will be added to the scene,
and when you press the **addCubes** button, five cubes will be added. The following
is an example demonstrating friction and restitution:

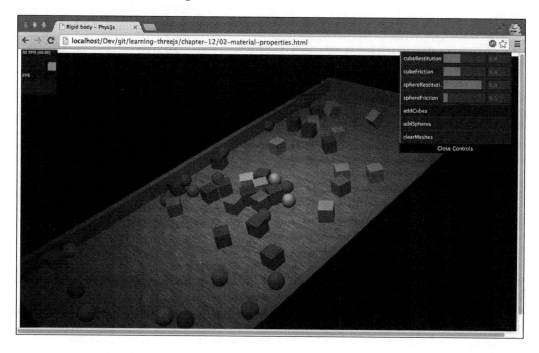

This example allows you to play around with the `restitution` (bounciness) and
`friction` properties that you can set when you create a Physijs material. If, for
example, you set **cubeFriction** all the way to 1 and add some cubes, you'll see that,
even though the ground is moving, the cubes barely move. If you set **cubeFriction**
to **0**, you'll notice the cubes sliding around as soon as the ground stops being level.
The following screenshot shows that high friction allows cubes to resist gravity:

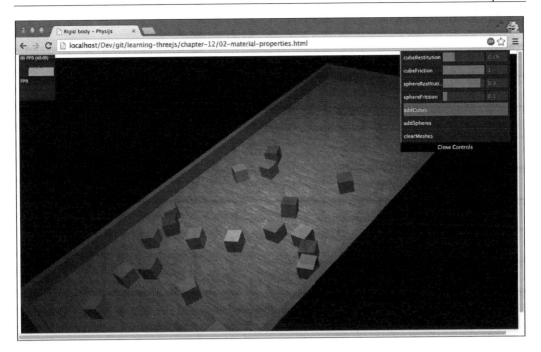

The other property you can set in this example is the `restitution` property. The `restitution` property defines how much of the energy that an object possesses is restituted when it collides. In other words, high restitution creates a bouncy object, and low restitution results in an object that stops immediately when it hits another object.

When you use a physics engine, you normally don't have to worry about detecting collisions. The engine will take care of that. It is, however, sometimes very useful to be informed when a collision between two objects occurs. For instance, you might want to create a sound effect, or when creating a game, deduct a life.

With Physijs, you can add an event listener to a Physijs mesh, as shown in the following code:

```
mesh.addEventListener( 'collision', function(
    other_object, relative_velocity, relative_rotation,
    contact_normal ) {

});
```

This way, you'll be informed whenever this mesh collides with another of the meshes handled by Physijs.

A good way to demonstrate this is using spheres, setting the restitution to 1, and clicking on the **addSpheres** button a couple of times. This will create a number of spheres that bounce everywhere.

Before we move on to the next section, let's look at a bit of code used in this example:

```
sphere = new Physijs.SphereMesh(new THREE.SphereGeometry( 2, 20 ),
    Physijs.createMaterial(new THREE.MeshPhongMaterial({color:
    colorSphere, opacity: 0.8, transparent: true}),
    controls.sphereFriction, controls.sphereRestitution));
box.position.set(Math.random() * 50 -25, 20 + Math.random() * 5,
    Math.random() * 50 -25);
scene.add( sphere );
```

This is the code that gets executed when we add spheres to the scene. This time, we use a different Physijs mesh: `Physijs.SphereMesh`. We're creating `THREE.SphereGeometry`, and the best match from the set of meshes provided is, logically, `Physijs.SphereMesh` (more on this in the next section). When we create `Physijs.SphereMesh`, we pass in our geometry and use `Physijs.createMaterial` to create a Physijs-specific material. We do this so that we can set `friction` and `restitution` for this object.

Until now, we've seen `BoxMesh` and `SphereMesh`. In the next section, we'll explain and show the different types of meshes provided by Physijs that you can use to wrap your geometries.

Basic supported shapes

Physijs provides a number of shapes you can use to wrap your geometries. In this section, we'll walk you through all the available Physijs meshes and demonstrate these meshes through an example. Remember that all you have to do to use these meshes is replace the `THREE.Mesh` constructor with one of these meshes.

The following table provides an overview of the meshes that are available in Physijs:

Name	Description
`Physijs.PlaneMesh`	This mesh can be used to create a zero-thickness plane. You could also use `BoxMesh` for this together with `THREE.BoxGeometry` with low height.
`Physijs.BoxMesh`	If you have geometries that look like cubes, use this mesh. For instance, this is a good match for `THREE.BoxGeometry`.
`Physijs.SphereMesh`	For sphere shapes, use this geometry. This geometry is a good match for `THREE.SphereGeometry`.

Name	Description
Physijs. CylinderMesh	With `THREE.Cylinder`, you can create various cylinder-like shapes. Physijs provides multiple meshes depending on the shape of the cylinder. `Physijs.CylinderMesh` should be used for a normal cylinder with the same top radius and bottom radius.
Physijs.ConeMesh	If you specify the top radius as 0 and use a positive value for the bottom radius, you can use `THREE.Cylinder` to create a cone. If you want to apply physics to such an object, the best fit from Physijs is `ConeMesh`.
Physijs.CapsuleMesh	A capsule is just like `THREE.Cylinder`, but with a rounded top and a rounded bottom. We'll show you how to create a capsule in Three.js later on in this section.
Physijs.ConvexMesh	`hysijs.ConvexMesh` is a rough shape you can use for more complex objects. It creates a convex (just like `THREE.ConvexGeometry`) to approximate the shape of complex objects.
Physijs.ConcaveMesh	While `ConvexMesh` is a rough shape, `ConcaveMesh` is a more detailed representation of your complex geometry. Note that the performance penalty of using `ConcaveMesh` is very high. Usually, it is better to either create separate geometries with their own specific Physijs meshes or group them together (as we do with the floors shown in the previous examples).
Physijs. HeightfieldMesh	This mesh is a very specialized one. With this mesh, you can create a height field from `THREE.PlaneGeometry`. Look at the `03-shapes.html` example for this mesh.

We'll quickly walk you through these shapes using `03-shapes.html` as a reference. We won't explain `Physijs.ConcaveMesh` any further since its usage is very limited.

Before we look at the example, we'll first have a quick look at `Physijs.PlaneMesh`. This mesh creates a simple plane based on `THREE.PlaneGeometry`, as follows:

```
var plane = new Physijs.PlaneMesh(new THREE.
    PlaneGeometry(5,5,10,10), material);

scene.add( plane );
```

In this function, you can see that we just pass in a simple `THREE.PlaneGeometry` to create this mesh. If you add this to the scene, you'll notice something strange. The mesh you just created doesn't respond to gravity. The reason is that `Physijs.PlaneMesh` has a fixed weight of 0, so it won't respond to gravity or be moved by collisions with other objects. Besides this mesh, all the other meshes respond to gravity and collisions, as you'd expect. The following screenshot shows a height field on which the various supported shapes can be dropped:

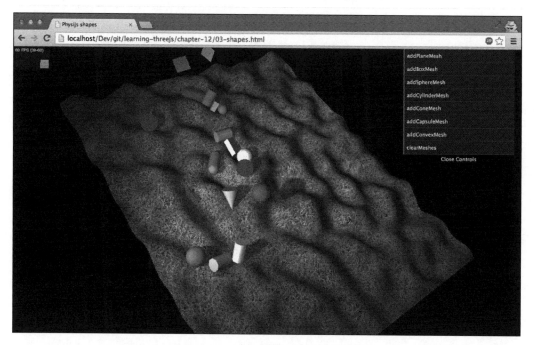

The previous image shows the `03-shapes.html` example. In this example, we've created a random height field (more on that later) and have a menu in the top-right corner that you can use to drop objects of various shapes. If you play around with this example, you'll see how different shapes respond differently to the height map and in collisions with other objects.

Let's look at the construction of some of these shapes:

```
new Physijs.SphereMesh(new THREE.SphereGeometry(3,20),mat);
new Physijs.BoxMesh(new THREE.BoxGeometry(4,2,6),mat);
new Physijs.CylinderMesh(new THREE.CylinderGeometry(2,2,6),mat);
new Physijs.ConeMesh(new THREE.CylinderGeometry(0,3,7,20,10),mat);
```

There's nothing special here; we create a geometry and use the best matching mesh from Physijs to create the object we add to the scene. However, what if we want to use `Physijs.CapsuleMesh`? Three.js doesn't contain a capsule-like geometry, so we have to create one ourselves. Here's the code for this purpose:

```
var merged = new THREE.Geometry();
var cyl = new THREE.CylinderGeometry(2, 2, 6);
var top = new THREE.SphereGeometry(2);
var bot = new THREE.SphereGeometry(2);

var matrix = new THREE.Matrix4();
matrix.makeTranslation(0, 3, 0);
top.applyMatrix(matrix);

var matrix = new THREE.Matrix4();
matrix.makeTranslation(0, -3, 0);
bot.applyMatrix(matrix);

// merge to create a capsule
merged.merge(top);
merged.merge(bot);
merged.merge(cyl);

// create a physijs capsule mesh
var capsule = new Physijs.CapsuleMesh(merged, getMaterial());
```

Physijs.CapsuleMesh looks like a cylinder but has a rounded top and bottom. We can easily recreate this in Three.js by creating a cylinder (cyl) and two spheres (top and bot) and merging them together using the merge() function. The following screenshot shows a number of capsules rolling down the height map:

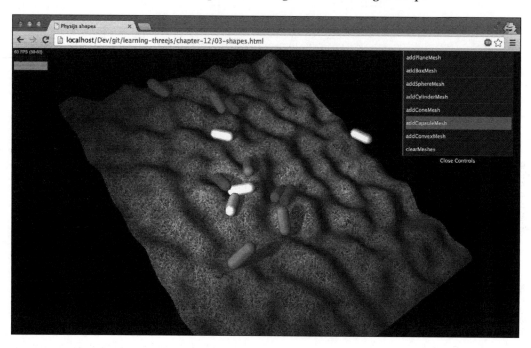

Before we look at the height map, let's look at the last of the shapes you can add to this example, Physijs.ConvexMesh. A convex is the minimal shape that wraps all the vertices of a geometry. The resulting shape will only have angles smaller than 180 degrees. You would use this mesh for complex shapes such as torus knots, as shown in the following code:

```
var convex = new Physijs.ConvexMesh(new
    THREE.TorusKnotGeometry(0.5,0.3,64,8,2,3,10), material);
```

In this case, for physics simulation and collisions, the convex of the torus knot will be used. This is a very good way to apply physics and detect collisions for complex objects, while still minimizing the performance impact.

The last mesh from Physijs to discuss is `Physijs.HeightMap`. The following screenshot shows a height map created with Physijs:

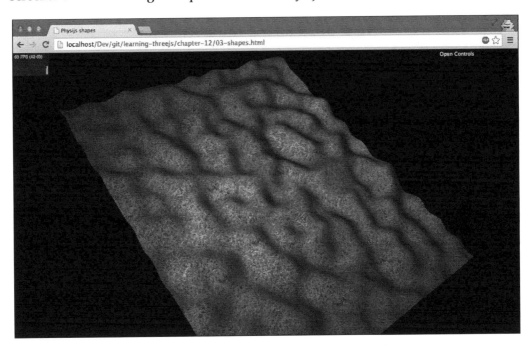

With a height map, you can very easily create a terrain that contains bumps and shallows. Using `Physijs.Heightmap`, we make sure all the objects respond correctly to the height differences of this terrain. Let's look at the code required to accomplish this:

```
var date = new Date();
var pn = new Perlin('rnd' + date.getTime());

function createHeightMap(pn) {

   var ground_material = Physijs.createMaterial(
     new THREE.MeshLambertMaterial({
       map: THREE.ImageUtils.loadTexture('../assets/textures
         /ground/grasslight-big.jpg')
     }),
     0.3, // high friction
     0.8 // low restitution
   );
```

```
var ground_geometry = new THREE.PlaneGeometry(120, 100, 100,
    100);
for (var i = 0; i < ground_geometry.vertices.length; i++) {
    var vertex = ground_geometry.vertices[i];
    var value = pn.noise(vertex.x / 10, vertex.y / 10, 0);
    vertex.z = value * 10;
}
ground_geometry.computeFaceNormals();
ground_geometry.computeVertexNormals();

var ground = new Physijs.HeightfieldMesh(
    ground_geometry,
    ground_material,
    0, // mass
    100,
    100
);
ground.rotation.x = Math.PI / -2;
ground.rotation.y = 0.4;
ground.receiveShadow = true;

return ground;
}
```

In this code fragment, we take a couple of steps to create the height map you can see in the example. First off, we create the Physijs material and a simple `PlaneGeometry` object. To create a bumpy terrain from `PlaneGeometry`, we walk through each of the vertices of this geometry and randomly set the z property. For this, we use a Perlin noise generator to create a bump map just as we used in the *Using the canvas as a bump map* section of *Chapter 10, Loading and Working with Textures*. We need to call `computeFaceNormals` and `computeVertexNormals` to make sure the texture, lighting, and shadows are rendered correctly. At this point, we have `PlaneGeometry`, which contains the correct height information. With `PlaneGeometry`, we can create `Physijs.HeightFieldMesh`. The last two parameters for the constructor take the number of horizontal and vertical segments of `PlaneGeometry` and should match the last two properties used to construct `PlaneGeometry`. Finally, we rotate `HeightFieldMesh` to the position we want and add it to the scene. All other Physijs objects will now interact correctly with this height map.

Using constraints to limit movement of objects

Until now, we've seen some basic physics in action. We've seen how the various shapes respond to gravity, friction, and restitution and how they affect collisions. Physijs also provides advanced constructs that allow you to limit the movement of your objects. In Physijs, these objects are called constraints. The following table gives an overview of the constraints that are available in Physijs:

Constraint	Description
PointConstraint	This allows you to fix the position of one object to the position of another object. If one object moves, the other will move with it, keeping the distance and orientation between them the same.
HingeConstraint	HingeConstraint allows you to limit the movement of an object as if it were on a hinge, such as a door.
SliderConstraint	This constraint, as the name implies, allows you to limit the movement of an object to a single axis, for instance, a sliding door.
ConeTwistConstraint	With this constraint, you can limit the rotation and the movement of one object to another. This constraint functions like a ball-and-socket joint, for instance, the way your arm moves in your shoulder socket.
DOFConstraint	DOFConstraint allows you to specify the limit of movement around any of the three axes, and it allows you to set the minimum and maximum angle that is allowed. This is the most versatile of the constraints available.

The easiest way to understand these constraints is to see them in action and play around with them. For this, we've provided an example where all these constraints are used together, `04-physijs-constraints.js`. The following screenshot shows this example:

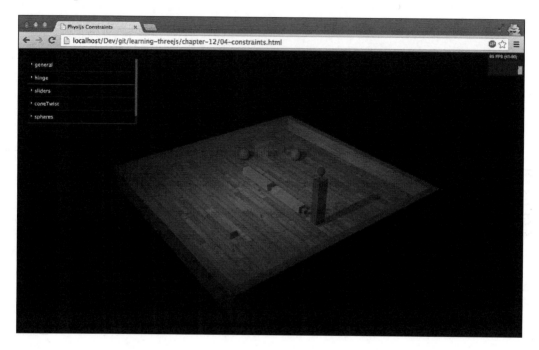

Based on this example, we'll walk you through four of these five constraints. For DOFConstraint, we've created a separate example. The first one we look at is PointConstraint.

Using PointConstraint to limit movement between two points

If you open the example, you'll see two red spheres. These two spheres are connected to each other using PointConstraint. With the menu in the top-left corner, you can move the green sliders around. As soon as one of the sliders hits one of the red spheres, you'll see that both of them move in the same manner, and they keep the distance between them the same, while still complying with weight, gravity, friction, and other aspects of physics.

PointConstraint in this example was created as follows:

```
function createPointToPoint() {
  var obj1 = new THREE.SphereGeometry(2);
  var obj2 = new THREE.SphereGeometry(2);

  var objectOne = new Physijs.SphereMesh(obj1, Physijs.
    createMaterial(new THREE.MeshPhongMaterial({color: 0xff4444,
    transparent: true, opacity:0.7}),0,0));

  objectOne.position.x = -10;
  objectOne.position.y = 2;
  objectOne.position.z = -18;

  scene.add(objectOne);

  var objectTwo = new Physijs.SphereMesh(obj2,Physijs.
    createMaterial(new THREE.MeshPhongMaterial({color: 0xff4444,
    transparent: true, opacity:0.7}),0,0));

  objectTwo.position.x = -20;
  objectTwo.position.y = 2;
  objectTwo.position.z = -5;

  scene.add(objectTwo);

  var constraint = new Physijs.PointConstraint(objectOne,
    objectTwo, objectTwo.position);
  scene.addConstraint(constraint);
}
```

Here, you can see that we create objects using a Physijs-specific mesh (SphereMesh in this case) and add them to the scene. We use the Physijs.PointConstraint constructor to create the constraint. This constraint takes three parameters:

- The first two arguments define which objects you want to connect to each other. In this case, we connect the two spheres to one another.

- The third argument defines to what position the constraint is bound. For instance, if you bind the first object to a very large object, you can set this position, for instance, to the right-hand side of that object. Usually, if you just want to connect two objects together, a good choice is to just set it to the position of the second object.

If you don't want to fix an object to another one, but to a static position in the scene, you can omit the second parameter. In that case, the first object keeps the same distance to the position you specified, while complying with gravity and other aspects of physics, of course.

Once the constraint is created, we can enable it by adding it to the scene with the `addConstraint` function. As you start experimenting with constraints, you'll likely run into some strange issues. To make debugging easier, you can pass in `true` to the `addConstraint` function. If you do this, the constraint point and orientation is shown in the scene. This can help you get the rotation and position of your constraint correctly.

Creating door-like constraints with HingeConstraint

`HingeConstraint`, as the name implies, allows you to create an object that behaves like a hinge. It rotates around a specific axis, limiting the movement to a specified angle. In our example, `HingeConstraint` is shown with two white flippers at the center of the scene. These flippers are constrained to the small, brown cubes and can rotate around them. If you want to play around with these hinges, you can enable them by checking the `enableMotor` box in the **hinge** menu. This will accelerate the flippers to the velocity specified in the **general** menu. A negative velocity will move the hinges down, and a positive velocity will move them up. The following screenshot shows the hinges in the up position and in the down position:

Let's take a closer look at how we created one of these flippers:

```
var constraint = new Physijs.HingeConstraint(flipperLeft,
    flipperLeftPivot, flipperLeftPivot.position, new
    THREE.Vector3(0,1,0));
scene.addConstraint(constraint);
constraint.setLimits(-2.2, -0.6, 0.1, 0);
```

This constraint takes four parameters. Let's look at each one in a bit more detail:

Parameter	Description
mesh_a	The first object passed into the function is the object that is to be constrained. In this example, the first object is the white cube that serves as the flipper. This is the object that is constrained in its movements.
mesh_b	The second object defines to which object mesh_a is constrained. In this example, mesh_a is constrained to the small, brown cube. If we move this mesh around, mesh_a would follow it around, still keeping HingeConstraint in place. You'll see that all constraints have this option. You could, for instance, use this if you've created a car that moves around and want to create a constraint for opening a door. If this second parameter is omitted, the hinge will be constrained to the scene (and never be able to move around).
position	This is the point where the constraint is applied. In this case, it's the hinge point around which mesh_a rotates. If you've specified mesh_b, this hinge point will move around with the position and rotation of mesh_b.
axis	This is the axis around which the hinge should rotate. In this example, we've set the hinge horizontally (0,1,0).

Adding HingeConstraint to the scene works in the same way as we've seen with PointConstraint. You use the addConstraint method, specify the constraint to add, and optionally add true to show the exact location and orientation of the constraint for debugging purposes. For HingeConstraint, however, we also need to define the range of movement that is allowed. We do this with the setLimits function.

This function takes the following four parameters:

Parameter	Description
low	This is the minimum angle, in radians, of motion.
high	This is the maximum angle, in radians, of motion.

Parameter	Description
bias_factor	This property defines the rate with which the constraint corrects itself after an error in position. For instance, when the hinge is pushed out of its constraints by a different object, it will move itself to its correct position. The higher this value, the faster it will correct its position. It is best to keep it below 0.5.
relaxation_factor	This defines the rate at which the velocity is changed by the constraint. If this is set to a high value, the object will bounce when it reaches its minimum or maximum angle of motion.

You can change these properties at runtime if you want. If you add HingeConstraint with these properties, you won't see much movement. The mesh will only move when hit by another object or based on gravity. This constraint, as with many others, however, can also be moved by an internal motor. This is what you see when you check the enableMotor box in the **hinge** submenu from our example. The following code is used to enable this motor:

```
constraint.enableAngularMotor( controls.velocity,
    controls.acceleration );
```

This will speed up the mesh (in our case, the flipper) to the specified velocity using the acceleration provided. If we want to move the flipper the other way, we just specify a negative velocity. If we didn't have any limits, this would cause our flipper to rotate as long as our motor kept running. To disable a motor, we can just call the following code:

```
flipperLeftConstraint.disableMotor();
```

Now the mesh will slow down based on friction, collisions, gravity, and other aspects of physics.

Limiting movement to a single axis with SliderConstraint

The next constraint is SliderConstraint. With this constraint, you can limit the movement of an object to any one of its axes. The green sliders in the 04-constraints.html example can be controlled from the **sliders** submenu. The following screenshot shows this example:

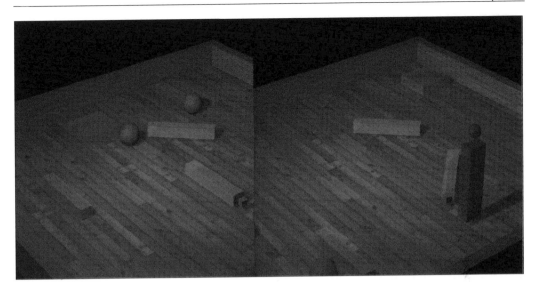

With the **SlidersLeft** button, the sliders will move to the left-hand side (their lower limit), and with the **SlidersRight** button, they will move to the right-hand side (their upper limit). Creating these constraints from code is very easy:

```
var constraint = new Physijs.SliderConstraint(sliderMesh, new
    THREE.Vector3(0, 2, 0), new THREE.Vector3(0, 1, 0));

scene.addConstraint(constraint);
constraint.setLimits(-10, 10, 0, 0);
constraint.setRestitution(0.1, 0.1);
```

As you can see from the code, this constraint takes three arguments (or four if you want to constrain an object to another object). The following table explains the arguments for this constraint:

Parameter	Description
mesh_a	The first object passed into the function is the object that is to be constrained. In this example, the first object is the green cube that serves as the slider. This is the object that will be constrained in its movements.
mesh_b	This is the second object, which defines to which object mesh_a is constrained. This is an optional argument and omitted in this example. If omitted, the mesh will be constrained to the scene. If it is specified, the slider will move around when this mesh moves around or when its orientation changes.

Parameter	Description
position	This is the point where the constraint is applied. This is especially important when you constrain mesh_a to mesh_b.
axis	This is the axis on which mesh_a will slide. Note that this is relative to the orientation of mesh_b if it is specified. In the current version of Physijs, there seems to be a strange offset to this axis when using a linear motor with linear limits. The following works for this version if you want to slide along: • The *x* axis: new THREE.Vector3(0,1,0) • The *y* axis: new THREE.Vector3(0,0,Math.PI/2) • The *z* axis: new THREE.Vector3(Math.PI/2,0,0)

After you've created the constraint and added it to the scene using scene. addConstraint, you can set the constraint.setLimits(-10, 10, 0, 0) limits for this constraint to specify how far the slider may slide. You can set the following limits on SliderConstraint:

Parameter	Description
linear_lower	This is the lower linear limit of the object
linear_upper	This is the upper linear limit of the object
angular_lower	This is the lower angular limit of the object
angular_higher	This is the upper angular limit of the object

Finally, you can set the restitution (the bounce) that'll occur when you hit one of these limits. You do this with constraint.setRestitution(res_linear, res_angular), where the first parameter sets the amount of bounce when you hit the linear limit and the second one sets the amount of bounce when you hit the angular limit.

Now, the complete constraint has been configured, and we can wait until collisions occur that slide the object around or use a motor. For SlideConstraint, we have two options: we can use an angular motor to accelerate along the axis we specified, complying with the angular limits we set, or use a linear motor to accelerate along the axis we specified, complying with the linear limits. In this example, we used a linear motor. For using an angular motor, take a look at DOFConstraint, which is explained later on in this chapter.

Creating a ball-and-socket-joint-like constraint with ConeTwistConstraint

With ConeTwistConstraint, it is possible to create a constraint where the movement is limited to a set of angles. We can specify what the minimum and maximum angle is from one object to the other for the *x*, *y*, and *z* axes. The following screenshot shows that ConeTwistConstraint allows you to move an object around a reference at certain angles:

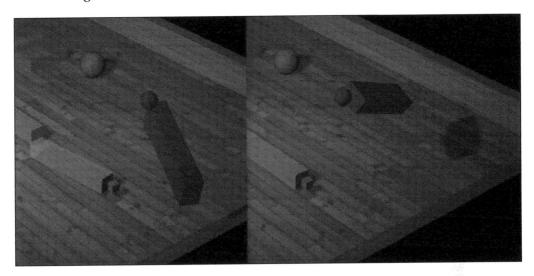

The easiest way to understand ConeTwistConstraint is by looking at the code required to create one. The code required to accomplish this is as follows:

```
var baseMesh = new THREE.SphereGeometry(1);
var armMesh = new THREE.BoxGeometry(2, 12, 3);

var objectOne = new Physijs.BoxMesh(baseMesh,
  Physijs.createMaterial(new THREE.MeshPhongMaterial({color:
  0x4444ff, transparent: true, opacity:0.7}), 0, 0), 0);
objectOne.position.z = 0;
objectOne.position.x = 20;
objectOne.position.y = 15.5;
objectOne.castShadow = true;
scene.add(objectOne);
```

```
var objectTwo = new Physijs.SphereMesh
  (armMesh,Physijs.createMaterial(new THREE.MeshPhong
  Material({color: 0x4444ff, transparent: true, opacity:0.7}), 0,
  0), 10);
objectTwo.position.z = 0;
objectTwo.position.x = 20;
objectTwo.position.y = 7.5;
scene.add(objectTwo);
objectTwo.castShadow = true;

var constraint = new Physijs.ConeTwistConstraint(objectOne,
  objectTwo, objectOne.position);

scene.addConstraint(constraint);

constraint.setLimit(0.5*Math.PI, 0.5*Math.PI, 0.5*Math.PI);
constraint.setMaxMotorImpulse(1);
constraint.setMotorTarget(new THREE.Vector3(0, 0, 0));
```

In this piece of JavaScript, you'll probably already recognize a number of concepts we discussed earlier. We start with creating the objects that we connect to each other with the constraint: objectOne (a sphere) and objectTwo (a box). We position these objects so that objectTwo hangs below objectOne. Now we can create ConeTwistConstraint. The arguments this constraint takes aren't anything new if you've already looked at the other constraints. The first parameter is the object to constrain, the second parameter is the object to which the first object is constrained, and the last parameter is the location where the constraint is constructed (in this case, it's the point around which objectOne rotates). After adding the constraint to the scene, we can set its limits with the setLimit function. This function takes three radian values that specify the maximum angle for each of the axes.

Just as with most of the other constraints, we can move objectOne using the motor provided by the constraint. For ConeTwistConstraint, we set MaxMotorImpulse (how much force the motor can apply), and we set the target angles the motor should move objectOne to. In this example, we move it to its resting position directly below the sphere. You can play around with this example, as shown in the following screenshot, by setting this target value:

The last constraint we'll look at is also the most versatile—DOFConstraint.

Creating detailed control with DOFConstraint

DOFConstraint, also called the degree of freedom constraint, allows you to exactly control an object's linear and angular movement. We'll show how to use this constraint by creating an example where you can drive around a simple, car-like shape. This shape consists of a single rectangle that serves as the body and four spheres that serve as the wheels. Let's start by creating the wheels:

```
function createWheel(position) {
  var wheel_material = Physijs.createMaterial(
  new THREE.MeshLambertMaterial({
    color: 0x444444,
    opacity: 0.9,
    transparent: true
  }),
  1.0, // high friction
  0.5 // medium restitution
  );
```

```
var wheel_geometry = new THREE.CylinderGeometry(4, 4, 2, 10);
var wheel = new Physijs.CylinderMesh(
  wheel_geometry,
  wheel_material,
  100
);

wheel.rotation.x = Math.PI / 2;
wheel.castShadow = true;
wheel.position = position;
return wheel;
}
```

In this piece of code, we just created a simple `CylinderGeometry` and `CylinderMesh` object, which can be used as the wheels for our car. The following screenshot depicts the result of the preceding code:

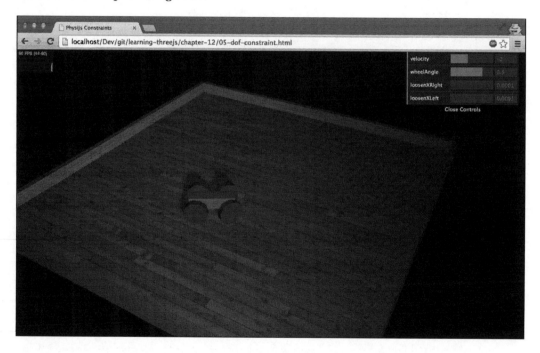

Next, we need to create the body of the car and add everything to the scene:

```
var car = {};
var car_material = Physijs.createMaterial(new THREE.
  MeshLambertMaterial({
    color: 0xff4444,
```

```
    opacity: 0.9,   transparent: true
  }),    0.5, 0.5
);

var geom = new THREE.BoxGeometry(15, 4, 4);
var body = new Physijs.BoxMesh(geom, car_material, 500);
body.position.set(5, 5, 5);
body.castShadow = true;
scene.add(body);

var fr = createWheel(new THREE.Vector3(0, 4, 10));
var fl = createWheel(new THREE.Vector3(0, 4, 0));
var rr = createWheel(new THREE.Vector3(10, 4, 10));
var rl = createWheel(new THREE.Vector3(10, 4, 0));

scene.add(fr);
scene.add(fl);
scene.add(rr);
scene.add(rl);
```

Until now, we just created the separate components that will have to make up our car. To tie everything together, we're going to create constraints. Each wheel will be constrained to body. The constraints are created as follows:

```
var frConstraint = new Physijs.DOFConstraint(fr,body, new
  THREE.Vector3(0,4,8));
scene.addConstraint(frConstraint);
var flConstraint = new Physijs.DOFConstraint (fl,body, new
  THREE.Vector3(0,4,2));
scene.addConstraint(flConstraint);
var rrConstraint = new Physijs.DOFConstraint (rr,body, new
  THREE.Vector3(10,4,8));
scene.addConstraint(rrConstraint);
var rlConstraint = new Physijs.DOFConstraint (rl,body, new
  THREE.Vector3(10,4,2));
scene.addConstraint(rlConstraint);
```

Each wheel (the first argument) has it's own constraint, and the position where it is attached to the car (the second argument) is specified with the last argument. If we ran with this configuration, we'd see that the four wheels hold up the body of the car. We need to do two more things to get the car moving: we need to set up the constraints for the wheels (along which axis they can move), and we need to configure the correct motors. First, we set up the constraints for the two front wheels; what we want for these front wheels is just to be able to rotate along the *z* axis so that they can power the car, and they shouldn't be allowed to move along the other axes.

The code required to accomplish this is as follows:

```
frConstraint.setAngularLowerLimit({ x: 0, y: 0, z: 0 });
frConstraint.setAngularUpperLimit({ x: 0, y: 0, z: 0 });
flConstraint.setAngularLowerLimit({ x: 0, y: 0, z: 0 });
flConstraint.setAngularUpperLimit({ x: 0, y: 0, z: 0 });
```

At first glance, this might seem weird. By setting the lower and upper limits to the same value, we make sure that no rotation is possible in the specified direction. This would also mean that the wheels can't rotate around their z axis. The reason we specify it like this is that when you enable a motor for a specific axis, these limits are ignored. So setting limits on the z axis at this point doesn't have any effect on our front wheels.

We're going to steer with our rear wheels, and to make sure they don't fall over, we need to fix the x axis. With the following code, we fix the x axis (set upper and lower limits to 0), fix the y axis so that these wheels are already initially turned, and disable any limit on the z axis:

```
rrConstraint.setAngularLowerLimit({ x: 0, y: 0.5, z: 0.1 });
rrConstraint.setAngularUpperLimit({ x: 0, y: 0.5, z: 0 });
rlConstraint.setAngularLowerLimit({ x: 0, y: 0.5, z: 0.1 });
rlConstraint.setAngularUpperLimit({ x: 0, y: 0.5, z: 0 });
```

As you can see, to disable the limits, we have to set the lower limit of that specific axis higher than the upper limit. This will allow free rotation around that axis. If we don't set this for the z axis, these two wheels will just be dragged along. In this case, they'll turn together with the other wheels because of the friction with the ground.

All that is left to do is set up the motors for the front wheels, which can be done as follows:

```
flConstraint.configureAngularMotor(2, 0.1, 0, -2, 1500);
frConstraint.conAngularMotor(2, 0.1, 0, -2, 1500);
```

Since there are three axes we can create a motor for, we need to specify the axis the motor works on: 0 is the x axis, 1 is the y axis, and 2 is the z axis. The second and third arguments define the angular limits for the motor. Here, we once again set the lower limit (0.1) higher than the upper limit (0) to allow free rotation. The third argument specifies the velocity we want to reach, and the last argument specifies the force this motor can apply. If this last one is too little, the car won't move; if it's too high, the rear wheels will lift off from the ground.

Enable them with the following code:

```
flConstraint.enableAngularMotor(2);
frConstraint.enableAngularMotor(2);
```

If you open up the `05-dof-constraint.html` example, you can play around with the various constraints and motors and drive the car around. The following screenshot shows this example:

In the next section, we'll look at the last subject we'll discuss in this book, and that is how to add sounds to your Three.js scene.

Add sound sources to your scene

With the subjects discussed until now, we have a lot of the ingredients in place to create beautiful scenes, games, and other 3D visualizations. What we haven't shown, however, is how to add sounds to your Three.js scene. In this section, we'll look at two Three.js objects that allow you to add sources of sound to your scene. This is especially interesting since these sound sources respond to the position of the camera:

- The distance between the sound source and the camera determines the volume of the sound source.

- The positions to the left-hand side and the right-hand side of the camera determine the sound volume of the left-hand side speaker and the right-hand side speaker, respectively.

The best way to explain this is to see this in action. Open up the 06-audio.html example in your browser, and you'll see three cubes with pictures of animals. The following screenshot shows this example:

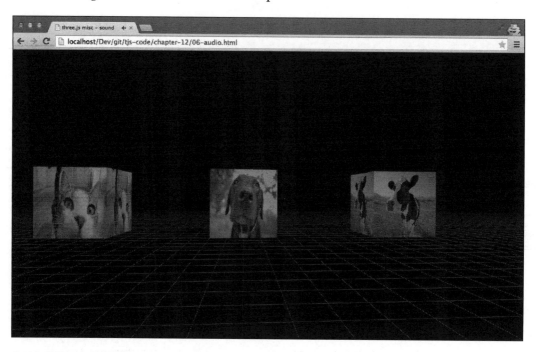

This example uses the first-person controls we saw in *Chapter 9, Animations and Moving the Camera*, so you can use the arrow keys in combination with the mouse to move around the scene. What you'll see is that the closer you move to a specific cube, the louder that specific animal will sound. If you position the camera between the dog and the cow, you'll hear the cow from the right-hand side and the dog from the left-hand side.

In this example, we used a specific helper, THREE.GridHelper, from Three.js to create the grid beneath the cubes:

```
var helper = new THREE.GridHelper( 500, 10 );
helper.color1.setHex( 0x444444 );
helper.color2.setHex( 0x444444 );
scene.add( helper );
```

To create a grid, you need to specify the size of the grid (500 in this case) and the size of the individual grid elements (we used 10 here). If you want, you can also set the colors of the horizontal lines by specifying the color1 and color2 properties.

Accomplishing this only takes a small amount of code. The first thing we need to do is define `THREE.AudioListener` and add it to `THREE.PerspectiveCamera`, as follows:

```
var listener1 = new THREE.AudioListener();
camera.add( listener1 );
```

Next, we need to create `THREE.Mesh` and add a `THREE.Audio` object to that mesh, as follows:

```
var cube = new THREE.BoxGeometry(40, 40, 40);

var material_1 = new THREE.MeshBasicMaterial({
  color: 0xffffff,
  map: THREE.ImageUtils.loadTexture("../assets/textures/
    animals/cow.png")
});

var mesh1 = new THREE.Mesh(cube, material_1);
mesh1.position.set(0, 20, 100);

var sound1 = new THREE.Audio(listener1);
sound1.load('../assets/audio/cow.ogg');
sound1.setRefDistance(20);
sound1.setLoop(true);
sound1.setRolloffFactor(2);

mesh1.add(sound1);
```

As you can see from this code snippet, we first create a standard `THREE.Mesh` instance. Next, we create a `THREE.Audio` object, which we connect to the `THREE.AudioListener` object we created earlier. Finally, we add the `THREE.Audio` object to the mesh we created and we're done.

There are a couple of properties we can set on the `THREE.Audio` object to configure its behavior:

- `load`: This allows us to load an audio file to be played.
- `setRefDistance`: This determines the distance from the object from where the sound will be reduced in volume.
- `setLoop`: By default, a sound is played once. By setting this property to `true`, the sound is looped.
- `setRolloffFactor`: This determines how quickly the volume decreases as you move away from the sound source.

Internally, Three.js uses the Web Audio API (`http://webaudio.github.io/web-audio-api/`) to play the sound and determine the correct volume. Not all browsers support this specification. The best support currently is from Chrome and Firefox.

Summary

In this last chapter, we explored how you can extend the basic 3D functionality from Three.js by adding physics. For this, we used the Physijs library, which allows you to add gravity, collisions, constraints, and much more. We also showed how you can add positional sound to your scene using the `THREE.Audio` and `THREE.AudioListener` objects. With those subjects, we've reached the end of this book on Three.js. In these chapters, we covered a lot of different subjects and explored pretty much everything Three.js has to offer. In the first couple of chapters, we explained the core concepts and ideas behind Three.js; after that, we looked at the available lights and how materials affect how an object is rendered. After the basics, we explored the various geometries Three.js has to offer and how you can combine geometries to create new ones.

In the second part of the book, we looked at a few more advanced subjects. You learned how to create particle systems, how to load models from external sources, and how to create animations. Finally, in these last couple of chapters, we looked at the advanced textures you can use in skinning and the postprocessing effects that can be applied after the scene is rendered. We end the book with this chapter on physics, which, besides explaining how you can add physics to your Three.js scene, also shows the active community of projects surrounding Three.js that you can use to add even more functionality to an already great library.

I hope you've enjoyed reading this book and playing around with the examples as much as I have writing it!

Index

G

geometries, loading from external resources
  about 220
  file formats 220-222
  importing, from 3D file formats 233
  Three.js JSON format, saving
        and loading 222
geometry
  functions 42-48
  properties 42-48
  using 41
geometry grouping and merging
  about 215
  multiple meshes, merging into
        single mesh 218-220
  objects, grouping 216-218
Git
  URL 7
  used, for cloning repository 7
git command-line tool 7
GLSL
  about 119
  URL 119

H

head-up display (HUD) 206
helper functions,
        THREE.ShapeGeometry 141
HingeConstraint
  about 367, 370
  axis parameter 371
  door-like constraints, creating with 370-372
  mesh_a parameter 371
  mesh_b parameter 371
  position parameter 371
HTML5 canvas
  particles, styling with 195
  using, with THREE.
        CanvasRenderer 195-197
  using, with WebGLRenderer 197-200
HTML skeleton
  creating 12, 13

I

iewebgl plugin
  URL 3
intersect function
  about 179, 184, 185
  demonstrating 186

J

JavaScript file, Physijs
  URL 352
JSON format 221

L

lens flares 89-93
light map
  about 294
  used, for creating fake shadows 294, 295
lights
  about 66
  adding 19-21
  basic lights 66
  special lights 84
  THREE.AmbientLight 66
  THREE.AreaLight 66
  THREE.DirectionalLight 66
  THREE.HemisphereLight 66
  THREE.LensFlare 66
  THREE.PointLight 66
  THREE.SpotLight 66
Literally library
  URL 310
lookAt function 18

M

material properties, Physijs
  about 358-360
  friction property 358
  restitution property 358, 359
materials
  about 95
  adding 19-21

W

Thank you for buying
Learning Three.js – the JavaScript 3D Library for WebGL
Second Edition

About Packt Publishing

Packt, pronounced 'packed', published its first book, *Mastering phpMyAdmin for Effective MySQL Management*, in April 2004, and subsequently continued to specialize in publishing highly focused books on specific technologies and solutions.

Our books and publications share the experiences of your fellow IT professionals in adapting and customizing today's systems, applications, and frameworks. Our solution-based books give you the knowledge and power to customize the software and technologies you're using to get the job done. Packt books are more specific and less general than the IT books you have seen in the past. Our unique business model allows us to bring you more focused information, giving you more of what you need to know, and less of what you don't.

Packt is a modern yet unique publishing company that focuses on producing quality, cutting-edge books for communities of developers, administrators, and newbies alike. For more information, please visit our website at www.packtpub.com.

About Packt Open Source

In 2010, Packt launched two new brands, Packt Open Source and Packt Enterprise, in order to continue its focus on specialization. This book is part of the Packt Open Source brand, home to books published on software built around open source licenses, and offering information to anybody from advanced developers to budding web designers. The Open Source brand also runs Packt's Open Source Royalty Scheme, by which Packt gives a royalty to each open source project about whose software a book is sold.

Writing for Packt

We welcome all inquiries from people who are interested in authoring. Book proposals should be sent to author@packtpub.com. If your book idea is still at an early stage and you would like to discuss it first before writing a formal book proposal, then please contact us; one of our commissioning editors will get in touch with you.

We're not just looking for published authors; if you have strong technical skills but no writing experience, our experienced editors can help you develop a writing career, or simply get some additional reward for your expertise.

Learning Three.js: The JavaScript 3D Library for WebGL

ISBN: 978-1-78216-628-3   Paperback: 402 pages

Create and animate stunning 3D graphics using the open source Three.js JavaScript library

1. Create and animate beautiful 3D graphics directly in the browser using JavaScript without the need to learn WebGL

2. Learn how to enhance your 3D graphics with light sources, shadows, and advanced materials and textures.

3. Each subject is explained using extensive examples that you can directly use and adapt for your own purposes.

WebGL Game Development

ISBN: 978-1-84969-979-2   Paperback: 418 pages

Gain insights into game development by rendering complex 3D objects using WebGL

1. Load and render complex 3D objects in WebGL using JavaScript.

2. Apply textures and lighting to game scenarios.

3. Load rigged 3D models and Skeletal Animations.

4. Add Physics Engines to WebGL games.

Please check **www.PacktPub.com** for information on our titles

Made in the USA
San Bernardino, CA
13 March 2017